The Life of Jesus

written and illustrated
by
Steven P. Thomason

The Life of Jesus

Steven P. Thomason

Published by:

Vibble Books

www.VibbleBooks.com

First printing
Hart Haus Resources, LLC ©2006

reprinted
Vibble Books © 2009

Special Thanks to:
Jeff Garrett, Carol Garrett, Linda Quackenboss, Leah Craig, Lona Thomason
Dave Schwarz, Mark Wooldrage
The Hart Haus Community

ISBN: 0-9840670-1-9
13-Digit: 978-0-9840670-1-5

Cover Artwork and Interior Illustration: Steven P. Thomason

Printed in the United States of America

Introduction

About This Study

This study was originally written in the fall of 2004 for a network of house churches called Hart Haus. Each week the members of the community would commit to spend 5 days studying the designated passage of scripture and then share what they learned with the group when they gathered in the various homes on Sunday.

Originally, this was designed to be a 15-week study, with 75 daily lessons, that leads you through all four Gospels. You may choose to follow the fast-paced, 15-week study, or you may choose to slow down and spread it out over a longer period of time. To facilitate a more flexible format, this version is structured around **Chapters**, **Sessions**, and **Lessons** rather than *Weeks* and *Days*. Feel free to use whatever method fits best with your group's needs.

About the Author

Steve Thomason is first and foremost a child of God that is committed to loving his wife and four children. He currently resides in the suburbs of Minneapolis, Minnesota.

Steve has two passions in life. The first is teaching people about God and how to grow in a relationship with the Creator. His second passion is art -- specifically cartooning and animation. Throughout his career he has sought to blend these two passions together to create visually interesting lessons that draw people closer to God.

From 1994-2002 Steve was in Adult Minstries at Central Christian Church in Las Vegas, Nevada. During those years Steve led small group ministries, adult education classes, and wrote curriculum for both settings. Along the way he earned a Masters of Divinity degree from Bethel Theological Seminary through their In-Ministry Program.

In 2002 Steve and his family joined with a group of friends to explore what it would look like to "do church" in a different way. For the next 5 years they experimented with being a community in a network of house churches called Hart Haus. During those years Steve wrote a daily Bible Study that combined cartoons and Bible Commentary.

In 2009 Steve set out on a new leg of his teacher/artist journey. He took the Hart Haus studies and used them as the foundation for creating Vibble Books. His desire is to see Vibble Books and VibbleSpace.com become a resource for his generation to engage with the reality of God's Love so that God's Kingdom can be realized in our world.

Experience the Life of Jesus Vibble

A VIBBLE is a **V**isual **I**nteractive **B**ible **B**ased **L**earning **E**xperience. You can supplement this study and experience the Life of Jesus study in full color, interactive video at *www.vibblespace.com/LOJ*.

If you are leading a small group, you can use the Session Videos as a nice introduction to the group study. They are short videos (5-8 minutes each) that talk through the full color illustration for each session. Log on today and begin the learning experience.

Table of Contents

An Invitation

Why another study on the life of Jesus? The story of Jesus is so old and has been told so many different times and in so many different ways, why in the world would we want to tell it again? For 2,000 years the most brilliant scholars in the world have analyzed the texts of the four Gospels in the New Testament, have written countless pages of doctoral theses about them, and have contrived a wide array of theological interpretations of their meaning. So why do we think we have anything to say about it?

Because stories were meant to be told. When we are children we love to hear the same story over and over again.

"Please, Daddy, read it one more time!"

Even as adults there are certain stories and movies that have woven their way into our hearts. These books and videos sit on the shelf like a trusted friend, ready to be brought down and revisited when we need a little comfort, motivation, or encouragement.

The amazing thing about stories is that they seem to take on a life of their own. They were written by one particular author, in one particular historical setting, yet, truly good stories tend to transcend their boundaries and speak to each new generation in a new way. Stories even speak to us as individuals in a new way each time we read them. We hear a story as a child and it affects us in one way. When we hear it as a young adult it seems to come at us from an entirely different angle. Then, as a middle-aged parent the story seems different.

Has the story changed? Not at all. What has changed is us. We have grown as individuals. Our culture has changed around us. Our perspective, and perhaps our receptivity, has developed and we are able to compare the story to so many new facets of reality that whole new layers of meaning become apparent to us.

The story of Jesus is just that...a story. It is not a dry theological textbtook written by crusty intellectuals in some far-off ivory tower. The story of Jesus is a real-life drama that has been recorded for us by four very real, very human men. Each of these four men, Matthew, the tax collector; Mark, the young man; Luke, the physician; and John, the fisherman/pastor writes the story of Jesus from his own unique perspective. Two of them, Matthew and John, were eyewitnesses and the close friends with Jesus. Two of them, Mark and Luke, were interviewers of and close friends with eyewitnesses and the close friends of Jesus. Each of them felt compelled to record this story in writing because they believed that Jesus' story would change the world.

Over 2,000 years the story has never changed. Jesus was a Jewish man, a carpenter/rabbi who lived in politically volitile times in Israel. The Jewish monarchy had sold out to the Roman Empire. The Jewish religion had become fractured and diluted by the influence of Persian, Greek, Egyptian, and Roman philosophies. The politics between government leaders and religious leaders had grown so complicated that the common man had become completely lost in the shuffle. The poor and the sick were all but forsaken. The glory of Israel and the physical evidence of Jehovah's power was now a 500-year-old-story, captured in a dying language on decaying scrolls. The talk of a Messiah, a great leader who would deliver Israel from its miserable condition was such a worn-out concept that most people had grown skeptical. "Messiahs" were a dime a dozen. They would raise up a rabble for rebellion and then the Romans would squash it. Every year it was the same.

Jesus entered into this arena as a 30-year-old man. He spoke some amazing words that had never been heard before. He performed some amazing miracles that caused even the religious leaders to stop and look. He interacted with the "wrong" crowd. He made bold claims about Himself, about His kingdom and His power, and then He allowed Himself to be executed like a criminal.

His story only lasted for three and a half years. He did what He did. He had a political and theological agenda. Those who wrote down His story had a political and theological agenda as well. That has not changed. And yet, the story has remained consistent for 2,000 years. Each generation and each culture has encountered and been confronted and challenged by this story. In fact, each generation and each culture has been transformed by this story. It is more than a trusted book that sits on a shelf. There is something about this story that is like a knife or a laser beam. It cuts through us. It penetrates our depths and challenges us at the core of who we are.

That is why we must tell this story again.

Come as you are

I am one man, in my mid-thirties. A husband, a father, an artist, and a pastor of a fledgling house-church ministry.

We live in the beginning of the twenty-first century. Our culture is shifting and reinventing itself every three to five years.

You are who you are, right now.

We need to hear this story again.

Who are you?

If you are a skeptic, I encourage you to be a skeptic. I invite you to read this story with skeptical eyes. Pick it apart. Barage it with questions. If it is false you will discover that and move on. If it is true, and if you are open to that possibility, you will be changed. That is not for me to decide. I merely invite you to bring who you are to this story.

If you are a Christian, I invite you to be careful. Be careful you do not let your Christianity get in the way of reading this story. The truth is, if you are honest with the story, you will discover that in our world, today, Jesus would not be very welcome in many of the churches claiming to bear His name. He was a radical. He did not play by the rules. He brought the unbridled truth of the Kingdom of God into clear focus for the world and the religious establishment to see. Be careful, please, to bring a humbled and open heart to this story.

If you are hurting, bring your pain. If you feel outcast and alone, come. If you were living in Jesus' day, He would have blown past the well-dressed, politically poised, religious people and come to see you first. He would have opened His arms and welcomed you to receive the truth of His Kingdom.

Be open to change

Whoever you are, I welcome you to journey through this story with me. Think of me as part tour guide, part traveling partner. As we travel through Jesus' story together, I will point out things along the way that will help you understand the story. I may tell you ways that this story has transformed me. I may tell you stories about others that have been transformed. I may even stop at times and challenge you.

Yet, don't just listen to me. The ultimate goal for this study is that you would encounter the story raw. That you would read it straight from the pages of your Bible, be "transported" to the streets of Jerusalem and the seaside of Galilee and see the preacher from Nazareth for yourself. Hear His brash teaching. Witness His powerful miracles. Watch the grueling execution. Be dumbfounded by His resurrected body. Then, let the story — the eternal story — get a hold on you on its own.

I welcome you to the journey. May these sessions be enriching and transforming for us all.

How the Study Works

This study on the life of Jesus is devided into 15 Sessions with five Lessons for each Session. The assigned readings for each lesson are a hybrid of the four Gospels, picking out the individual stories of each Gospel and piecing them together into one flowing chronological sequence. That means that you may be reading from one, two, three, or even all four of the Gospels in one lesson. You may read the same story four times. It also means that the sequence of the stories may be altered from the original author; for example, you may read Matthew 18 before you read Matthew 16.

Before you start accusing me of rewriting Scripture, there are a couple things that should be made clear regarding the nature of this study and the nature of the Gospels themselves:

1. No portion of the Gospels have been added or subtracted from this study (if you find one, it's a typo!) At the end of the study you will have read every word of each of the four Gospels. I am merely taking whole sections, intact, and piecing them into a chronological order.

2. This is how the Gospel writers themselves wrote their stories. When Matthew, Mark, Luke, and John sat down to put the story of Jesus to ink and papyrus, they were faced with a serious editing challenge. Jesus had done so many amazing things in His short three and a half years that it was impossible to record them all. Also, in those days, the writing of history was not as much about capturing an accurate chronology as it was about making a point. So each of the writers, bringing their own perspective and agenda to the project, selected key stories from the pile of choices and wove them together to present a portrait of Jesus that was accurate, yet skewed to his own agenda.

   In our study, we have an agenda as well. Being twenty-first century westerners, we have a need to see history as a sequence of events in linear time; I have attempted to order the stories of Jesus in such a way. Also, we want to study the life of Jesus in a manageble length of time so we have created 15 divisions. It is impossible to know if the sequence of events is exactly right, since that was not the greatest concern to the original authors, but the readings you will be doing seem to be in a good order of events.

3. There are risks involved in studying Jesus' life this way. By rearranging the stories from the order that the original author intended, you automatically lose some of the intended meaning. Yet, the only way to truly study

the meaning in that respect is to look at each Gospel separately, as a whole.

While this is a risk, I believe it is one worth taking and one that will bring about great return. By synthesizing the Gospels we will gain a much broader perspective on Jesus' life and see it in a fresh way. If you are familiar with the Gospels then they will seem fresh to you placed together in this manner.

In each session there will be six major sections to the study.

Illustration

An illustration will try to encapsulate the main point of that section in the story. These illustrations will correlate to the DVD used in the small group.

Introduction

This section will outline pertinent historical information and context that will help frame the picture of the session's reading for you.

Reading Assignments

Each lesson there will be assigned sections to read from the gospels. Please remember that these sections will jump around a bit because we are attempting to construct a chronologival account of Jesus' life based upon all four gospels.

Study Questions

First, read the assigned section on your own. Second, read and answer the questions. These questions are designed to help you look a little closer at the text and perhaps see things you may have missed the first time.

Food for Thought

After you have answered the Study Questions, read the "Food for Thought" section to get one particular commentary and insight on the passage.

Kid's Questions

There are few better ways that parents can train their children for their own relationship with Jesus than to demonstrate an authentic excitement about Jesus and His story. These questions are designed to help adults interact with children concerning the daily reading.

The Master Illustration

This illustration is designed to give a bird's eye view of the Life of Jesus. If you begin in the upper left corner you see how Jesus descended from being the Eternal Word of God to the lowly state of being human. Moving from left to right you will follow the ups and downs of his ministry. At first he extended the invitation to enter the Kingdom of Heaven to Israel. They rejected him as their Messiah and Herod had John beheaded.

After this Jesus changed the tone of his mission. He withdrew to pagan regions surrounding Israel. His teaching became pointed and his mission became laser focused. The only way for him to successfully bring about the Kingdom of Heaven was to allow the religious leaders of Jerusalem to execute him. Only then would the final victory over the real enemy — death itself — be won.

Introduction

What is a word? At first you may think, "That's an easy question, and a silly one, too." Maybe, but think about it for a second. What is a word? There are two ways that we encounter words. The first is in a written form. Right now your eyes are encountering a series of words. What are they? They are nothing more than black marks arranged on a piece of paper or a computer screen. The second way that we encounter words is through sounds. Vocal cords or the diaphragm of a speaker vibrate and send sound waves through the air. Those sound waves hit your eardrum, which then sends signals to your brain. Your brain then interprets those signals into symbols which we call words. The fact that I speak English and that you read English and that we share enough common cultural experiences and agree upon a standardized language makes it possible for these marks or sounds to have meaning. If this same message were typed in Chinese, it would most likely look like chicken-scratch to you.

A word is more than marks on paper or sound waves in the air. A word is even more than a language. These things are merely physical vehicles to deliver something much deeper, something much more abstract and much more real. Ultimately there is something in the universe that is behind everything that we consider to be real. When we look around we see the physical objects that make up our lives — the sun, the moon, our houses, the computer, the people around us. We observe the hustle and bustle of everyday life and listen to the news of world events. There is so much going on and so much complexity to all of it, that even though it may seem like so much random chaos, deep down inside we know there must be some sort of mastermind or driving idea behind all of it. There must be, or else none of it could exist.

The ancient Greeks thought about this kind of stuff all the time. They knew that there was an abstract idea that governed the entire universe. They called it the Logos. In English we translate it "Word." There's that word again. The Word represents the abstract idea behind everything that exists. Every worldview, whether it is religious or secular, has an idea about what the Word may be. Pantheists believe it to be a non-personal "force" that binds everything together. Naturalists and scientists call it "Nature." Religions call it God. The ancient Greeks called it Logos.

In the opening pages of our story about the life of Jesus we encounter the Word in its purest form — raw creative power. "In the beginning was the Word." The amazing thing about this story is that the Word does not remain in an abstract, enigmatic form. The miracle of all miracles happens. The Word becomes flesh. The Creator becomes the created. The infinitely abstract becomes the finitely concrete.

As you work through the readings this week, and as you observe the illustration, you will notice a transformation take place. The Word will transform from abstract concept to a spoken proclamation to a potential potentate, to a physical person. The first characters on the left of the picture will encounter the Word through the proclamation of a messenger from God. The Word will be presented as a promise fulfilled and the prospects of a child. Astrologers from Persia will encounter the Word as signs in the heavens declaring the coming of a mighty king. The shepherds in the field will encounter the Word as a joyful chorus of redemption for the oppressed. Mary will encounter the Word as the painful reality of a child passing through her birth canal. Joseph will encounter the Word as the responsibility of a scandalous pregnancy and the role of a surrogate father. Herod will encounter the Word as a threat to his political power.

On the right side of the picture, after 30 years of normal human development, we will encounter the Word in the form of an adult male from the city of Nazareth. His name is Jesus. The prophet in the desert proclaims that He is the Lamb of God who will take away the sins of the world and cut down the unproductive tree of Israel. Prophets proclaim Him and common fishermen are willing to follow Him.

We will see that the Word is purified by water and by fire. He passes through the waters of baptism, as a symbol of cleansing, and the fire of temptation

in the desert, passing the test of integrity. These two events serve as the coronation and commissioning of the long-awaited King of Israel, the Messiah, to confront the Kingdom of Israel that man has constructed and replace it with the Kingdom of Heaven that God has in mind. That will be presented next week.

For now, we get to see the formation of the abstract mind of the universe being translated into black marks on paper, sound waves in the air, the physical parameters of a human being, culture, and language. We get to see the deep, infinitely complex truths of God pop into focus as it is communicated through a language we can understand — the story of a single man.

Lesson 1

- John 1:1-5
- Luke 1:1-80

Study Questions

What was Zechariah's reaction/response to the message that Gabriel brought to him?

What was Mary's response to the message that Gabriel brought to her?

At what point in the timeline did Mary "prophesy" and sing her praise song to God?

At what point in the timeline did Zechariah "prophesy" and sing his praise song to God?

How would you summarize the difference between the reactions of Mary and Zechariah?

Food for Thought

How do you feel when you get those phone calls informing you that you have just won a trip to the Caribbean or some exotic place? "What's the catch?" right? In our culture we have been so inundated with fast-talkers and wheeler-dealers that we have a hard time believing that anything good could ever be given to us.

As we journey through the life of Jesus we will encounter again and again people who are presented with an incredible proposition. If we are open to it, we, too, will be offered an outlandish proposition. The God of the universe — the eternal, infinite "mind" or "word" that brought all things into being — actually cares about you. Not only that, but that Word took on human existence and entered into this messy, dangerous, dark place in order to shine a beacon of hope and guide us home safely.

Sounds too good to be true, doesn't it? It's a myth, right? Is it a hopeful tale made up by starry-eyed dreamers who were too weak to deal with the brutal realities of life? Perhaps. Then again, perhaps not.

In the reading today we see two people who were presented with outlandish propositions from one rather alarming messenger. The messenger of God named Gabriel brought two similar messages to two people in Israel. The messenger told Zechariah that he and his wife would have a miracle baby in their old age and that their son would be the Elijah-figure that the nation had been waiting for more than 500 years. To Mary he said that she would become pregnant through the Holy Spirit and that her son would be the Messiah that would save God's people from their bondage. How did these two respond?

Zechariah said, "Yeah right. Prove it to me." Mary said, "How can it be?... May it be so." In these two stories we find the two typical responses that we tend to have toward the proposition of God's outlandish truths. Some of us are Zechariahs, squinting our eyes with the gaze of a skeptic. Others are Marys, bowing our head in humble submission. Which are you?

If you are willing to hear them, you will be presented with some messages of God throughout this study. Even if you are already a "Christian," God has things to say to you as you examine the life of this Word-made-flesh. The question is, how will you respond?

Notice what happened to these two. They both ended up "prophesying" and praising God. To prophesy is to speak truth boldly. Mary's prophecy happened right away, because she openly and humbly accepted the gift that God had given her.

Zechariah, on the other hand, had to wait for nine months without the ability to speak at all before he was able to prophesy and praise God. It took some proving before Zechariah came around. Two things had to happen to him before he woke up to the truth of God's amazing gift in his life. First, he had to see it in action for himself. Second, he had to suffer the consequences of disbelief for a while.

It's easy to be skeptical when you are offered a gift that is too good to be true; of that there is no doubt. The great thing about the message that was offered to Zechariah and Mary — and to you — is that it is the truth. Whether we believe it or not, truth is always the truth and it will always bring itself about. If you are open to it, whether you go the Mary route or the Zechariah route, may the truth of God's wonderful gift get a hold of your heart in the course of this study.

Kid's Questions

How do you feel when your parents give you a wonderful gift on your birthday or at Christmas?

That is how Mary must have felt when she was told that she was going to be the mother of Jesus.

When she found out the good news she sang a beautiful song about it. Spend some time as a family and either sing one of your favorite praise songs or try to write a praise poem that thanks God for His wonderful gifts to us.

Lesson 2

- Matthew 1:1-25
- Luke 3:23-38
- Luke 2:1-40

Study Questions

What was at stake for Joseph? What risk was he willing to take by accepting a pregnant woman as his wife?

How did the shepherds respond to the message of the angels? What did they do with the information?

Summarize the message of Simeon and Anna. What do you think was the purpose for their piece of the story?

Food for Thought

There are three short lessons from today's reading: a risk-taking stepdad, the enthusiastic fringe, and the temple pair.

A risk-taking stepdad. One of the most unsung heroes in the story of Jesus' life is his stepdad, Joseph. Here is a guy who was asked to do something that betrayed everything his training had taught him was decent and good. And he was asked to do it by God, no less.

In those days a man and woman were betrothed (engaged) at a very young age. The whole deal was set up by their parents. The arrangement wasn't about love and romance; it was about creating good political ties between families. Honor, respect, and carrying on the family name to the next generation was the name of the game in the matchmaking arena. The betrothal was considered a legally binding agreement that would be consummated at the wedding feast and by the marriage bed. Sexual purity and fidelity were cornerstones of the whole arrangement.

So it was with Mary and Joseph. For Joseph to discover that his Mary was pregnant was the worst possible scandalous news that he could possibly hear. What would their parents think? What would the village think? This disgrace would tarnish their families' honor for generations. Nobody's going to believe the whole "the Holy Spirit did it to me" story. The only option Joseph had was to divorce her and quietly move on to a more noble situation.

Enter Gabriel once again. Joseph is now our third recipient of God's preposterously wonderful gift. Gabriel tells him "Joseph, Mary's telling the truth. This child is the Son of God. You are being asked to bear the weight of potential disgrace in order to bring the hope of the world into action." Yikes! What would you have done in that moment? Everything that Joseph held dear was hanging in the balance. He could potentially lose everything if he accepted the weight of this gift. That's why he's a hero. Joseph said, "Bring it on."

The enthusiastic fringe. One of the recurring themes of Luke's version of the story is God's special affection for the fringe of society. Here we see the most amazing event in the history of mankind happening in Bethlehem, and who gets to witness the Hallelujah chorus? Shepherds. After 2,000 years of Sunday school Christmas pageants watching little children gather around the manger with towels wrapped around their heads, the significance of this scene tends to slip away from us. Shepherds were the fringe. Shepherds were stinky. Shepherds lived out in

9

the fields with their sheep and were not readily welcome in the mainstream of society.

So why did God send His choir to perform for these nobodies? Why didn't He drag the king out of bed and rattle the cage of the Roman emperor, announcing that their days were numbered? Because that is how God works. God uses the ways of the simple to confound the ways of the wise. Here's a pretty good rule of thumb: if it's slick and polished, has great pedigrees, comes from the top down, and is readily accepted by the status quo, then it is probably not from God. Throughout the Bible, and highlighted here, we see God use the shepherds of society to be the bearers of the truth.

Notice what the shepherds did when they heard the news. They ran through the streets shouting about it. They wanted everyone to know that the day Israel had been waiting for so long had finally arrived. You see, they were able to unashamedly proclaim the message of Good News in the streets because they had nothing to lose. Their political position and place of high regard would not be tarnished if they were seen shouting bold "nonsense" in the public forum.

The question we need to ask ourselves is whether God would send the choir to us. Would we be willing to share the Good News like they did, or would we stand to lose too much?

The temple pair. Finally we see some straightforward truth about Jesus in this passage. There were two people in the temple — Simeon and Anna — that had been promised by God they would see the Messiah before they died. When Mary and Joseph brought the baby to the temple to have Him circumcised and dedicated (which was the custom for all boys) Simeon and Anna knew, without a doubt, that this little boy was the Messiah that had been promised. It doesn't get much clearer than that. According to both a male and female prophet of Israel, Jesus, Mary's son, was the long-awaited Messiah, the Savior of Israel. In the testimony of Simeon, Anna, and John (whom we will meet Lesson 4) we bridge the gap between the Old Testament and the New Testament. In the Old Testament, God spoke to His people through messengers called prophets. Typically the nation didn't listen to the prophets and got itself into all sorts of trouble. Now the time had come for God to put an end to the prophetic era and bring His own Son to be the prophet that would not only proclaim the words of truth to Israel but would be the Word of truth in the flesh.

Kid's Questions

How do you think the shepherds felt when the angels showed up in their field?

What did the angels tell the shepherds?

What did the shepherds do when they heard the news?

In what ways could you spread the news the way the shepherds did?

Do one of the following activities:

1. Draw a picture of the angelic choir singing for the shepherds.
2. Act out the scene of the angels singing to the shepherds.

Lesson 3

- Matthew 2:1-23
- Luke 2:41-52

Study Questions

What prompted the Magi to journey to Jerusalem?

What did they expect to find when they got there?

Who was Herod? What was his response to the message of the Magi?

What was Joseph forced to do because of Herod?

What was the twelve year old Jesus' attitude toward His parents?

Food for Thought

Today we see a foreshadowing of the power struggles that will come in Jesus' life. In this story we see a beautiful contrast between the right and wrong way to handle the message of the coming King and the authoritative power of Jesus' presence in your life. In the story we see two different kings being confronted with the potential of that reality. Remember, there were no armies entrenched around their palaces. No Jesus didn't — and doesn't — invade that way. At this point Jesus was just a toddler, less than two years old. To this point of the story the Word/King was simply a sign in the stars that rang the warning bell. Let's observe how these two kinds of rulers reacted.

The Magi. The text simply calls them "wise men from the east." Here we must speculate that it is most likely these men were astrologers/philosophers, political leaders from Persia. (Please note that astrology meant something different at that time than it does today.) Persia was once the most powerful empire in the world. It was in Persia that Daniel saw his vision as he served in the royal court. It was Persia that granted permission for Zerubbabel, Ezra, and Nehemiah to rebuild Jerusalem. It was Persia that strongly influenced Jewish theology. When Alexander the Great conquered Persia with his Greek culture, he did not wipe them out. In fact, he was enamored with Persian culture and incorporated much of it into Greek. When the Romans took over they left cultures intact, so the Persian wise men were symbols of great power in the world and in Israel.

So how did they react to the invasion of Jesus? They embraced the concept of a new King. They bowed to Him and brought Him gifts.

Herod, on the other hand, was a different story. Herod was not the rightful heir to the throne in Israel. He was placed in power by the Romans because he was a political and cultural sell-out. He didn't care for the Law of Moses or the integrity of the holiness of Israel that God had required. He was more of a Greek thinker and Roman politician than a Jewish king. He kept his "power" because he was willing to cater to the oppressive Roman Empire.

Here he is confronted with the potential of the true king of Israel showing up — the one that was prophesied about 500 years earlier. How did he react? "No way!" He couldn't let this happen. He had too much to lose. Instead of embracing the King, he tried to kill him.

Today we have been reminded of one aspect of Jesus that we must never lose sight of...Jesus is a conquering King. One vital component of His mission was to establish His throne and rule in the world. A throne is a symbol of authority and power. He did not come to cohabitate with the rulers of the world; He came to establish His throne over all others. Although you may not be the king of a nation, you do have some level of authority and power over something. At the very least each one of us likes to perceive of ourselves as the king or queen of our own mind and space. Jesus, the invading king, has come to tear down that throne and establish Himself upon it. The wise men and Herod represent the two categories of people that we will see in the story and that still exist today. There are those who embrace the King and there are those who resist, protecting their assets and trying to kill the Word. Where are you today?

Kid's Questions

Think of a game that you are really good at. Let's pretend that you are the champion of that game and that for a long time you have beaten everyone who plays you.

Now let's pretend that a new kid comes along and tells you that someone is coming who is better at that game than you are and that he will now be considered the new champion. How would you feel?

That's kind of what happened to King Herod. He had been the King of Israel for a while. When the wise men showed up and told him that the true King of Israel had been born, he got pretty mad and tried to kill Him.

The wise men were rulers, too, but they didn't get mad. How did they respond to the news of a new King?

Which kind of person do you want to be like toward Jesus: Herod or the wise men?

What kind of gifts can you bring to Jesus?

Lesson 4

- Matthew 3:1-12
- Mark 1:1-8
- Luke 3:1-20
- John 1:6-34
- John 3:22-36

Study Questions

Create a comparison chart.

In what ways is John described the same in all four Gospels?

What is a unique part of his story in each Gospel?

In your own words, what was John's message?

Summarize the purpose of John's ministry.

Food for Thought

In order to understand John the Baptist we must understand the role of the prophet in the Old Testament. Throughout the stories of God's interaction with His people in the Old Testament He used people called prophets to communicate His message of truth. The very first prophet was Moses. Through this man God delivered the blueprint for the freed slaves to become a bona fide nation by establishing laws and a code of ethics for everyday living. God's perfect plan for the people was to be able to live without a human political ruler and allow the law of God to govern their hearts and lives from the inside out. The people were not up to that challenge and begged God to give them a king. He did, and from the moment King Saul was anointed there was a human ruler that governed the people. The king, however, did not carry the voice of God. In fact, the king, more often than not, led the people down wicked paths and got the nation into all sorts of trouble.

Enter the prophet. The way God dealt with his wayward kings was to call out a prophet, give him a message, and send him to the king. The message usually went like this: "Hey king, you are way out of line. If you continue doing the wicked things you are doing you are not only going to hurt yourself, you are going to drag all of God's people into destruction with you. The enemy is at your door, ready to destroy you. If you don't repent you will be crushed by them. Is that what you want? Please turn back to God now, and we can all live happily ever after."

Almost always the king rejected the words of the prophet and sometimes killed him. Inevitably the words of the prophet would come true and the nation would be dragged into war, slavery, oppression, and desolation of some sort or another.

Many of the words of these prophets were written down and you had better believe that the common people listened to them. One common theme from all of the prophets was that someday God would put an end to this cycle of failures of fallible rulers and would bring a King that would deliver the people from oppression once and for all. This coming ruler was called the Messiah. In Hebrew the word means "anointed one," the king of all kings. In the Greek language the word Messiah is translated "Christ." It was prophesied that a prophet would come before the Christ appeared who would be like the earlier great prophet Elijah. Elijah was the bold prophet who had confronted the wicked king Ahab and his evil queen Jezebel. The people were waiting for the Elijah-like prophet to be the voice calling out in the desert, "prepare the way of the Lord."

For 500 years the people of Israel had been waiting, living under the oppressive rule of the Babylonians, Persians, Greeks, Egyptians, and Romans. God's voice had been silent during that period. The Jews knew that no Scripture had been penned since the prophecies of Malachi 400 years earlier. It seemed as if there was no hope. God appeared to be absent. The "king" was more wicked than ever. The people were divided between warring ideological factions. And the Romans were taxing the people into poverty.

Then one day a man named John came out of his desert home with the Essene monks and began to preach a message of repentance. He called the people to come out of the city and walk away from their hedonistic, corrupted ways, and enter into the cleansing waters of baptism. Baptism was a Jewish ritual of ceremonial cleansing that demonstrated a heart was willing to come back to God and get on the right path that He had marked out for them. John warned the people to be ready for the coming of the Messiah. He warned the rulers of Israel to be prepared because they had led the nation into moral bankruptcy and the day of accounting was upon them. The Messiah was coming and He had an ax in his hand, ready to cut down the withered tree of a corrupt and wayward establishment and plant the true Kingdom of God. The Messiah was coming with the empowering Spirit of God and the relentless fire of truth.

John was the bridge between the Old Testament day of the prophet and the New Testament day of the Kingdom of God, the rule of the Messiah. John's coming was necessary for a few reasons.

1. It fulfilled prophecy. God always keeps His promises. Jesus couldn't start His job until John did his.

2. It demonstrates for us the attitude that we should have when we are proclaiming the message of Jesus. John modeled three things that we should imitate. First, he was not afraid to speak the message boldly and directly. Second, he was not afraid to be falsely accused, imprisoned, and ultimately killed for speaking the truth. Third, he realized that the message was not about him. He was willing to fade away from the public arena in order to people to focus on Jesus.

3. He reminds us all that the real, bottom line message of Jesus is to repent because the Kingdom of God is at hand. We will explore that more next session.

Kid's Questions

Draw a picture of what you think John the Baptist looked like.

Why do you think John was so different from the average person?

Was John afraid to speak the truth about Jesus to everyone?

What happened to John as a result of his courageous preaching?

Even though this may be a scary topic, we all need to ask ourselves, "Would I be willing to be made fun of, or arrested, or even killed for the truth of Jesus?"

Spend some time talking about the kind of challenges we face from people who don't like our message.

Lesson 5

- Matthew 3:13-17
- Matthew 4:1-11
- Matthew 4:18-22
- Mark 1:9-20
- Luke 3:21-22
- Luke 4:1-13
- John 1:35-51

Study Questions

What happened when Jesus was baptized?

Who led Jesus into the wilderness to be tempted? (read carefully)

How did Jesus defeat the temptations that were brought to Him?

What did it cost the disciples to follow Jesus?

Food for Thought

There are two things we need to look at today. First we need to see the preparation that Jesus went through before He started His work. Then we need to see what happened when Jesus called His first followers.

Water and Fire

Today we read that Jesus was baptized by water, but He was also baptized by fire. The word "baptism" means to be dipped into a liquid until the point of transformation. Quite literally, a cucumber is baptized to become a pickle. The raw vegetable is soaked in vinegar until the constitution of the vegetable is unalterably transformed into the state of being a pickle.

The key word here is transformation. Jesus encountered two transforming events. He entered into the waters of baptism and He passed through the fires of temptation. As we discussed yesterday, water baptism was a Jewish custom that represented a ceremonial cleansing — a washing of mind, spirit, and body. It demonstrated that the individual was ready to "come clean" with God and get on the right track. It was a symbol of repentance — the process of turning away from one way of thinking and acting and moving toward a new way of thinking and acting. By being baptized, Jesus was accomplishing two things.

1. He was demonstrating to the world the first step of entering into the kingdom that He was going to establish. Unless a person decides to turn away from their self-rule and self-absorption, pursuing the things that don't last, they will never be able to move toward the life and joy that Jesus' kingdom has to offer.

2. He was repenting. Are your theological red flags going up? How could Jesus repent? He didn't sin. True, Jesus didn't sin. However, He had lived the past 30 years of His life in obscure normalcy. He was the son of a carpenter. He was the member of the village of Nazareth. He was just a common Joe who blended into the crowd. Now, He was turning away from the comfortable, common life, and taking on the task for which He was sent. By being baptized He was decisively repenting — turning in a new direction — and stepping into active ministry. At that moment we see the synergy of the Trinity — the Father, the Son, and the Holy Spirit — focusing its purpose of establishing its kingdom on earth.

Once He had decisively begun His movement toward a purposeful life it was time for a deeper form of baptism. He had to pass through the fire of temptation. When a goldsmith wants to create pure gold he places the gold into a crucible and subjects it to enormous amounts of heat. The heat separates the pure gold from the impurities, allowing them to be removed and thrown away.

Here are some observations about Jesus' temptation:

1. He had to enter the desert. If you study the Bible you will discover that anytime God intends to use someone to accomplish His work He leads that person into a time of desert living. In the desert we are stripped of all the creature comforts. We are faced with the reality of our own mortality and the prospect of eternity. If you are experiencing a difficult season in your life, it may be that God is preparing you for something of significance for Him.

2. He was attacked in His areas of potential weakness. Satan, the accuser, is very good at knowing where we are weak. Jesus had not eaten in 40 days, so He was extremely hungry. Satan Hit him in the belly, "Don't you want a little bread?" Jesus was the Lord of all Heaven and had power at His fingertips. These were His natural abilities. God's plan was for Jesus to give up that authority in order to establish His Kingdom, so Satan hit him in the area of pride. "Come on Jesus, strut your stuff and call the angels." God's plan was for Jesus to suffer in order to establish His kingdom and take away Satan's dominion. The path of pain was difficult, so Satan hit Him in the area of comfort. "Come on Jesus, you don't have to suffer, just bow to me now and I'll give it to you...the easy way." Isn't this where we get hit every day — our belly, our pride, and our comfort?

3. He was victorious. The fire of temptation exposed the reality that there was no impurity in Jesus' heart. Had he not gone through that fire, we would not have known if He was the one, the pure one who is able to go the distance and deliver His people from the power of oppression.

The truth is that every one of us must pass through these same two baptisms. Jesus only had to do it once. After all, He was the ONE. Our process, however, takes a little longer. We have all kinds of junk in our hearts that needs to be cleaned up and burned out. As we grow spiritually we will experience new and deeper seasons of water and fire. The Holy Spirit will point out different aspects of our lives and say, "It's time to baptize that area now. Repent from it and wash it away." Then at other times He will lead us into times of spiritual dryness and testing in order to refine our purpose and resolve.

While God's process of refinement for us never stops, it does begin. There does come a point where each one of us is faced with the choice: "Will you move in this direction or not?" If you have not yet made the first step, perhaps it is time.

Calling the Crew

We end our session reading the story of the first round of followers that Jesus called. This is an appropriate thought to follow up the previous section on baptism. Notice what happened when Jesus called these men. They did not just say, "Yes, Jesus, we agree that you are the Messiah. Hope you have a great ministry." Instead, they dropped their nets and followed Him. For these men their nets represented their very livelihood. They were fishermen. Without nets how would they provide for their needs? When Jesus called them, they left everything they knew to be safe and secure and walked with Him.

Coming to the end of this first session perhaps you have noticed that encountering the story of Jesus is not just a casual pastime. From the outset we are confronted with Jesus. He does not mess around. Jesus calls us to Him. He calls us to commitment, dedication, and purpose. Why? Because He wants to be a task-master and make our lives miserable? No. He invites us to this high calling because He has His eyes fixed on what is real. He knows that if we are willing to take Him up on the invitation and follow Him along the way, that He will lead us to places of love, joy, and truth that we never dreamed possible in our limited experiences. I hope that you are ready to follow Him along the rest of this journey.

Kid's Questions

Today we are going to do a fun experiment that will spill into the weekend.

Begin with a raw egg.

Pour enough vinegar into a jar to completely cover the egg.

Make sure the egg stays submerged in the vinegar.

Let it sit for 24 hours.

Tomorrow night, take out the egg from the vinegar and notice any changes that have taken place. Hold the egg about a foot off a hard floor. Drop it and see what happens.

In the story today we see that Jesus was baptized. Read the section of the grown-ups devotional that explains what that word means.

Being baptized is a symbol that you are ready to give your life to Jesus and follow in His footsteps. Talk to your parents about whether you are ready to be baptized.

Chapter 1 - Session1: The Message of the Kingdom

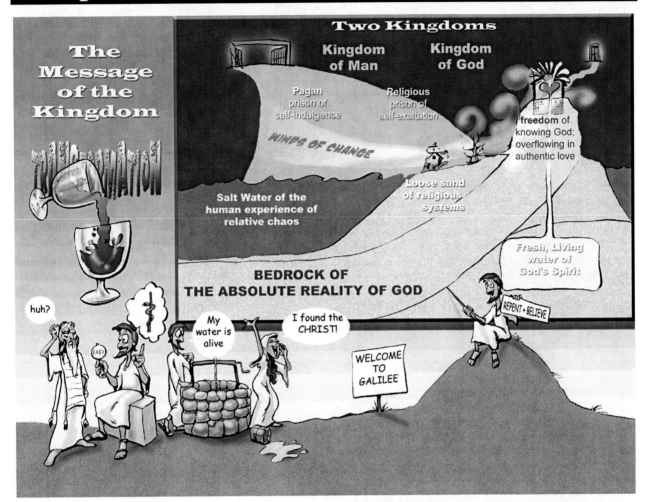

Introduction

Extreme Makeover: Kingdom Edition

In the illustration this session you see that there are two things going on. Along the left we see the storyline. In the upper right is the message.

The Story Line

John begins his story of Jesus' ministry with a scene at a wedding party. After much coaxing by His mother, Jesus turns water into wine. This miracle sets the stage for the entire story and burns an image into our minds that describes what Jesus' message and His kingdom is all about. In a word, it's about transformation. Jesus can turn simple, ordinary water into the choicest wine. He can turn dried up, sin-scorched hearts into thriving fountains of life-giving water. He can turn broken dreams into fulfilling realities. As Jesus begins preaching to the people of Israel and inviting them into the Kingdom of God He is announcing His plan to renovate the hearts of his people and make them brand new.

The next two scenes show an interesting contrast. First, Jesus tries to explain the renovation project to the wisest of the wise. He sits down with Nicodemus, a prestigious teacher of the law and leader of Israel and explains that it requires a new birth, a complete spiritual overhaul to be able to enter the kingdom of God. All this wise man can say is, "huh?"

Next, Jesus encounters the lowest of the low. He runs into a Samaritan woman living in adultery.

19

In those days it doesn't get much lower on the socio-economic scale than that. Jesus explains the renovation project to her, describing how it requires drinking from the well of Living Water and spiritual renewal to enter the Kingdom. This woman caught onto it and saw that Jesus could actually make her life new. She got so excited she told the whole town.

These two stories provide a foreshadowing of coming events. The "wise" of Israel will reject the invitation to the Kingdom. Only the outcast will be willing to tap into the reality of Jesus' life-giving water.

The Message

In our last three lessons, we will sit at Jesus' feet and hear the message of the Kingdom as He delivers the Sermon on the Mount (Matthew's version) and the Sermon on the Level Place (Luke's version). These two messages are a primer to the basic structure of the Kingdom of God. As you can see in the illustration, Jesus contrasts two Kingdoms: the Kingdom of Man and the Kingdom of God. In the Kingdom of Man there are two types. On the one side is the "pagan" kingdom that is based upon human experience. The actual experience of daily human existence is one of chaos. In our world we hear people refer to it as relativism and the absence of any foundational anchor point for "truth." They believe that life is chaotic and is the byproduct of chaotic happenstance. At one very practical level, they are right. Much of the human experience is like living in a constant state of flux, being blown here and there by the winds of change and the power struggles of self-indulgent humans.

On the other side is the "religious" Kingdom of Man. Here we see humans trying to make sense out of the chaos and bring order to it by constructing an externally focused set of rules and regulations that will insure their place in eternity. Religion is a false foundation and is like building a house on sand. It looks good on the outside, but it has nothing of true substance upon which to withstand the chaotic blowing of the wind. It is a bad tree with no roots that cannot produce good fruit.

Jesus came to cut through all the malarkey. He came to tell the world that there is, in fact, a bedrock of absolute truth. That truth, however, is not found in our religious systems. The truth is the reality of God — the reality of a God that is so much deeper, so much more vast and real than any puny theology can hold. It is the reality of a God who is so real that He is the essence behind the seeming chaos of life. There couldn't even be a chaotic sea of human experience if there wasn't a solid basin beneath it in which to contain it.

The truth of the Kingdom of God is like an outcropping of bedrock that pushes through the rubble of religiosity and holds within it the life-giving spring of living water that flows from the Spirit of God. To reach the summit is not an easy climb. It's behind a narrow gate. It's not a beach party, but a mountain expedition of discipline and truth. Yet, it is real. To follow the way of Jesus is to cut through the smoke-blowing hoopla of ritual and prestige, to bypass the mind-numbing intoxication of self-indulgence, and get to the heart of God's selfless truth and love. To follow Jesus is to anchor deeply into the eternal, mysterious, reality of God, be changed from the inside out, and to overflow with authentic love. It is being a good tree, rooted in good soil, to produce good fruit. It is to be transformed from the inside out.

This is the message that Jesus was presenting to His people. We will see that most people rejected it. However, the offer still stands. This is the message of the Kingdom of God. It is open for all who willingly receive it. Simply put, Jesus' message could be boiled down to this simple statement, "The Kingdom of God is here, repent and believe the Good News." That was the message then, and it is the message now.

Lesson 1

- John 2
- John 3:1-21

Study Questions

What impact did the miracle at the wedding have on Jesus' disciples?

Why was Jesus upset at the temple? What did He do about it? How do these actions match up with your image of Jesus?

To what does Jesus compare the Spirit and those born of the Spirit? Why?

According to John 3:17, what was the purpose for the Son's coming to the world?

What is required to receive what the Son has to offer?

Food for Thought

Extreme Makeover

Today we read about three events that, according to John's version, begin Jesus' ministry. He turned water into wine, thrashed the temple, and taught a teacher about truth. In all of these events there is a common theme...Jesus came to make some serious changes.

For the Jews, Jerusalem had been the center of religious and political life. One thousand years earlier, King David established it as the seat of royal power. King Solomon had built his magnificent temple there to replace the mobile tabernacle and to establish this city as the center of religious life. It is appropriate, then, that Jesus began His mission in Jerusalem. This "holy city" had fallen into a trap that seems to be a pattern in human history — as soon as you anchor down God's presence, centralize the authority over His people, and systematize worship of Him, things go amuck. The people of Jerusalem had forgotten that God's relationship with Abraham was built on just that, a dynamic relationship based on faith and power. They had forgotten that God led Moses with a pillar of cloud and fire and that the Law was intended to establish a code of ethics that would lead to a transformed heart. By the time Jesus got there, 1,400 years later, the Law had become nothing more than a set of rules used to control the lower classes and manipulate God into dispensing blessing. The temple had become a mockery of God and the teachers didn't know who God was anymore.

For one thousand years God had been struggling with His people, sending them prophets to teach them the truth, allowing them to be disciplined by their own bad choices, and waiting patiently for His people to return to His heart. Now Jesus had come to set things right. He came to make things new. He came to set the religious system upside down.

When Jesus sat down with Nicodemus He spelled it out clearly. He said that it's not about what you do on the outside that matters; it's about who you are on the inside. The people, including Jews, were in the dark. They needed the light of Jesus, the light of the truth of God's reality to shine on them.

Here are some observations about Jesus' message to Nicodemus.

1. **Jesus didn't come to condemn, He came to invite.** His wasn't a mission of saying, "You are dirty, rotten sinners; why don't you

get right so God can love you?" Rather, He said, "You are lost in the woods and in the dark. God loves you so much that He sent me to shine the light so you can find your way home." Do you see the difference in these two approaches? One is motivated by self-righteous vindication; the other is motivated by selfless love. What is your attitude toward people who have not yet experienced the love of God?

2. **God's truth is not containable.** That's what the problem was with Nicodemus' theology. It was airtight. He had all the answers. There were no more questions. He had created a box, concretized by the temple itself, and placed God in it. Jesus said that God's truth is like the wind. You can't see it, but you can see the evidence of it when it is working. You can't predict it or control it. You can only yield to it and harness its power.

As inheritors of two thousand years of Christian traditions and theological boxes, perhaps it would do us well to listen to this carpenter's son from Nazareth with fresh ears and allow him to examine the physical boxes and religious systems we have built for him.

Kid's Questions

Get a jar, like a peanut butter jar. Now get your pillow. Try to stuff your pillow into the jar (make sure it's clean first, OK?)

Were you able to get the pillow in there? Why?

Were you able to get any part of the pillow in there?

Was the part of the pillow you got into the jar 100% your pillow? Was the part of the pillow you got in the jar 100% of your entire pillow?

Imagine that the jar is like the human mind and the pillow represents God. For a puny human to try to understand the infinite God is like trying to stuff you pillow into the jar. You can't do it. You can get some of it in there, and the part that you get in there is really pillow, but there is no way you can get it all in there.

When Jesus was talking to Nicodemus he compared God to the wind. You can't see the wind or catch the wind, but it is real and powerful. The problem Nicodemus had was that he thought he could completely understand and predict God. He thought he had the whole pillow in the jar.

Let's remember that the things we know about God are true and accurate and trustworthy, — from the Bible — but that we don't and can't know everything about God. We get to spend the rest of our lives and the rest of eternity learning more and more about the love of God. Isn't that great!

Lesson 2

- John 4:1-54
- Mark 1: 14-15, 35-39
- Matthew 4:12-17, 23-25

Study Questions

What did Jesus offer to the woman at the well?

What was her response?

In John 4:26, what does Jesus claim to be?

In John 4:34-38, what attitude does Jesus have toward the people in the village?

According to Matthew 4:17 and Mark 1:15, what is the basic message of Jesus? Restate this message in your own words.

Food for Thought

Living Water

Today we see a wonderful example of a "truth encounter." On His way to Galilee, Jesus passes through Samaria and stops for a drink of water. To grasp the full weight of this story it is important to know a little bit about the history of the Jewish/Samaritan relationship. Basically, the citizens of Judea thought that the citizens of Samaria were dogs. They were half-breed mutts that God would not even give the time of day; so why should they? This deep-set prejudice stemmed from the days of the divided Kingdom and the fall of the Northern Kingdom of Israel 700 years earlier. (See 2 Kings for the details.) The Kingdom of Israel was the same plot of real estate that was called Samaria in Jesus' day. When the Assyrian Empire destroyed Israel, they took the Israelites and forced them to intermarry with their pagan neighbors, thus polluting the bloodlines and destroying the 10 tribes of Israel forever. When the Judeans saw the Samaritans it reminded them of the disgrace of their past. They blamed the Samaritans for God's punishment on them and accused them of being heretics because they did not worship God at the temple.

In light of that, it was not just a big deal that Jesus was talking to a woman in public. It also wasn't just a big deal that Jesus was talking to a Samaritan woman. Those were both big deals, but the really big deal was that Jesus was in Samaria at all. Most Jews hated the Samaritans so much that when they wanted to travel north to their Jewish brothers in Galilee, they would cross over the Jordan to the east side, travel north along the east bank, and cross over at the mouth of the Sea of Galilee, just to avoid that territory.

Imagine His disciple's thoughts when He announced their departure for Galilee and headed straight north. "No, master, you must have your bearings wrong. You're heading into...that place." "I know. Do you have a problem with that?" "Oh no...of course...not."

Let's face it, for many of us sharing the message of hope with people is a scary prospect. Jesus' conversation can serve as a great example of how to have truth encounters with people. Here are some key points to keep in mind:

1. **Jesus intentionally broke out of the established comfort zone.** As we have already discussed, Jesus wasn't supposed to be there. How often are we willing to talk and take an alternate path in our daily lives in the hopes that we might encounter someone with whom we could share the message of hope?

2. **He began with a common point of interest.** They were standing next to a well. She had a bucket. To ask for a drink was a natural question. God is evident in everything around us. Talking about the weather, the war, the victorious sports teams, these are all places where people are willing to start. Open up a conversation about anything. If you are open to it, and have an open heart, you may be surprised how quickly people are willing to discuss the mysteries of life.

3. **He presents the truth quickly.** In this story Jesus moves quickly from "give Me physical water" to "I can give you spiritual water." He does not beat around the bush and waste too much time on building common ground. Why? Probably because He was so convinced that the information He was about to present to her was the truth and that she desperately needed it.

4. **He cuts to the chase.** Very quickly Jesus got to the heart of the matter: He talked about her sin problem. This wasn't a theological discussion; this was a heart-condition discussion. This woman was trapped in a lifestyle of bad relationships with men. We don't know if she was a prostitute, a sexual addict, or co-dependent with abusive men. Whatever the reason, she had a long line of failed marriages and was currently "living in sin." What she needed was a spiritual bath. She was thirsty with a soul-level thirst that was not being satisfied by chasing fulfillment with men. She needed to feel the freedom that comes only after a good scrub with the fresh water of God's grace and forgiveness.

5. **He is not derailed by attempts at distraction.** Ironically, people in need of a scrub are often not readily willing to receive a free bath. Perhaps they don't trust that there is such a thing as a free drink of living water. Perhaps they don't want to let go of their cherished sin. Most often, when we get to the heart of the matter, people will send up a smokescreen and try to deflect the heat of the truth. The woman does just that by throwing the old, "Where should I worship?" tactic. This would be like a person throwing the 500-year-old Protestant/Catholic, or baptism debate in your face when you start talking about Jesus. Learn this lesson well. Jesus did not get sucked into that quagmire of worthless argument. He simply said, "Wrong question. It's not about where, it's about how. Now, let's get back on task, shall we?" When people ask those kinds of questions 99% of the time they are trying to get out from under the spotlight of God's truth.

6. **He oozes with compassion.** When His disciples saw that Jesus was involved in a conversation with a Samaritan woman, they quickly came to "rescue" Him. "No," He said, "my food is to do the will of Him who sent me. Can't you see that we are standing in a ripened field? I love these people so much that I can't walk away until they are clean."

Kid's Questions

Tell about a time when you were really thirsty.

How would you have felt in that moment if someone came up to you and said that they had a nice big bottle of cold water?

Jesus told the woman at the well that He had water for her to drink that would make it so she would never be thirsty again. What was He talking about?

Get two glasses. Label one glass "Living Water" and the other glass "Worldly Water."

Now fill the glass labeled "Living Water" with fresh cold water.

Fill the glass labeled "Worldly Water" with lukewarm water and stir in two tablespoons of table salt.

When you look at the water, do they look the same?

Now, taste the water. Do they taste the same?

These two cups are a reminder for us that there are two choices set before us every day. We can either drink from the cup that Jesus offers or from the cup that the world offers. Which will you choose today?

Lesson 3

- Matthew 5:1-6:15

Study Questions

When Jesus sat down on the mountainside, to whom was He speaking?

Make a list of the kinds of people that Jesus considered blessed.

What was Jesus' attitude toward the Law of Moses?

Make a chart that has two columns. On one side write, "you have heard that it was said..." on the other side write, "but I say to you." List these contrasts as you read through chapter 5.

What does God require? (Matthew 5:48)

Food for Thought

The Kingdom Message

For the rest of this session we will be looking smack into the heart of the message that Jesus brought to the world. Many times, when people think of Jesus, their thoughts are dominated by His execution and subsequent resurrection. While these events are obviously extremely important, they are not the dominant features of the Gospel stories. Jesus didn't come just to die. Jesus came to live and to teach us how to live the life that we were intended to live.

The lessons found in Matthew's Sermon on the Mount and Luke's sermon on the level place can be thought of as "the best of" anthology of Jesus' teaching. Here, in this early phase of Jesus' ministry, while He was extending the invitation of the Kingdom to the people of Israel, these Gospel writers packaged His teaching into a concise primer on the true Kingdom of God.

As Jesus sat down to deliver this message, it's as if He is a new Moses coming down from the mountain with the Law in His hand. This message could have been titled "Rules for Radicals" or, "How to Fly Right Side Up in the World When Religion Has Turned You Upside Down." He was not doing away with the Law of Moses; He was reminding the people what the Law of Moses was truly all about. He said that He did not come to abolish the Law, but to fulfill it. You see, the law was designed to capture the hearts of the people and change them, maturing them to a point that they would not need the law, but behave like God would, reflecting His nature of love. Instead, the law became externalized, ritualized, and petrified. Jesus came to fulfill the law by exemplifying a heart of absolute love that works from the inside out.

The sermon can be divided into two parts.

1. How to Be
2. How to Do

We will look at part one today and part two next time.

Part 1: How to Be

vv. 3-12 The first section of the message has the repetitive phrase "Blessed are the..." This has been referred to as the beatitudes for many years, literally meaning "supreme blessedness or happiness." For our purposes we could think of these as the BE-attitudes. How should we *be* if we are in the Kingdom of God? We should be poor in spirit, sorrowful, meek, hungry for righteousness, merciful, pure in heart, peacemakers, and persecuted for righteousness. That's how.

vv. 13-16 Jesus goes on to say that we should be salt and light in the world; being, by our very nature, agents of preservation and hope for a world that is rotting and dark.

vv. 17-20 After opening with bold BEING statements, it's as if Jesus is answering this unspoken challenge, "Yes, Jesus, but what does this have to do with the Law of Moses? We thought that keeping the law is what was required to be included in the Kingdom." His answer, "I'm not questioning the law, I'm intensifying it. I'm deepening it. I'm getting to the heart of it. Here let me explain to you what the Law of God really requires of you..."

vv. 21-47 It's not about the external act of murder; it's about harboring hate *in your heart*. It's not about the external act of adultery; it's about lust *in your heart*. It's not about a wife pleasing a husband; it's about a husband loving his wife with *his whole heart*. It's not about swearing on this or that with verbal words; it's about being a truthful person *to the core of your heart*. It's not about retaliation; it's about *unconditional love*.

In a nutshell, what is required of you to enter into the Kingdom of God is...perfection. **Perfection?!?!** What does He mean? How could anyone possibly enter into the Kingdom of God if we are to be perfect? No one is perfect!

There are two ways we should look at this.

1. You're right; you can't be perfect. That's the point. There is no way you can earn your way into the Kingdom of God through external behaviors of "goodness." What we need is a heart transformation from the inside out. We need the kind of heart surgery that only the Holy Spirit can perform in us when we yield control and let Him do His business with us.

2. The word translated 'perfect' is the Greek word 'telios'. It means having the sense of being brought to a place of completion, having a sense of maturity and fullness; of consummate human integrity and virtue. In other words, to be telios is to be the opposite of hypocritical. It is to be the same on the inside as you are on the outside. What God wants is a heart that is authentically seeking after his heart and not worried about performing a religious dog and pony show to try to convince the world that it is "good." God wants more than "goodness"; He wants "telios."

The question for today is, "Where is the Law for you today?" Is your concept of God all about pleasing Him with an external performance, hoping you can score high enough to be considered "good" Or, is the law of Jesus seeping past the tough exterior and, by God's grace, changing you from the inside out?

Kid's Questions

When you hear the word "perfect," what do you think of?

Do you think that you could ever be perfect?

When you hear the word "mature," what do you think of?

Do you think that you will ever become a mature adult? Is it possible?

Jesus said that we are to be perfect. What do you think of that? The Greek word can also be translated "mature." That is what Jesus wants from you. He wants you to grow to become a mature adult.

What are some things that you need to be doing in your life as a kid, to prepare for becoming mature?

Lesson 4

• Matthew 6:16-7:29

Study Questions

What are the three activities that Jesus describes in Matthew 6:1-18? In what manner are those activities to be practiced?

Draw a square around the times Jesus uses the phrase "do not." Make a list of the things we are not to do.

What are we to do according to Matthew 6:33?

What two analogies does Jesus use to describe the contrast between those who follow His words and those who do not? What is the point of these two analogies?

Food for Thought

Part 2: What to do

Today we look at the second half of the Kingdom message. Last time Jesus taught us how to be. Today He talks about what that being looks like in practice.

There are 3 Do's and 3 Don'ts

3 Do's

1.   Do Giving...in secret.

2.   Do Prayer...in secret.

3.   Do Fasting...in secret.

Are you detecting a theme here? Here's what's going on. The religious system of the Jews considered these three disciplines — giving alms to the poor, prayer, and fasting — to be very valuable for the "spiritual" life. Indeed they are. However, over time these disciplines had become distorted and had lost their original intent. "Religious" people had entered into two dangerous attitudes. First, they believed that their ability to practice the spiritual disciplines elevated them to a higher status than "those people" who were obviously cursed by God because of their poverty, sickness, and ignorance. Second, they believed that their practice of the disciplines won them favor in the sight of God. As a result of these attitudes they had turned the spiritual disciplines into a public performance, standing in the street, blowing trumpets to announce to everyone that they were giving, praying and fasting.

Jesus said, "Hold on just a minute. The Kingdom of God is about your heart. It's about the hidden person that no one can see but you and God. God doesn't care how well you can put on a show and impress other people. He sees right to the core of your being. You can't fool Him, so stop trying. The spiritual disciplines are very important. Giving to the poor helps you remember that all riches belong to God and you are simply a steward of them. Praying is vital because we need to have an intimate relationship with the Father and lover of our souls. We need to be open and honest with Him and daily keep our minds focused on His Kingdom and His plan. Fasting is important because it helps us remember that there is more to life than filling our bellies and physical contentment. It clears our minds and our bodies for sharper and more efficient living. These things are good, but if they get distorted into becoming some sort of spiritual one-upsmanship, then they lose all of their potency and actually become toxic to your soul. In light of all that, introduce a new discipline to the mix. Try practicing the discipline of silence and keep your spiritual exercises to yourself. Starve your pride and don't allow people to see what you are doing. That way you will know that your motivation is truly to please and love God, not to be revered by other people."

Good advice.

3 Don'ts

1. Don't horde wealth...it's going to burn anyway. What Jesus is really talking about here is focus. Seek first God's Kingdom and the rest will fall into place. If your eyes are focused on gaining material security — bad eyes filling the body with darkness — then you will miss the light of God's reality which brings truth and joy. Unfortunately, many people in our culture bow to the god of money everyday. We either have it and are consumed with trying to protect it, or we don't have it and are consumed with trying to get it to dig ourselves out of the pit of debt that we have dug. If we stop worrying about the finances, focus on fulfilling God's plan and the passion He has placed in us, and be good stewards of what He provides, then our lives will be full of light and fulfillment.

2. Don't worry...you aren't in control anyway. It has been said that worry is being preoccupied with things that you cannot control because if you could control them you would have already changed them to be the way you want them to be and would have no need to worry. The key to not worrying is to realize that you can't control it, to acknowledge that God is in control, to focus on changing the things that you can control (like your attitudes), allow God to be in control, and trust that He has your best interest in mind. Hey, if He cares enough for little birds and a bunch of grass, don't you think He notices the needs that you have? Give it up!

3. Don't judge...you can't change people anyway. As humans we seem to be consumed with the pastime of trying to change others. Why can't my husband be more like this? Why can't my children be more like that? Why can't our government do more of this? Why can't my church stop doing that? There is one simple reason why we do this. It is much easier to look at someone else's problems than it is to look into the mirror of God's truth and see one's self. Imagine what would happen if every person stopped trying to change everyone else and got serious about letting God change them. If that happened then everyone would be transformed from the inside out. We would be filled up with God's love and begin to overflow into the lives of everyone. Eventually everyone else would be basking in the life-giving, life-transforming grace of God and the things we were trying to change in the other person would either be washed away or exposed to us as not the sin we thought it was. Either way, it isn't our job to change them; it's God's.

Have you ever wondered what the whole thing about the dogs and pigs is all about? In the context of not judging others it seems that Jesus is saying, "Don't waste your time trying to change dogs and pigs (people resistant to the truth) into saints. You can't do it. Besides, it's not your job anyway. Spend your time being transformed by God and spilling into areas that He has asked you to spill. This ties into the parable of the sower that we will read about later. Some people are hard soil, they are dogs and pigs, and do not want to hear the truth. That's OK; let God deal with them while focusing on cultivating and harvesting the good soil."

The Big Do (A Mountain Do, perhaps?)

In section one, Jesus summarized the BE-Attitudes with a simple phrase; be perfect. Today He summarizes the Do section with another simple phrase. "Do to others as you would have them do to you." It's that simple. If you want to be loved, then love others. If you want to be treated fairly, then be fair. If you want respect, then respect others. The list goes on and on. If we could just live by this "Golden Rule" then things would turn around in our world.

The Invitation to the Kingdom

Now that Jesus has spelled out the nature of God's Kingdom, He throws open the doors and invites everyone to come in. He tells us that entering the Kingdom is as easy as saying, "Please." Ask for it; seek it out; knock on the door. He is waiting and ready to receive anyone who wants to drink deeply from this fountain of truth and ultimate reality.

Be warned, however, that the door He will open is not an easy one. It is a narrow gate. It's not that He has made a lot of religious hoops for you to jump through in order to please God. This doesn't mean that Jesus is trying to weed out everybody and only wants a few to be in His elite club. It's not that kind of narrowness. No, when Jesus speaks of the narrow gate He is acknowledging the fact that the Kingdom of Man is incredibly intoxicating and a difficult force from which to break free. The pervasive current of human systems is so strong that it seems like it is the only reality. It is hard to break away from pride, self-indulgence, self-glory, power, fame, riches, physical pleasure, and the safety of comfort. While those things are ultimately a lie and a shadow of the truth, they are the broad gate and the easy path that takes no effort to follow. Most people may look at the narrow gate and the loving eyes of Jesus as they float by on the lazy river of complacency, but they are too intoxicated by their own baggage to reach out for Him. Whoever does, He will snatch them up and pull them out of the muck in a heartbeat.

The Kingdom of God, the very heart of the absolute reality of the eternal creator, is a reality of truth, love, mystery, and adventure. It will not be easy, but it is real. It is the only bedrock into which we can anchor our hearts that will enable us to withstand the raging storms of our chaotic human existence. The passage is free. The door stands open. You simply must choose to enter.

Kid's Questions

Let's do a little experiment. You will need two people for the experiment, person A and person B.

Give an object to A. It should be something soft that won't break, like a teddy bear.

Person A really loves the bear. Pretend like you love it.

Have B come up and grab the bear from A's hand and take it to the other side of the room.

How does A feel? Why?

Have A stomp over to B and slap A (not for real, just pretend)

How does B feel? Why?

Now, reset the stage so that A has the bear back and is loving it. Have B come up to A and say, "that is a very nice bear, may I see it for a moment?"

How does A feel? Why?

This is a simple exercise, but it demonstrates one of the most important principles that Jesus ever taught. He said that we should do to others the way we want others to do to us. Many people have called this the Golden Rule.

If B wanted to share and didn't want to get slapped, B should not have grabbed. It's that simple.

Spend some time writing a list of the ways that you like people to treat you. Now, circle every one that is a description of how you typically treat other people. One key to living in God's Kingdom is getting everything on your list circled. The way to be treated nicely is to treat others nicely.

Lesson 5

- Mark 4:21-23
- Luke 8:16-18
- Luke 6:17-49

Study Questions

Compare Matthew 5:3-10 with Luke 6:20-26. What is similar; what is different?

In Luke 6:31 we read what has been called the "golden rule." In vv. 32-38 Jesus gives examples of this rule in action. Restate His explanation in your own words.

According to Luke 6:45, what is the real measure of a man's "goodness"?

Food for Thought

Who's right?

Today we see Luke's version of the Kingdom message. At this point it would be good to address the issue of the differences between the Gospels. Many skeptics point to apparent discrepancies (like the fact that Matthew says the sermon was on a mountain and Luke says it was on a level place) as proof that the Bible is inaccurate and therefore an unreliable source. There are two kinds of defense against this kind of accusation.

The first defense is to see that both Gospels are literally correct, but are taking a different angle on the story. The main objective of this approach is to maintain the integrity of the accuracy of the Gospel record in its literal representation of the events as they happened, as if it were a video tape or a transcript of the event. Let's use the sermon we are studying as an example. Matthew says the sermon was delivered on a mountainside, but Luke said it was delivered from a level place. Proponents of the first type of defense would say that the level place that Luke refers to is actually a level place on the mountainside, thereby making both Gospel writers accurate.

The skeptic's rebuttal to this would be the fact that, even if you can explain the location issue, there is still great disparity between the words recorded by Matthew and Luke. Specifically, Luke includes a whole section on the "woes" after the list of the "blessed" while Matthew doesn't even mention it. Also, huge sections of the sermon are missing from Luke. Don't worry; there is another, equally valid explanation.

The second type of defense is to recognize that the individual authors were not as interested in accurate details as we would be in the modern era, but were more interested in major themes. In the example of our sermons at hand, the argument would be that neither of these sermons was a specific event that happened only one time. Both Matthew and Luke used the fact that Jesus preached all the time and in many different places as a background setting for the compilation of a message that represented the essential teaching of His early ministry. The Sermon on the Mount and the sermon on the level place are Matthew and Luke's attempt to distill and communicate the quintessential Jesus — His bare bones message of the Kingdom of God. It doesn't really matter if it was on a mountainside or on a level place. It doesn't matter if He said the blessed phrases only, or followed them up with the "woes." The fact is that He probably said both things a lot of times and in a lot of different ways. When

Matthew sifted all of Jesus' teachings through his own filter, the 'woes' slipped through. Luke's filter caught the woes and made them part of the essential package.

Both defenses have strong value. The truth is that they both are correct in different areas of the Gospels. The most important thing to remember, and the reason we are even talking about it in the first place, is to know that there is no validity to the arguments of the skeptics saying that the Gospels are not accurate and therefore unreliable. When the Gospels were written they were 100% accurate according to the common standards of biographies in the first century.

Rich beware

We need to set one thing straight; Luke had an agenda about the rich. I'm not saying that he is misrepresenting Jesus by any means, nor am I saying that the other writers didn't share his perspective on Jesus' attitude toward the wealthy; I'm simply pointing out that Luke was obviously passionate about this aspect of Jesus' message. As you read through the story over the next few weeks, and are comparing the four Gospels, keep your eye out for this bias in Luke's accounts and see if I'm correct in my assessment.

We would do well to tune into Luke's frequency on this topic. Notice how he emphasizes it in his version of the Kingdom Message. He is different than Matthew. Matthew focuses more on the positive side, emphasizing who is blessed, and leaving the opposites out...not off the hook, just subtly unmentioned. Not Luke. He just blurts it out. Blessed are the poor. Notice that he does not say 'poor in spirit,' leaving the possibility for the rich to spiritualize this phrase and make it more about an attitude than an economic condition. Nope. Luke says, "Blessed are the poor and woe to the rich." BAM! In your face, no holds barred. "Woe to the well-fed, the "happy," and the well thought of. You guys are no better than the ear-tickling false prophets in the Old Testament."

The brashness and hard truth of Luke's direct approach cuts quick and stings. If you are a middle- or upper-class North American reading this (as I am), there should be a cold shiver running down our spines. It should make us squirm in our seats. Here we sit in our comfy chairs, under the protection of a solid roof over our heads, with a well-stocked refrigerator in the kitchen, and hot water in our faucets. We get frustrated when the on/off button on our remote doesn't work and we have to walk across the room to turn on the TV. We get angry when our landscaper misses a section of our manicured lawn. We get mean when the person in front of us has 21 items in the

20 items or less line at the grocery store. All the while there are billions of people — men, women, and children — who will go to sleep tonight on the hard ground, unfed, ridden with disease, and unloved.

Does that sound like a heavy-handed guilt trip? Yup. I'm only expressing the attitudes of Luke. To say "Woe to you!" is not the stuff of diplomacy; those are the words of war. Throughout the Gospels we will see Jesus making a frontal assault on the aristocracy. Why? Is it because it is evil to be rich? No. However, it is extremely difficult to not be lulled into the complacency and false sense of security that comes when the bills are paid and there is excess in the bank.

Does that mean that we should all give everything away and plunge ourselves into abject poverty? Not necessarily. If that is what it will take for you to die to the need for material wealth and security, then yes. Better to starve on the side of the road and be a righteous man than to be separated from God forever because you had a great financial portfolio. Once again, it all comes down to the heart. The truly blessed are those who, in the world's eyes, are poor. They may have nothing to speak of in the arena of money, fame, power, or creature comforts, but they do have plenty of room in their hearts to be filled with the presence of God.

It's all about overflow

It would be easy to read the previous section and get on a high horse about the evil of money and how everyone should give everything away. If we went on this campaign and really sold it well, we might actually get a bunch of people convinced that they need to give away all that they own in order to enter the Kingdom of God. Do you know what the truth of that scenario would be? Many of those people wouldn't be any closer to the Kingdom of God than they were before they gave away their material possessions. Here's why. It isn't about having or not having wealth. It isn't about giving things away or not giving things away. It isn't about praying or not praying. It isn't about going to church or not going to church. Luke sums up the whole deal very well in Luke 6:45, "The good man brings good things out of the good stored up in his heart, and the evil man brings evil things out of the evil stored up in his heart. For out of *the overflow of his heart* his mouth speaks." Doing things does not make you good or bad. What you do is the evidence of who you are. The Kingdom of God is not about establishing external rules of do's and don'ts that turn people into religious clones; it's about allowing the reality of God's Spirit to soak deep into your inner being and transform you from the inside out, creating in you a clean heart that can't help but reflect the nature of God.

Kid's Questions

You will need a tube of toothpaste, or some kind of squeeze dispenser for this exercise.

I'll assume you have a toothpaste tube.

Take a piece of construction paper and cut it to a size that will allow you to wrap it around the toothpaste tube as if the construction paper were a new wrapper. Make a new wrapper, decorating it as if it were a wrapper for a tube of squeezable peanut butter. Have fun with this and make an exciting wrapper. Attach the wrapper to the toothpaste tube and try to cover up any hint that it is a tube of toothpaste.

Now get two pieces of bread and some jam.

Make a peanut butter and jelly sandwich with your tube of squeezable peanut butter.

What? You don't want to? Why not?

Jesus taught us that it doesn't matter what people look like on the outside. They can pretend to be good Christians and do all the right things, but if they are not genuinely loving people on the inside and if God is not truly living in them, they are still a bunch of toothpaste.

Jesus said it is the overflow of a person's heart that reveals who they really are. If there's peanut butter inside, then you will squeeze out peanut butter. If there is toothpaste you will squeeze out toothpaste. If there is bitterness or hatred on the inside, then you will squeeze out bitterness and hatred.

What's inside of you?

Introduction

The Power is in the "Put"ting

In our world of politicians, telemarketers, and televangelists, it is very easy to become jaded and skeptical about the verbal claims that people make. It seems that everyone is a talker. "Our product is the best." "No new taxes." "I'll have that to you by next Thursday, I promise." Yeah right.

Every day we are bombarded by messages from people — some real, some synthetic — who are spewing words to us. We hear the words on the radio as we drive to work. We read the words on the billboards and in the newspaper. We listen to our coworkers and customers bantering and bickering all day. Our friends and family use words to get us to do the things they want us to do. We watch countless hours of verbose dribble on the television. You even read hundreds of words in this study each week.

So what? We don't want to hear words any more. We won't believe someone is the real deal until we see some proof — some real teeth behind their verbiage. That is what this session reading is all about. Last time we read about Jesus saying a lot of words. He laid out a new game plan for God's people and revised the structure of the kingdom of God. Everyone who heard him speak commented that He spoke not as the spineless, wishy-washy teachers they had grown accustomed to, but as one who had authority behind his words. Great. Lots of words. So prove it.

This week we will see that Jesus did not only present the preaching of the kingdom of God, He brought the Power to back up the words. There are five areas in which we see Jesus demonstrate His power. Each lesson's reading will deal with one of them.

1. **Power over sin.** When a paralyzed man crashed the party by being lowered through the ceiling by his friends, he was expecting his body to be made well. Jesus took it a step further. In the presence of the teachers of the law, Jesus claimed to be able to forgive this man's sins — an act only God has the right to do.

2. **Power over demons.** Sprinkled throughout the stories we see demons — evil spirits — popping up in Jesus' path. The irony of these characters is that they are some of the first to proclaim the absolute truth about Jesus' true identity. They knew He was the Son of God and they were powerless against Him. Jesus gave them a gag order knowing that He did not need their kind of publicity.

3. **Power over nature.** While on the boat with His disciples Jesus encountered a fierce storm. No problem. The man who made the storms can simply tell them to calm down.

4. **Power over sickness.** One of the greatest ministries Jesus had was to heal the physical illnesses that He encountered in the people around him. Jesus is not just interested in the "spiritual," He cares deeply about our physical health as well.

5. **Power over traditions.** At the end of the week we will see that Jesus liked to stir the pot and get under the skin of the religious elite. He was constantly challenging the humanly created religious restrictions and pushing the envelope of the traditions of the Jews. This is what eventually got Him in trouble with the leaders.

Where's the Center?

This week there is a significant event that takes place that could be easily overlooked. Jesus officially sets up His base of operation in the city of Capernaum. Choosing this fishing village to launch off the kingdom of God is an example of how simple geography can speak volumes about the heart of Jesus.

If your mission was to come to God's chosen people — the nation of Israel, present yourself as their long-awaited Messiah, and extend to them an invitation to enter into the true Kingdom of God, don't you think you would set up shop in the heart of their kingdom at the center of power — in Jerusalem? Perhaps we would, but that is why we aren't the Messiah. Instead of that plan, Jesus chose a little village on the northern-most border of the Jewish lands. Capernaum was just across the river on the west bank of the Jordan, across from an area occupied by Greek people called Trachonitus and the Decapolis. Just to the north of Capernaum were the regions of Phoenicia and Syria. To the Jews these areas were cesspools of human waste and not even worthy of mention. To Jesus these were fields that were ripe for the harvest.

If you look at a map of Palestine in Jesus' day and compare the location of Jerusalem with the location of Capernaum, you will discover exactly why Jesus set up base camp in this seemingly obscure village. Jerusalem was centrally located in the region of Judea. Capernaum, on the other hand, was centrally located for the entire region, reaching down to Egypt and up past Syria. This location was a foreshadowing and an indication that Jesus was bringing a radical, earth-shattering "shift-of-center" to the Kingdom of God. Jesus did not intend to bring salvation to only the Jews; He came to bring the Kingdom of God to all nations.

Of course He did since this has been the plan from the beginning. God created humanity for the purpose of love. The divisions of nations, tongues, and cultures is a human construct that is the result of sin in the world. From the time of Adam to the time of Abraham, God was continually reaching out to humanity but humanity was continually running away fromHim and worshipping the creation instead of the creator. In an attempt to reach the entire world, God chose one man — Abraham — and made him a promise. He told Abraham that He would make him into a great nation and that through that nation *all nations would be blessed*. (Read about it in Genesis 12.) The nation of Israel was designed to be a conduit of God's love and grace to the entire world, drawing all nations into the loving arms of God. Instead, Israel took their "special" status and interpreted (distorted) it to mean that they were the only people God loved and that the rest of the world could go to hell. This attitude tended to clog up the conduit allowing very little of God's grace to flow out.

Jesus' mission, based in this border village, was to set the record straight, flush the grace pipes, and reorient the Kingdom back to its original mission.

Lesson 1

- Matthew 8:1-4
- Mark 1:40-45
- Luke 5:12-24
- Mark 2:1-12
- Matthew 9:1-8

Study Questions

Why did the friends lower the paralytic through the roof? What were they hoping to accomplish?

What did Jesus offer the man?

By offering this to the man, what was Jesus claiming about Himself?

Why did this cause controversy among the teachers of the law?

Food for Thought

Sickness and sin

In today's reading we meet two men that were healed by Jesus. Notice what happens to each man. The first man is healed from leprosy and Jesus instructs him to go to the temple and perform the necessary sacrifices and ceremonies that are required by the Law of Moses. You can read about these laws in Leviticus 13-14.

In the Old Testament, in the days when Moses led the rag-tag group of newly-freed slaves out of their bondage in Egypt, God gave the people a set of laws. The vast majority of these laws were related to issues of sanitation and health. Back then there was no running water, no antiseptic or antibacterial soap. It was common for killer diseases to ravage through villages and wipe out everyone. God loved His people so much that He gave them laws to keep them safe from disease. Leprosy (or some sort of infectious skin disease in general) was one of the great killers of the ancient world. The Law of Moses stated that lepers were to be kept outside the camp until they either died or were healed. If they were healed they had to come to the Tabernacle, make an offering for sin to be forgiven, and be ceremonially cleansed with water. This way they were well and whole, and safe to reenter normal society. This was a law of love and protection for everyone.

Through the centuries the law had become distorted. The lepers were cast out and forgotten. They were accused of being sinners and that their sickness was God's wrath being poured out on them. The law that was intended for love and protection had been twisted to make them outcasts and eternally condemned. It would be safe to say that few lepers were ever healed and actually reentered the temple to make the necessary sacrifices and cleansing to reenter society.

Notice why Jesus sends the healed leper to the temple. He was sent as a testimony. It's as if Jesus was using this healed leper to say to the priests at the temple, "Guess what, boys, God loves lepers. When God's love is the order of the day, lepers get healed, not forgotten. Lepers can and will be reintroduced into healthy society. Pull out those old, dusty laws regarding the reassimilation of the leper that you haven't used for ages and let this poor man back in."

Now, look what happens to the second man who is healed. Jesus is in the company of many teachers of the Law. They are no doubt there to see if He is, in fact, preaching heresy. The room is so crowded that the friends of the paralyzed man have to lower him down through the roof in order to be seen by Jesus. Jesus has compassion on the man. Notice, however, that He does not first heal him. He forgives his sins. "Blasphemy!" Say the teachers. Only God can forgive sins. Exactly. In this moment Jesus is saying a few things.

1. He is God and therefore has the right to forgive sins.

2. Since He is the author of the law, He is bypassing the law that we discussed earlier and making it possible for this man to be physically healed and spiritually cleansed simply through his faith in Jesus and the authority of Jesus' words.

3. His sacrifice at the end of the story is what will satisfy the "letter of the law" and make this kind of physical/spiritual healing possible. (Jesus didn't necessarily say that in this specific event, but I am interjecting it at this point, having read the whole story since it is appropriate to the lesson.)

Kid's Questions

If your mom called you to the dinner table and she saw that your hands were filthy, would she kick you out of the house and tell you that you could never be a part of the family again? What would she say for real? Why?

Would she make you wash your hands because she is a mean old ogre and loves to see you do things you hate to do? Of course not. Your mom makes you wash your hands because she loves you and doesn't want you to get germs on your food that might hurt you.

In Jesus' day people thought that sick people were sick because they were sinners. They called them unclean. That is kind of like your hands that we talked about in the example. Do you know how the unclean people were treated? They were thrown out of the city and told never to come back again. Do you think that was very nice?

Jesus came to show that God doesn't treat unclean people that way. God treats them like your mom would treat you if you had dirty hands. God makes them wash their hands, and when they aren't able to wash their own hands, he washes them. Do you know why? It's because God loves everyone so much that he wants everyone to have clean hands so they can sit at His dinner table.

The next time you see people that are dirty or on the street or sick, how will you look at them? Will you turn in disgust, or will you see if they want to have Jesus clean them up?

Lesson 2

- Luke 4:14-30
- Matthew 13:53-58
- Mark 6:1-6
- John 2:12
- Matthew 8:5-13
- Luke 7:1-10
- Mark 1:21-28
- Luke 4:31-37

Study Questions

In Luke's account of Jesus reading from the scroll in the synagogue, what part of His speech got them angry?

According to Matthew and Mark, why was Jesus not able to do many miracles in Nazareth?

What request did the centurion make of Jesus?

What was the centurion's attitude toward Jesus?

What was Jesus' reaction to the centurion's attitudes and behavior?

Compare the attitude of the people of Nazareth toward Jesus with that of the centurion.

Food for Thought

A contrast of vision

Today we see another interesting contrast. We have the people of Nazareth, Jesus' hometown, contrasted with a Roman centurion in the city of Capernaum.

Let's set the stage in Nazareth. By this time Jesus has been teaching and doing some amazing miracles around the country and word has gotten back to His home town about it. Now Jesus is home in Nazareth on the Sabbath. Of course they would expect a noted rabbi as Himself to stand in front of the synagogue to read the assigned text for the day, then sit down and comment on it. This was how the Sabbath was observed every week, and when a guest rabbi was in town, it was assumed that he would do the honors. So, Jesus stood to read the passage assigned for that day. It just so happened (wink, wink) that it was the passage from Isaiah that talked about the coming ministry of the Messiah. This was a passage about freedom for the oppressed, healing for the sick, and victory over bondage.

"Uh, huh. We've heard this passage a thousand times," the people thought. "I wonder what he's going to say about it?" They watched as He assumed the normal seated position of a teaching rabbi. They were not quite prepared for what came out his mouth.

"Today," he said, "this scripture is fulfilled."

Stunned silence. "Well, that is interesting," they thought to themselves. The baker who occupied the storefront next to Mary and Joseph's carpenter shop leaned over to the farmer and said with a wink, "Isn't this Joseph's son? What a fine boy, what gracious words he speaks." They all nod in doting approval, completely blind to the cosmic-shattering truth that had just been uttered in their presence.

Jesus stares back at them in disbelief. "You blind, close-minded, nearsighted people. You don't get it. When you look at Me, all you can see is the son of a carpenter. You see the boy who played in the streets with his brothers and sisters. Look closer. I am not the son of Joseph. He was a good foster parent, but he is not my father. I am the son of God. I am the Messiah who has come to set the world free. If you are this blind then you are like the people in the days of Elijah and Elisha. The people of their day were so stubborn that God sent those two great prophets outside of Israel to bring healing to the gentiles. So it will be with Me. If you represent the attitude of Israel toward their coming Messiah, then I will go to the gentiles."

At this the people became outraged and ran the poor boy out of the very streets in which He grew up. For the human side of Jesus, this must have been a dark day. It's never fun when your closest friends and family turn you out for standing up for the truth.

Jesus then moved on to Capernaum. (Read the introduction to this session to learn more about Capernaum.) In this fishing village Jesus receives a welcome of an entirely different sort. Jesus is approached by a centurion. I wonder if Jesus flinched a little when he saw the soldier approaching. It was never good when a centurion approached you. After all, these men were not just soldiers; they were commanders of 100 soldiers. They were strong leaders of Roman troops. They represented everything that was evil and wrong in Israel. The only time one of these men approached you was to bring a heavy hand of oppression.

What the centurion said must have been a shock to Jesus and his disciples. "Sir, my servant is sick. Please heal him. You are a busy man and I am not worthy to eat up your precious time. Just say the word, and I know you can heal him, right where you stand." Out of the mouth of this icon of evil comes some of the purest, most raw and fresh morsels of truth that anyone has yet uttered in the story to date. The eyes of this Roman see Jesus for exactly who He is — the Lord who has authority and is able to bring about great power and healing with the simple breath of a word. Now that's more like it! You can almost hear Jesus turning cartwheels when He sings the praises of this pagan man. "I have not found faith like this in all of Israel. People like this man will be welcomed in My kingdom from any place, while the blind "chosen" ones will miss the boat completely."

Kid's Questions

Let's pretend that you are the star of a play. It's the first night of your performance and you know that your friends and family are going to be there. What do you hope your friends and family will say after the show?

How would you feel if they came up to you and said, "That was awful; you should get off the stage"? Why?

Now imagine that there is a big bully that lives across the street from you that picks on you and makes fun of you every day. If he came to your show, what would you expect him to say after he saw it?

How would you feel if the bully came up to you and said, "Wow! That was really cool. You did a great job!" ? Why?

In today's story we saw that Jesus was rejected by his family. How do you think he felt? We also saw that he was accepted by a Roman centurion. The Roman is like the bully in our example. How do you think Jesus felt when the centurion accepted him?

Let's make sure that we treat Jesus like the centurion did, not like his friends and family.

Lesson 3

- Matthew 8:14-27
- Mark 1:29-34
- Luke 4:38-44
- Mark 4:35-41
- Luke 8:22-25

Study Questions

What happened to Jesus and the disciples while they were on the boat?

How did the disciples react?

How did Jesus react?

What accusation did the disciples direct at Jesus when they found him napping?

What was Jesus' attitude toward the disciples when He saw their fear?

Food for Thought

Stormy weather

It is a short story but it really packs a punch. Jesus and his disciples get in a fishing boat and head out across the Sea of Galilee to continue their mission in the gentile lands across the water. As they go, Jesus nestles down for a little nap. Suddenly, as was common on this body of water, a storm swooped down on them and threw the boat around like a child's toy. "Jesus, save us! Don't you care about us?!?" the disciples wailed. Blinking with sleepy eyes, He looks at the storm, looks at their faces, and says, "Boys, boys, you still don't get it do you?" With a soft word He hushed the storm and probably went back to napping. The disciples were left scratching their heads in bewilderment.

Here are some observations about the scene and some analogies that can be drawn to our own lives.

1. **The storm was real**. The waves and the wind that were crashing down on the boat were not figments of the disciples' imagination. The storm posed the threat of real physical harm to them. Many times, in our world, people try to convince us that the pain we are experiencing — the storm that is raging in our lives — is not real. They want us to believe that we suffer simply because we don't have a positive attitude, that pain is a figment of the imagination. Wrong! Sometimes really bad things happen to people. Houses burn. Spouses bail. Partners betray. Kids rebel. Assailants attack. Burglars steal. Stuff happens, and it's for real. In an attempt to bring comfort or advice, let's never downplay the severity and reality of the pain and suffering at hand.

2. **The disciples became distracted**. Think about this for a minute. These men had given up their livelihood in order to follow Jesus because they believed He was the glorious Messiah that would deliver their people from darkness. They had witnessed Him turn water into wine, heal the sick, cast out demons, and speak with the authority of God that no man had ever claimed before. They believed that He was on a divinely ordained course and had hand-picked them to help Him complete his mission. And yet, in spite of all this experiential knowledge, when faced with physical peril, they freaked out. Not only

were they scared — anyone would be scared in that situation — but they actually accused Jesus of not caring.

Isn't that just like us? Everything is all fine and dandy when we are walking in the shadow of Jesus' power and authority. We can take on the world. Then, when the winds blow and the waves crash, and it seems like Jesus is taking a nap, we freak out and hurl accusations at God about being distant and uncaring. How quickly we forget.

3. **Jesus was always present**. Jesus was taking a nap. From the disciples' perspective it could seem that Jesus was disinterested and couldn't care less if the disciples were suffering. From Jesus' perspective, on the other hand, He was so deeply entrenched in his faith that God was completely in control that no matter what happened there was no need to panic. Did you catch that? No matter what happened. Perhaps they would die in the storm. So what. That would have been part of the plan. If they live and make it to the other side, then that is a strong indication that they are to continue the mission at hand. Jesus could be at peace because He was resting in the sovereignty of God. Jesus didn't abandon them; He was always there, so deeply that He did not need to worry.

4. **Jesus calmed the storm**. He didn't have to calm the storm, but He saw that the disciples were so freaked out that they needed it to be gone. Work with me a little as I make a speculation. Could it be that Jesus' desire for His disciples (and for us) is that they would grow in such faith and confidence in God, Jesus, and their role in life, that the disciples would not need Him to calm the storm? Oh sure, He can calm the storm. After all, He created weather itself. That's not the real miracle. The real miracle would have been if the disciples had such deep faith in God that they would have been napping with Jesus instead of freaking out. Too many times we want to see a big, dramatic show from God. We want to see the power of God manifested in our lives through physical healing, speaking in tongues, crying statues, whatever it may be. We want to do great things in the physical world, yet the greatest feat of God's power is when a heart is transformed into the image of Jesus and has such deep faith that skies don't need to part and the waves don't need to stop crashing.

Where are you today? Are you pacing at the bow of the ship, worrying about the storm that is crashing in on you? Yes, it's real. No, Jesus is not sleeping in disinterest. The question is, do you need Him to wake up and calm the storm, or are you ready to lie down and take the nap of faith that He is taking. God is in control. He'll get you to the other side.

Kid's Questions

Let's act out this story.

Have one person play Jesus.

One person be the special effects guy and stand by the light switch.

Have everyone else be the disciples.

Pretend that the couch is a boat and have Jesus and the disciples all get on the boat and set out for sea.

Jesus takes a nap.

Then a storm hits (cue the lightning person at the switch.) Flash the lights!)

The disciples are afraid. Show fear. Jesus is sleeping.

Discples say, "Jesus, don't you care that we drown?"

Jesus looks at the storm and says, "Quiet! Be still!"

The disciples are amazed.

Good acting.

What kind of storms do you have in your life? What makes you scared?

Just remember that Jesus is able to make any storm calm down and He can take away our fear if we ask him to.

40

Lesson 4

- Matthew 8:28-34
- Mark 5:1-20
- Luke 8:26-39
- Matthew 9:9-13
- Mark 2:13-17
- Luke 5:27-32

Study Questions

Describe the man that Jesus encountered when they reached the shore of Gadarene.

What attitude did the demons have toward Jesus?

How did Jesus treat the demons?

Why were the villagers angry?

At the end of the story what mission did Jesus send the man to complete ?

Food for thought

Getting the story straight

Before we dive into a discussion about the meaning or implications of these stories, let's clear up a possible technical issue. When you compare Matthew's version of Jesus' encounter with demons at the tombs with Mark and Luke's, you will notice a glaring discrepancy. Matthew says there were two men while Mark and Luke speak of only one. So, which is it?

Many skeptics point to this as another example of inconsistencies in the Bible. However, it is not. Both accounts can be accurate. Just because Mark and Luke speak of only one it does not mean that there were not two. When Matthew tells the story, he only mentions the exorcism and the angry farmers and leaves it at that. Mark and Luke, however, seem to have a different purpose for telling the story. They focus on the actions of the man after he was healed and the subsequent mission that Jesus set before him to return home and be a witness. It is very likely that only one of the two men that were healed from demon-possession ended up being grateful and following Jesus. Mark and Luke didn't want to waste time talking about the other man when he did not ultimately get his life turned around in the end. For more about dealing with apparent discrepancies see lesson 5 in session 1.

What about demons?

Scattered throughout the story so far, we have encountered characters called demons but have not addressed them at all. Today's spectacular story of Jesus' encounter with a legion of demons living in one man affords us a great opportunity to deal with the general topic of demons.

Here are some basic observations and comments that may help you process the question of demons and how we should handle the subject.

1. Demons are real. If you believe that the Bible is the truth and if you believe that the stories in the Bible are historical narrative and not fantastic fiction or mythical legend, then you must accept the fact that Jesus encountered beings that were called demons. (Please note: I am running on the presupposition that the Bible is, indeed, a reliable piece of historical narrative. I have come to this conviction through much study, not just because I want it to be true. If you are not at that place yet, it's OK. However, when reading the Gospels, it is important to remember that the writers and original readers of these documents

believed them to be true accounts and not mythological or fantastic fiction.)

While it is important to believe that there are such things as demons, it is also important to note that there is very little actual biblical data to be able to construct an authoritative description of the nature of demons. What we do know is that, according to the description found in the Bible, demons are described as evil spirits that have the ability to inhabit humans at some level and have influence upon their behavior.

From that brief description we see that there are three things to note concerning the nature of demons. First, they are spiritual. They exist in a realm that is different than our own. They are not physical creatures, but spiritual realities. Given the fact that we really don't know much about the spiritual realm, it is difficult to describe what a demon (or an angel for that matter) really is. Second, demons are evil. To be evil is to be opposed to the purposes and nature of God. It does not necessarily mean vicious or grotesque. The horned heads and split tongues found in the TV shows Buffy the Vampire Slayer or Angel are simply fantasy. In fact, if demons did manifest in physical form, they would most likely be very beautiful and sensual. For some reason, demons delight in the obstruction of the human ability to receive God's love. Thirdly, demons can interact with human beings. How the spiritual can affect the physical is a mystery beyond our current ability to understand. Yet, it happens.

2. Demons know the truth. Getting back to the story of Jesus, have you noticed a very interesting reoccurrence? The most verbal witnesses to the true identity of Jesus are the demons. The humans are struggling with understanding who He is, but the demons know right away. "Oh no, here comes Jesus, the son of the Living God. He's gonna kick our tail! Please, Jesus, don't throw us into the abyss." The demons were so loud about the truth that Jesus put them under a gag order. He didn't need that kind of publicity!

3. The line between demonic activity and physical ailment can sometimes be blurry. In the ancient world, almost all physical ailments were attributed to demonic activity. In the pagan cultures, every aspect of life had a spirit attached to it. There were the household spirits of the hearth and the threshold. There were the spirits of the highways and the spirits of the woods, water, and air. One couldn't do anything without encountering a spirit. Some were evil, some were good. (It is important to note that this was the culture in which Jesus was operating, and that prevailing worldview would have definitely impacted and influenced the authors of the Gospels.) In our day, standing on this side of the Renaissance, the industrial revolution, and the development of modern medicine, it is easy to look at those times as steeped in the superstitious beliefs of unenlightened minds and throw out the entire idea of demons altogether.

This leaves the modern follower of Jesus in a bit of a bind. It seems that there is a line that has been drawn in the sand on this issue. It appears that we must choose between modern medicine and the accuracy of the Bible. I would like to propose that this line may be more blurry than we think. While it is true that not every sickness has spiritual roots, it is also true that the human being is a physical/spiritual creature. There are non-tangible elements—our mind and our spirit—that cannot be measured in a test tube, yet they exist. The spirit needs the body and the body needs the spirit. In the same way the spirit affects the body and the body affects the spirit. The bottom line of this discussion is that it is entirely possible that many of our sicknesses, even today, may be linked to spiritual issues.

4. Jesus has absolute authority over demons. Here's the point of the whole issue. Jesus had absolute authority over every demon He encountered, including Satan when Jesus was tempted in the wilderness. Jesus is not in a cosmic struggle between good and evil. The only reason evil exists is because God is a loving God that created us with free choice. If God wanted to do so, He could eliminate all evil in a moment, without batting an eye. If He did, though, He would destroy the things he loves — us. So, demons can run amuck, taking advantage of the grace of God. Yet, when they come across Jesus' path, they can do nothing other than tremble in fear. They run like the shadows run from a newly rising sun. Darkness has no power over the light. Rest assured that when you are fully submitted to Jesus, putting on the armor of God as Paul talked about in Ephesians 6:10-18, then you have nothing to fear from the evil spirits of the world.

Can Christians be "possessed?"

The Apostle Paul said in Ephesians 4:26-27, "In your anger do not sin" do not let the sun go down while you are still angry, and do not give the devil a foothold." He was speaking to followers of Jesus. It seems that it is possible to open ourselves to sin and in so doing allow evil to grow a root in our heart. It's like a flower garden. The seeds of weeds are constantly blowing in. If we do not nip them in the bud, and take care of unconfessed sin quickly, then negative thoughts and feelings can bubble, brew, and fester into the cancerous tumors of bitterness, resentment, rage, and depression. The question is, are these things evil spirits that are active in our lives, or are these simply negative attitudes that we personify with demon-talk? The answer is, does it matter? Does it have to be one or the other? What if they are the same thing? Either way, these are attitudes of the heart that are contrary and counterproductive to the Kingdom of God that Jesus came to present to the world and they need to be rooted out through the power and authority of Jesus. Aren't you glad that he loves you so much that he has made his authority available to you at any time? You need simply to ask.

Kid's Questions

What is a demon?

Draw a picture of what you think a demon looks like. Why do you have that picture in your mind?

This week we have been studying about how powerful Jesus is. He is stronger than sickness, sin, and storms. Do you know what? Jesus is even stronger than evil. In a lot of the movies you see or stories you read the bad guy seems pretty powerful and he gets into a big struggle with the good guy. Sometimes it seems like the bad guy might even beat the good guy. That is often true in stories, and about humans, but there is one important truth you must remember about Jesus...evil has no power over Jesus.

Take a little piece of paper and crumple it up into a ball. Set it on the table. Now, flick it with your finger as far as you can. Was it easy?

That's what the fight between Jesus and evil is like. Evil is nothing more than a piece of crumpled up paper to Jesus.

When we put our faith in Jesus can flick the evil away from us with no effort at all. You can take comfort in the strength of Jesus.

Lesson 5

- Matthew 9:14-17
- Mark 2:18-3:6
- Luke 5:33-39
- Luke 6:1-11
- Matthew 12:1-14

Study Questions

What was Jesus doing that caused the teachers to be upset with him? Why?

What was Jesus' response to their objections?

What parables did Jesus use to explain His actions? Write down each one, and next to it, write what you think they meant.

Food for Thought

Of patches and skins

Today's study ends our week of looking at the power of Jesus and that He brought it to authenticate his Kingdom. We've seen that He has power over sin, sickness, nature, and demons. Today we see that Jesus had power over traditions.

We read about two scenes where Jesus goes head-to-head with the teachers of the Law over matters concerning the observance of Moses' Law. In the first scene Jesus seems to be neglecting the age-old discipline of fasting. Then, in the second scene, He has the audacity to pick some grain on the Sabbath. Let's look at each scene again briefly, and then we can make some observations about Jesus' attitude toward tradition.

Scene 1. John's disciples are fasting quite often. The Pharisees and teachers of the law are also fasting regularly. In those days, when they fasted it was more than just abstaining from chocolate bars for the afternoon. For them, the fast was a time of mourning and sadness. It was a time to dress in sackcloth and sit in ashes. It had the smell of a funeral dirge. Originally, the fast was intended to be a discipline that would bring about a state of repentance from sin and a realignment of the faster's heart to the will of God. The problem with the Pharisees was that...well...they didn't think they had sin. For them, fasting had become a symbol of "holiness" and bred an attitude of "holier-than-thou" in their hearts. It had become a discipline that one does because good people do it, so they did it in the middle of the street, in the full view of everyone, ensuring that everyone would see how good they were. John's disciples did it partly out of tradition, like the Pharisees, and partly because their teacher had been thrown in prison and they were bummed.

So, here they are, sitting around in sackcloth and ashes, being all "holy," listening to their bellies grumble, while they look over and see Jesus, the supposed "Messiah," having a party with His disciples. "Hey, how come they have all the fun, while I'm sitting around in this stinking pile of ashes?"

Scene 2. In this scene we see Jesus and His disciples walking through a grain field on the Sabbath. In the original law that God gave to Moses, God commanded,

"Observe the Sabbath day by keeping it holy, as the LORD your God has commanded you. Six days you shall labor and do all your work, but the seventh day is a Sabbath to the LORD your God. On it you shall not do any work, neither you, nor your son or daughter, nor your manservant or maidservant, nor your ox, your donkey or any of your animals, nor the alien within your gates, so that your manservant and maidservant may be able to rest, not just the wealthy." On the Sabbath day everyone was equal and no one served anyone else. The Sabbath was a gracious gift of God given to people who had been worked 24/7 as slaves for over 400 years. Now, God said to them, "Hey, if I can rest, then you can rest. Slow down; take a day to rest in My presence. Let Me heal you so that you can live a long and prosperous life without burning out." God knows that the propensity of humanity is to work too hard, stress out, and ultimately burn out. So, like any good parent, He enforced this law with penalties because He believed that a regular day of rest was a necessity for the people he had created.

By the time Jesus came on the scene, the teachers of the law had completely distorted the Sabbath. They had become so afraid of breaking the law of the Sabbath that they scrutinized the definition of the term "work." "What does work mean?" they would ask each other. "If I walk from my house to the barn, is that considered work? If I take a drink of water, is that considered work?" In an effort to obey the law of the Sabbath they had turned the Sabbath into a time of stress, worrying about whether or not they were breaking it.

When these Sabbath-worriers saw that Jesus was strolling through the grain field (the first Sabbath violation), and picking heads of grain to eat (the second Sabbath violation) they were outraged. According to the Law of Moses, Jesus and his disciples should be stoned to death for this infraction.

In both scenes Jesus is accused of paying no regard to the Laws of Moses and is therefore regarded as a sinner. In response Jesus gave them two analogies. He said that you don't sew a new patch onto old clothes, otherwise the new patch will shrink in the wash and rip the old garment even worse. He also said that you don't put fresh, effervescent wine into an old, rigid wineskin. It would burst open and the wine would be wasted. Instead, you need a new shirt and a new wineskin.

Here's what Jesus was saying to the disciples.

"Look, guys, you have lost sight of the core truth behind the law. God did not give you the law as a means by which you could perform a little dog and pony show and earn his favor and love. You don't score brownie points every time you obey a law and lose them every time you disobey. God gave you the law because He *already* loved you and wanted you to be safe from harm. He knew that if you obeyed His guidelines that you would be protected from the harmful affects of idolatry,

sexual promiscuity, overworking, unsanitary living conditions, envy, and the like. You have forgotten that the law was intended to bring life. You have twisted the law and made it into a fear-based tool used to manipulate people into submitting to your earthly power and to control their lives. You have turned the clothes into old rags and made the wineskins rigid. I am not disobeying the law; I am living authentically and dynamically in the presence of the law-giver. There is a time and place where it may be necessary to break the rules, as long as they are broken out of an authentic obedience to God and carry the spirit of true love. There is a time to fast, and a time to party. Right now it's time to party. There is a time to rest, and there is a time to feed the hungry and heal the sick, even on the Sabbath.

Here's the bottom line. I am bringing the Kingdom of God into full view. People will now have the opportunity to know the giver of the Law personally and will have His Law written on their heart, not on a piece of paper that is strapped to their foreheads. I am bringing new wine, and in order to do so, I will be establishing a new set of parameters in which to hold that wine — The Law of Love and Grace."

Imagine what the teachers must have thought. These were the words of a radical. These were dangerous words. When you open the law to that level of interpretation, imagine how much abuse people could give it and the liberties they could take. No. We must control the people and not allow heresy to slip in. How dare this man say these things. Only one person could have the authority to deal with the law in this way, and that is God himself.

It was at this point that the plot against Jesus began to simmer among the leaders of Jerusalem. Jesus' teaching was becoming a threat to the Pharisees and they determined that it must be eliminated.

Today, we are faced with a question. How do we view God? Is God a list of rules that must be followed? Is He a dictator that runs His kingdom through fear and intimidation, controlling every movement of his subjects? Or, is God a loving Father who has set guidelines for His children to follow and is intimately involved in their lives?

I believe that Jesus is presenting to us an image of God where He is the kind of Father that is more interested in the training of a child through real life experiences for the purpose of cultivating maturity than He is interested in His children being automatons that obey every command to the letter, with no spark of life. God is interested in life, not death.

Which picture of God is more prevalent in your world? How does that affect your everyday life?

Kid's Questions

Let's say that your parents made a rule that you were not to get out of bed after the lights were turned out, and if you got out of bed that you would get a spanking.

What would happen if you got out of bed in order to peek in on what they were doing? You would get in trouble, right? Yes, because you broke the rules and disobeyed them.

Your parents made that rule because they love you and know that you need to get your sleep in order to stay strong and healthy. They had to put a consequence to your disobedience in order to train you to do the thing that is good for you.

Now, let's imagine that the lights have been turned out and you are lying in bed. As you lay there you start to smell smoke. Then the smoke alarm goes off. Your house is on fire. What do you do? Your parents told you not to get out of bed after the lights go out. If you run downstairs and outside to escape the fire you will be disobeying your parents. If you don't run outside, you could get trapped in the fire.

In that moment, what do you think your parents would want you to do? Why?

You see, that's how God is. God gave laws to his people in the Old Testament because he loved them and wanted them to do the things that he knew would be best for them. When Jesus came, the people had forgotten that God loved them and thought that he was only interested in having them follow the rules, no matter what.

Remember this. God loves you. He is not waiting for you to mess up so that he can zap you; neither are your parents. The rules that they have made for you are really for your own good. The goal is that someday you will not need to have any rules because you will be responsible enough to do what is good for you without being told. The better you obey the rules now, the less you will need them when you are older.

Introduction

Over the past two weeks we have been able to see and hear some amazing things coming from a simple carpenter's son from Nazareth. He preached up a storm and made bold claims about who He was and what His Kingdom was all about. To back up His words he performed great miracles, demonstrating His power over both the physical and spiritual universe. You would think, after all this wonder-working, the people of Israel would come flocking to Jesus, declaring that their Messiah had finally arrived. You would think. But, as is often the sad reality of head-strong humans, they did not.

In the readings this week we will see that a shadow begins to form over Jesus' ministry. People are beginning to question Him. The Pharisees haven't liked Him from the beginning, so their accusations don't surprise us. This week their hatred for Him intensifies as they actually accuse Him of being a demon, or at least being in league with Satan. While that does not surprise us, we are caught off guard by the questions of John the Baptist. From prison John has heard about how Jesus is wandering the countryside, staying away from Jerusalem, and healing the sick and dying. John sends some of his disciples to ask if Jesus really is the Messiah, or if we should be looking elsewhere for the great Savior of Israel.

The constant rejection and resistance to Jesus' invitation to enter His Kingdom indicates that the hearts of the people of Israel are hardened. This calloused-heart condition leads Jesus to begin to teach in parables. A parable is a simple analogy, using everyday items and circumstances to teach deep spiritual truths. If a person is tuned into Jesus' frequency, then the parables make sense.

If a person is not tuned in, then the parables make it sound like Jesus is speaking nonsense, and He is easily dismissed.

We will spend Thursday and Friday studying one of the most famous analogies that Jesus used to describe the Kingdom of God — a seed. Through this simple analogy Jesus will teach us many important truths about what the Kingdom is and what it isn't.

Lesson 1

- Mark 3:13-19
- Luke 6:12-16
- Luke 7:11-35
- Matthew 10:1-4; 11:1-19

Study Questions

What was Jesus' purpose for choosing 12 disciples?

What designation was given to the 12 chosen disciples? What does this word mean? (You may wish to consult a Bible Dictionary)

What question did John the Baptist ask Jesus?

What was Jesus' response?

How did Jesus describe John in Luke 7:28?

How did John describe Jesus' coming ministry in Matthew 3:1-12 (from week 1)? In what ways is it the same and in what ways is it different from the way Jesus described His own ministry in Luke 7:22-23?

Food for Thought

Today there are two important topics to look at.

The Dynamic Dozen

The passages in Mark 3:13-19 and Luke 6:12-16 are so short that they could be easily overlooked. They are anything but insignificant, however, because here we see Jesus choosing 12 men from of the larger group of His disciples. Here are a few observations and thoughts about the choosing of the 12.

1. **Twelve is a significant number.** In the flow of the story we are on the verge of a major shift in the trajectory of Jesus' ministry. Dark clouds of doubt are gathering in the sky as Jesus senses more and more that the people of Israel will not receive His Kingdom as the legitimate reign of the coming Messiah. Because of their rejection Jesus is going to have to reconfigure the hard drive of God's Kingdom on earth and start a whole new operating system. The old system was built upon the family of Abraham, Isaac, and Jacob. Jacob had 12 sons and these sons became the leaders of the twelve tribes of Israel. Old system — 12 tribes. New system — 12 disciples. Get the picture? Jesus was building the new Kingdom on the backs of these twelve men. Hopefully they will turn out better than Jacob's boys.

2. **Infused with purpose.** It would do us well to define two very important terms. Every person who follows Jesus is called a disciple. The word simply means one who learns. Every teacher has disciples. Plato had disciples. John the Baptist had disciples. Mohammed had disciples. The disciples of Jesus were those who followed Him around and adhered to His teaching. From the larger group of disciples Jesus chose twelve men and designated them as Apostles. The word apostle means a messenger, or, one who is sent out. Jesus gave these twelve men the charge to go out and bring the message of the Good News to the people. To be an apostle is to be a disciple, but to be a disciple is not necessarily to be an apostle. The role of the apostle is very specific. Apostles are people on a mission. They go and push the envelope, cutting new paths in the uncharted territory so that everyone else in the group can follow behind them and establish camp.

3. **The formula for success.** There is a recurring pattern in Scripture that needs to be highlighted every time it is encountered. If you want to be successful in doing God's

work, you need to first be focused on being in true relationship with God. The "being" must precede the "doing," We see it here in a simple phrase in Mark 3:14: "He appointed twelve — designating them apostles — that they might be with Him and that He might send them out to preach." Their first purpose was to be with Jesus, then, and only then, would they be filled and equipped enough to go out and preach. As disciples of Jesus (whether we have the gift of apostleship, teaching, encouragement, or service) we must always remember that we must first come and drink deeply from the living water that comes only from time spent with Jesus, before we will be filled enough to use our gifts in a way they will be effective in the lives of others.

Two views of the Kingdom

In Luke 7:18-33 we encounter a somewhat confusing passage. To be honest, it's one of those passages that is very tempting to gloss right over and pretend it's not there. Yet, I think there is a rich nugget of truth for us to find here.

At this point in the story John the Baptist has been in prison for a while. The only thing that keeps him going are the periodic reports from his disciples on the latest happenings of Jesus. Let's try to see this story through John's eyes. He was most likely an Essene, which means that he lived in a secluded village with a group of monks. These monks were so disillusioned with the corruption of Israel, and specifically its capital city, Jerusalem, that they could no longer mingle with the people there. They believed that Jerusalem was destined for the destructive retribution by the wrath of God. Not only was John an Essene, he was also the one chosen by God to be the "voice of one calling in the desert, 'make way the path for the Lord.'" Do you remember what the basic gist of his message was to the people? He told them to repent because the Messiah was bringing a big ax to cut down the rotten tree of Israel. He was bringing an ax, a winnowing fork, and fire so that He could weed out the nasty elements of Israel and make it all brand new.

These are pretty violent and aggressive images of wrath and destruction. It may be that John saw in Jesus the fulfillment of what the Essenes believed was coming for Jerusalem.

So there he is, sitting in prison, anxiously awaiting the glorious day when Jesus whips out His cosmic ax and brings the heat to the sinners of Jerusalem. He waits and waits. Reports keep coming. "No, sir, He's not in Jerusalem yet. He's been spending most of His time in Galilee. We heard that He spent a few days in Samaria.

Most of His time is spent healing the sick and teaching people that they are supposed to love their neighbors and not judge others."

"Galilee?! Samaria!? Loving enemies?! Where's the ax? Where's the brimstone? It's supposed to be like Sodom and Gomorrah. He's supposed to be in Jerusalem, not out in the boonies."

"You two, come here. Go to Jesus. Ask Him if I got my story straight. I thought He was the one to bring the heat. Ask Him if He is the Messiah, or if we are supposed to look for a more aggressive leader."

Jesus responds to John's inquiry by quoting Isaiah, "The blind see. The lame walk. The infected are clean, the deaf hear, the dead are alive, and the poor have hope. I hope I'm not leading anybody off course here, but the last time I checked this was how Isaiah said it was going to be."

Jesus then turned to the crowd and said that John was indeed a great prophet, just like Elijah, yet he was still not as great as the least in the Kingdom of God. What did Jesus mean by this? Perhaps this is what He was saying: "John was the last of the Old Testament prophets. John prepared the way for the Kingdom, but he did not get to taste of the Kingdom himself. He came to bring only condemnation. That is so Old Testament-thinking. I did not come to condemn, I came to save. I came to bring the Good News of new life. Yes, there will be justice served, but not right now. The Father is not going to destroy Jerusalem when the vast majority of the people living there are victims of bad leadership. The Kingdom of God is all about freeing the oppressed and liberating the outcast. John's perspective of the Kingdom is limited in its scope."

Now for the final piece. Jesus then turns to the Pharisees and says, "What shall I say about you? You are like children. When will you grow up? You are so stubborn. The Father sends you a funeral dirge in the death message of John and you fold your arms and say, 'no, we won't do the funeral thing.' Then the Father sends Me to you and I play the flute and invite you to dance with Me. You fold your arms like a spoiled brat and say, 'no, we don't want to dance either. We want to be the ones to decide. If we can't have it our way, then we are going to take our toys and go home.'"

"GROW UP!"

You see, both aspects of the Kingdom are accurate. God will judge those who disobey. But, Jesus has opened the gate for all who want to escape that wrath to run into the loving arms of a forgiving

Father before it's too late. The Pharisees wouldn't have any of it. Their hearts were hard and their eyes were blind. This hardening of their hearts leads to a new path of teaching that Jesus uses for them to understand.

How many times do we develop stubbornness like that in our hearts? Have you ever been passionate for something and then been shown that you were wrong? How did you react? Many times, in that circumstance, we are not willing to admit that we are wrong and would rather deny the truth than admit that we were wrong. Perhaps we are embarrassed at being so passionate about something that was wrong, and now we feel stupid. Or maybe we feel that showing fallibility will be a sign of weakness and our enemies will use it against us. Whatever the motivation, the end result is still the same. If we have stubbornness toward obvious truth, then through the hardness of our hearts, we will miss out on the joy and freedom that only truth accepted in humility can bring. Ask God to expose to you any areas where your stubborn pride is keeping you from accepting the truth that Jesus is revealing to you.

Kid's Questions

(Note to parents: many of the stories are repeated one, two, and sometimes three times in one day's reading assignments. You may want to choose only one of them when reading with your children. This will help to keep them focused.)

Let's pretend that there are a group of kids getting together at the playground. Some of the kids want to play soccer, some of the kids want to play basketball, and some of the kids want to play on the playground equipment. What do you do? How do you make decisions?

What would happen if the soccer players took on an attitude that said, "If we can't play soccer then we would rather not play anything at all"? And then they cross their arms and sit on the ground with a big frown on their faces. How would the rest of the kids feel? Would their friendship grow stronger? Would that convince all the kids to want to play soccer? What do you think would happen?

In our story today we see that Jesus, John the Baptist, and the Pharisees ran into a similar situation. All three of them had different ideas about what God's Kingdom should be like. John thought it was going to be intense and a time for mourning and repentance. Jesus thought it should be fun and a time for rejoicing. The Pharisees, on the other hand, folded their arms and said, "We don't like your games. We want to play our way or we won't play at all." Jesus said that this kind of attitude will lead only to pain and death.

So this week, try not to have the selfish attitude of the Pharisees. Let's be more like Jesus and try to work out our disagreements by listening to each other and showing love, even when we disagree.

51

Lesson 2

- Matthew 9:27-34
- Mark 3:20-30
- Matthew 12:22-37
- Luke 11:14-28

Study Questions

What miracle did Jesus perform?

How did the crowd interpret Jesus' ability to perform miracles?

How did the Pharisees interpret Jesus' ability to perform miracles?

Food for Thought

Calling good evil and evil good

Up to this point in the story the Pharisees have been doing a bit of a dance with Jesus. It has been obvious that they don't like Him very much. They have been following Him around, trying to figure out where He is coming from and to what end He is aiming. Today the dance takes a sharp turn and gets downright ugly. Jesus has just done two amazingly beautiful miracles; He healed blind men and cast out demons. He demonstrated His power to free people from both physical darkness and spiritual darkness, showing that He truly is the light. His actions elicit two very different responses. The crowds rave about His glorious deeds and think He is the greatest thing since sliced bread. And then, on the other hand, the Pharisees step into the foreground. Teeth clenched, veins popping out of their necks, they point their finger in Jesus' face and say, "You cast out demons by the power of Satan."

You can sense the stunned silence that must have come over the crowd when they heard this wild accusation.

Jesus lowers His eyes for a moment to gather His thoughts. How do you respond to such a bold and frontal assault?

Looking up from under His brow He fixes His eyes on His accusers. Beginning softly so as to build to a crescendo, He says, (allow Me to paraphrase) "Gentlemen. Let's look at the logic of your accusation for a moment. Would Satan really drive out Satan? Can darkness really drive out darkness? No. A house divided against itself cannot stand. Satan doesn't want to lose and he is not about to start beating up his own team; it just doesn't make sense.

What does make sense is that I am doing what I'm doing by the power of God and in the full light of truth.

Allow Me to draw a deep line in the sand right now. There is no middle ground in the Kingdom of God. You are either for Me or against Me. If you are not for Me, then you are against Me.

I'm going to spell out this one principle again. It is what is inside a man that makes him good. Bad trees can't produce good fruit. Satan can't heal and shed the light of truth; he's a bad tree. I, on the other hand, am a good tree, and can only produce good fruit.

You, on the other hand are a pack of venom-spitting snakes, (hear the crescendo) and are so blind that you cannot even see the light of truth when it is shining in full brilliance right in front of you.

Today you have crossed the line. It's one thing to mess with Me, the Son of Man and misunderstand Me. That can be forgiven. It's an entirely different thing when you see the obvious power of God's Spirit working right before your eyes and call it Satan.

In the words of Isaiah as recorded in Isaiah 5:20

> Woe to those who call evil good and good evil, who put darkness for light and light for darkness, who put bitter for sweet and sweet for bitter.

You will be judged by your words, you can count on that."

After this encounter we see the beginning of Jesus' change. In tomorrow's study we will see Jesus pulling away from the people and beginning to regroup for a different approach to the hard-hearted Israel.

There is a lesson for us today. The problem with the Pharisees was that they had become so much in love with the god that they had created that they had become completely blind to the truth. The tricky thing was that the god they had created was based upon the very same documents that the true God had inspired and handed to His people to be used as a guide to His heart. Through centuries of political power-struggles, theological syncretism (blending two things into one) with foreign belief systems, and basic human pride, the Pharisees had constructed a god that was not accurate, and were casting judgment on everyone else for not worshiping their god in the proper fashion. When the true God showed up in the flesh, they thought it was Satan. Now that is some upside-down kind of thinking.

Here in the 21st century, we have 2,000 years of Christian tradition pushing behind us. In those 2,000 years the "church" has evolved through many phases. It has been formed, polluted, reformed, and polluted again many times and in many ways. Theological debates that never existed in the New Testament have arisen and divided the church. In many ways the forms and traditions that we hold to as deeply "Christian" have nothing to do with Jesus. They are man-made rules and beliefs that quite often stifle the power of the Holy Spirit in the life of an individual. I'm afraid that if Jesus were to show up, in the flesh, in our culture and come to some of our churches, He would be thrown out and accused of being a deranged outcast — maybe even possessed.

It is the job of every generation to look intensely at the life of Jesus and use it as a mirror to be held up to our own model of the church. Do we match up to His teaching? Are we a good reflection of Him, bringing life to the spirit of those who were once dead? Or are we making it extremely difficult for people to see the Kingdom of God because our preconceived notions and theologies are standing in the way?

Kid's Questions

Let's pretend that you are on a soccer team and that you have been the best player for a long time. Everyone looks to you to be the star. Then one day a new kid moves to town and joins your team. She is really good. She's better than you are and all the kids start cheering for her and looking for her to be the leader of the team. How would you feel toward the new kid?

Now let's imagine that you got so jealous of her, and couldn't believe that someone could actually be better at soccer than you are, that you started accusing her of cheating. You said that she had made a deal with the coaches and the referees to make it easier for her to look good. You said that she was a big fake.

How would the new kid feel? How would people feel about you if you did that? Why?

That is what the Pharisees did to Jesus. They were so angry about the fact that people were starting to listen to Jesus' teaching and that He had the power to do amazing things — like healing the sick — that they starting looking for ways to make Him look bad. In today's reading they stooped to an all-time low and said that He was not from God, but was actually working with Satan.

That's what envy and jealousy can do to a person. It can make him or her say and do things that don't make any sense. Remember this: there will always be someone who is better at something than you are, or who has more cool stuff than you have, or gets to do more cool things than you do. When you meet a person like that, don't push them away. Instead, be happy for them. Perhaps, if you are happy with what you have, and don't feel like you have to outdo the other kid, then together you guys could have even more fun than you ever thought possible.

Lesson 3

- Luke 7:36-50
- Luke 8:19-21
- Mark 3:31-35
- Matthew 12:38-50
- Matthew 12:15-21

Study Questions

In Matthew 12:15-21, in what ways did Jesus' ministry fulfill Isaiah's prophesy?

Compare and contrast Simon the Pharisee with the woman who anointed Jesus' feet. Why was she favored and Simon not?

What was Jesus' attitude toward His biological family? Why? What is His definition of family?

What miraculous sign did Jesus promise to give to the Pharisees?

Who did Jesus say would judge the Pharisees? What do these people have in common? What was His point?

Food for Thought

What is a family anyway?

Loneliness. Disconnection. These are feelings that plague a large percentage of our population. We are an uprooted society. Fewer and fewer people are actually native to where they currently live. The typical family has relatives scattered to all corners of the country. Many of the families that do share a geographical location have been splintered by the ravages of divorce or deep disagreement.

So, we live our lives in isolation. We go to work and try to stay out of people's way. If we are introverts we come home and slip into our little sanctuary of solitude and cozy up with our favorite friends on the sitcom. Those friends are safe. They don't talk back. They don't make things uncomfortable. If we are extroverts, we lose ourselves in masses of people, parties and activities, staying busy enough to avoid having to get too deep with anyone. After all, it's just safer that way.

Deep down inside we wonder if there is such a thing as a good family. What does that mean? What would it feel like to have people who really love us for who we are and are not trying to get us to perform according to their standards?

These thoughts are what Jesus addresses in our stories today. In many ways Jesus can relate to the feelings of disillusionment that many people feel toward their own families. Jesus was born into a Jewish family and culture. His leaders were supposed to be righteous men that were passionate for God and shepherds of his people. His own mother, brothers, and sisters were supposed to be supportive of Him through thick or thin. When He began to step out of the norm and begin proclaiming His message of truth and the Kingdom of God, his family abandoned Him. They ridiculed Him and walked away.

In Matthew 12:15 we see that Jesus reacted to the rejection of His family by moving away from them. Where did He go? He went to the people who received Him and needed Him. In the story of the woman anointing His feet, we see that Jesus was drawn to those who received His gift of forgiveness and loved Him back. All the Pharisees could do was to criticize His theology and attack His character in order to discredit Him. So Jesus pulled away further. Later, His biological family came for Him. The sense we get about the nature of their visit was that they had reached their point of tolerance and had come to collect their crazy brother so that He could leave all the nice people alone. They did not see Him for who He was, they saw Him how they wanted to see Him and they were embarrassed. So, He questioned, "Who is my family?" It certainly wasn't the family He had been born into. His family was the people who received Him for who He was and shared a common goal of bringing glory to the Father.

I'm sure the human side of Jesus found sadness in the rejection He experienced from His birth family. Perhaps you can relate. Perhaps the reason you hide from people is that the people in your past you thought were supposed to be safe were the first to hurt you. Perhaps the people in the church you were part of ended up being the most vicious accusers you had. If you are feeling that way today, be encouraged. It doesn't have to be that way. Just because you have a biological family or are in a particular church, doesn't automatically mean that they way those people behave is sanctioned by God. They are just people that are as messed up as you are. To be in a family or to be in a church does not automatically place you in the Kingdom of God. The God's Kingdom is a place where the balance between truth and love is the order of the day.

Many times entering into the Kingdom requires moving away from some human relationships and forming new ones. The church is designed to be the family of God, not an oppressive dictator. Our Father and Leader is God Himself, not a human being. God is a good Father who loves us and desires nothing but the absolute best for us. He gives us everything we need to thrive. Our true brothers and sisters are the people who share our love for God and desire to be a community that creates an environment in which each member can be encouraged and equipped to grow in the grace of God and become what God wants him or her to be, not what others demand. In this kind of family there is patience and a nurturing environment that is ruled by speaking the truth in love with the goal of unity and mutual edification. In the family of God there is no failure, there is only opportunities to grow and learn. There is no condemnation; there is only exhortation and equipping to become more like Jesus. Jesus calls us to strive for this ideal. May you find the people who will become your true family as you share the common purpose of loving your Dad.

It is possible.

Kid's Questions

What is a family?

How are families supposed to treat each other?

Is your family like that most of the time? No family is perfect. People get upset sometimes and do things they wish they hadn't. Is your family the kind of family where everyone loves each other, and when you do make mistakes you ask for forgiveness and make things right with each other?

If it is you need to be very thankful to God.

If it isn't and your family has a lot of problems, then you need to hear this. Maybe your dad left you and your mom and that has made you sad and confused. Maybe your mom has some problems and nobody is willing to talk about it. Maybe people in your family say or do mean things to you and you feel alone and scared.

If you feel that way, remember this: Jesus understands exactly what that feels like. His family treated Him that way. Jesus taught us that there is a family that we can be part of where our real Father is God Himself. God loves you so much and would never hurt you. In God's family we can live with no fear and we can experience the kind of love where we know we are accepted for who we are and will be well-fed and taken care of so that we can grow strong and healthy. No matter how bad your situation may be, God will always be there for you, and you can call him "Dad."

Lesson 4

- Mark 3:7-12
- Matthew 13:1-23
- Luke 8:1-15
- Mark 4:1-20
- Mark 4:24-25

Study Questions

Create a simple chart with two columns and four rows. Label the left column *soil*. Label the right column *description*. Fill in the chart based upon Jesus' description and explanation of the four soils.

Why does Jesus teach in parables?

Food for Thought

Good soil?

Today we examine one of Jesus' most well-known parables. Remember, a parable is a simple story using everyday images that demonstrates a deep spiritual truth. As we have seen over the past three days, the rejection of Israel toward Jesus' teaching has become very apparent. They just don't get it. He spoke very plainly to them in the Sermon on the Mount, and it was like speaking to a brick wall. Now Jesus starts closing the blinds on the window of the Kingdom because they are not ready to hear. The window is still open and anyone who realizes they just have to lift up the blinds is welcome to come in. Unfortunately, not many do. All they see is the opaque blinds of Jesus' seemingly meaningless drivel.

Of course, His stories were anything but meaningless drivel or the cutesy tales of a nice storyteller. Jesus was a master teacher who spoke volumes of truth by painting simple word-pictures. Let's spend a little time looking at one of His most brilliant paintings: the parable of the sower.

Soil samples

In the parable there are four types of soil upon which the seed falls: hard-packed, rocky, thorny, and good. The seed that falls on the hard-packed soil doesn't germinate and is carried away by the bird. The seeds in the rocky and thorny soil start, but are killed off. The good soil receives the seed and it thrives and grows into a bountiful harvest.

Jesus explains the meaning of the parable for us. The seed is the message of the Kingdom that Jesus is bringing. There are four kinds of people represented by the four kinds of soil. Let's look at the middle two first.

Rocks and thorns

The rocky soil represents people who hear the Good News of the Kingdom and are really excited about it. They go to an evangelistic rally (i.e. Billy Graham crusade, Christian concert, seeker-church service, etc.) and hear the fact that Jesus loves them and can save them. "Sign me up," they say, "Who wouldn't want a piece of that?" So they pray the prayer and get baptized. And that's it. There is no training. There is no discipleship. No one helps them to remove the rocks from their lives in order to let the water of the Spirit get down inside of them and spring up some new life. Eventually, without deep roots, a strong wind blows and the Kingdom is gone and they are lost.

It dies of neglect.

In the thorny soil people may be trained, but they are not nurtured. They live in a briar patch of hustle and bustle surrounded by the worries of the make-ends-meet world and a life full of pain. No one takes the time to help them sort out their mess and weed the garden of their hearts. Their situations seem too overwhelming and they cannot take their eyes off the problem long enough to see the solution. In the end they are buried; they are choked out by worries and the Kingdom of God dies within them.

What is good soil?

The next two soils may seem easy to interpret at first glance. Good people receive the seed, bad people reject it. Right? As we study Jesus' life it seems that just the opposite is true. Good soil was bad people and hard soil is good people. When Jesus sowed the seed He found that the hardest soil created the people that were considered to be "good." Let's tie this back to the story of the woman who anointed Jesus' feet. Jesus told Simon the Pharisee a parable about two people who were forgiven a debt. One was forgiven little; one was forgiven much. The first person — who was "good" — was forgiven little and therefore loved little. The one who was forgiven much — the bad person — was overflowing with thankfulness and was open and receptive to the leadership of the forgiver. The good person was hard-packed soil, while the bad person was rich, soft, receptive soil, eager to have life planted in it.

As you go through life you will discover that the most difficult people in the world with whom to share the Gospel are people who are considered "good" and are very secure in their situation. They have a good job, they are respected in the community, they give to charity, and, perhaps, they even go to church. Everything seems to be going their way. Their comfort level has made their hearts packed down hard toward the message of the Kingdom. After all, everything is going great for them, why would they need anyone's help? They definitely don't need to be saved from anything.

Jesus started His ministry going to those kinds of people. He offered the Kingdom to Israel — the good kids. As some of His seeds bounced off the good people's hearts and fell into the place where the "bad" people lived, the seed took root and began to sprout there while it was carried away from the good people. The truth is that many times people who are not secure in society are most receptive to the message of the Kingdom. They have nothing to lose and everything to gain. Their lives are in turmoil and they are struggling to find a sense of direction in a maelstrom of chaos. The chaos has tilled the soil of their hearts and they are soft and open to hear the message of true north: the Kingdom that Jesus brings.

When you think about sharing your faith, whom do you "target?" Do you go after the influencers of society? Do you go after the movers and shakers by reasoning that if they make a commitment to Jesus that their influence will impact a lot of people? Nine times out of 10 those people are hard soil. Yes, God loves them. He loved the Pharisees too. Yes, God wants them to enter the Kingdom. However, their own sense of self-righteousness is often the bird sent by Satan to steal the seed of the Kingdom from their heart before it ever has a chance to grow. Perhaps we would be better off using a different standard to evaluate a proper "target" for sharing the hope of the Kingdom of God. Who needs it most? It is those who have no hope. It is the hurting, the outcast, the leper, the prostitute, the AIDS patient, the orphans, the widows. Those who have been dismissed by the "good" and are without hope in the world are the ones who are most often the good soil. The soil of their hearts is ready to receive the hope of the Kingdom. When you spread the seed in that soil and water and fertilize it regularly it has room to grow and will flourish.

There are two questions for us today:

1. What kind of soil are we? Are we too good (hard) to be challenged by Jesus' teaching? Are we not willing to be discipled and trained (rocky), content to be a spiritual infant forever? Are we too worried about the circumstances around us (thorny) that we lose sight of the giver of life? Are we just plain old, unpretentious dirt (good) that is thoroughly tilled by the cultivating blade of the difficulties of life and open to receive whatever God wants to give us and do in us?

2. How much seed are we wasting by throwing it on hard-packed soil? Perhaps we should spend more time helping to cultivate the rocky and thorny soil, and bringing the seed to the people who are really ready to receive it.

Kid's Questions

Today we will begin a science experiment that will take a few weeks to develop.

Get four paper cups. Label one "HARD," label another one, "ROCKY," label another one, "THORNY," and label the last one, "GOOD."

If you have clay, pack some into the bottom of the cup labeled "HARD." If you don't have any clay, then get some dirt from the yard and pack it down as hard as you can into the bottom of the cup. Now cut the cup so that the lip is only about ¼" taller than the level of the hard-packed soil.

Fill the cup labeled, "ROCKY," with mostly rocks and a tiny bit of dirt.

Get some potting soil (or some good soil from the back yard) and fill the other two cups with it.

Now you will need some seeds. Drop some seeds onto the top of the hard-packed soil. Drop some seeds into the pile of rocks. Do not add water to these cups.

Now, in the "THORNY" cup, drop some seeds on the top of the soil. Then go in the back yard and see if you can find some dandelions that have turned to seed. If you can't find those, pull some weeds and bring them in. Sprinkle weeds all over the top of your seeds. Do not add water to this cup.

In the "GOOD" soil, make a little hole about ¼" deep and place two or three seeds in it. Cover the seeds and water them.

Place all the cups outside in a place where they will get adequate amounts of sunlight and shade. Do not water any of the cups except the one with the "GOOD" soil. Keep watering the good soil for several weeks and watching all four cups. Keep notes on what you observe.

Here's the point. When we allow our lives to become filled with so many activities that we don't have time to sit and read the Bible, pray, and spend time with our church family, then we will be like the hard, rocky, and thorny soil. There will be no way that the Kingdom of God can grow inside of us. In the same way that it will take some effort to see the seed that you planted grow in the cup, so it is with the Kingdom of God. Make sure you are spending time fertilizing and water the soil of your heart every day.

Lesson 5

- Matthew 13:24-52
- Mark 4:30-34

Study Questions

A parable is a story or a metaphor that draws an analogy between an everyday thing and a deep, eternal truth. Make a list of the different analogies that Jesus uses in today's reading to describe the Kingdom of God. What is His explanation for each one?

Food for Thought

Take the good with the bad.

Make sure you are alone when you read this today, because you don't want anyone to hear your answer to this question. It could get you in trouble. So, shhhhhh. Here's the question: Have you ever looked at the church and said, "Why is there so much evil in the church? Doesn't God see this? Why doesn't He do something about it?" Let's face it, the church is a pretty messed-up place. Historically the church has been the perpetrator of some of the most heinous crimes known to man. In the name of Jesus babies have been slaughtered, races have been shunned, and adultery has been covered up. Today many of our churches are looking more like the money-grubbing, success-driven corporations that run our economy and dictate our society by feeding us propaganda to keep us buying their products. Does God condone this? If He doesn't, why does He allow it? As is the answer to most questions about God, it boils down to His love.

In the parables that Jesus presents today we see the answer to that question. Here are some observations from today's reading regarding the nature of the Kingdom of God.

1. **It is valuable beyond comparison**. Jesus said that the Kingdom was like a field that had a treasure in it. When a man found it, he sold everything he had to buy the field, knowing that the benefit of owning the field would far outweigh the sacrifice of selling everything. In today's church it seems that we may have forgotten about the treasure in the field. Why do people wallow around in the muck of the world when they claim to be in the Kingdom of God? Perhaps it is because they don't really believe that the treasure of eternal life with God, both now and forever — is real. It is much easier to enjoy the guaranteed comforts of today than it is to give them all away in exchange for the promise of unseen treasure.

2. **It grows**. Growth is by definition a process of dynamic changes, therefore it is important to realize that the Kingdom of God is not a static institution that is safe and predictable. Rather, it is a living organism that is constantly changing as it perpetuates the process of life. It begins as a seed. In the tiniest seed there is all the genetic information to form an enormous tree. The seed is the potential for growth and when it falls on fertile soil it will burst into action. The cycle starts by first sending down roots for nourishment, then sprouting up tall and strong, next producing

fruit, and then, finally producing more seeds to be sown into the fertile soil. Each time it grows anew it is unique and dynamic. No two stalks of wheat are identical. They are the same in that they are wheat, yet they are uniquely shaped and that shape is unpredictable. So it is with the Kingdom. When it germinates in one person's heart it may grow three heads of grain; when it germinates in another's it may grow one. Both are right; both are vital; both will reproduce. It is our job to cultivate it and to be thrilled with the excitement of seeing how it is constantly changing, developing, and unfolding within us.

3. **It is infected**. Jesus used two parables to teach this point. In one He says that the enemy sows weed seeds of evil in the field. In the other He says that in the catch of fish there are both good and bad. Here we answer our original question. Why does God not pull the evil weeds out of the field? The field represents God's Kingdom on earth. The last thing Satan wants is for that Kingdom to become powerful and be the dominant force in the world. So, he infects it with the weeds of the world's systems. He tempts church leaders to believe that they deserve the power and privilege they possess and that they have the right to have the perks of position. He tempts church members to relinquish their responsibilities to the "pastor" and let him do all the spiritual work while they just sit and observe him do his thing. He tempts Christians to become self-righteous and develop an attitude of fear and hatred toward the "sinners." So the weeds spring up and the Kingdom is tainted. Why doesn't God pull them? He doesn't do it because He does not want to damage any good wheat. He would rather allow evil to remain in order to protect the good wheat, even if it means that He could be misunderstood and accused of being easy on the weeds.

It is much like the story of Sodom and Gomorrah. Abraham begged God not to destroy the city. "If there were only five righteous people in the city, would you spare it then?" he bargained. "Yes," God replied, "for only a handful of righteous I would spare scores of the wicked." You see, in every church there is the good and the bad. In every denomination of churches that claim to follow Jesus there is the corruption of human systems and human pride. It is in every one of them, including your own. Yet, in every one of them there is also the seed of the Kingdom of God. Jesus is there and He can be fostered and nurtured and the Kingdom can grow. Even if there is only one person that authentically lived

in the Kingdom of God in a church of a thousand, God will spare that church. In fact, He will not only spare that church, he will use that church to spread more seeds.

Here's the bare-bones take-home for today. It seems that one of our favorite pastimes as Christians is to sit around and say how messed up that "other" church is down the street. "They do this, and they don't do that," we whine. "Their theology is whacked in this area." Let's just stop it and agree that we are all whacked in one way or another and get on with the business of following Jesus and not some humanly constructed system.

I want to be crystal clear on this. I am not advocating that we should just allow sin to run rampant in the church. Not at all. I am saying that we need to check our hearts and our motivations before we start being the "weed police." If God Himself is not willing to pull the weeds right now so that no wheat will be damaged, then perhaps it is not our responsibility to do it. Each of us needs to be more concerned with the field of our own hearts, making sure there are no weeds there, than we are about how messed up everyone else is. And, if we let God be concerned with the big field of His global church by realizing that there will be a harvest day when justice will be served, then perhaps the wheat would become so strong that the weeds would die of natural causes.

Kid's Questions

Take either a napkin or a piece of cloth that your mom doesn't care about getting dirty.

Now drop something on it that will stain it — like grape juice, or ink, or ketchup. Don't put too much on it. Just put enough to make a little stain right in the middle of the clean cloth.

Now try to get the stain out. As you rub and rub on the stain, what happens to the thread around the stain? Some of the good thread that isn't stained gets damaged in the process.

Here's a question. Have you ever been disappointed by someone you really trusted? Maybe your parents hurt your feelings, or a teacher embarrassed you in front of the class, or a coach yelled at you. How did you feel?

Many times, when things like that happen, people can get angry at God and ask Him, "How could you let bad things like this happen? Why don't you punish these bad people?"

Jesus told a parable to answer that question. It was about a field that was full of weeds. The farmer didn't want to pull the weeds so that he wouldn't hurt some good wheat in the process. It's like the cloth that you stained. Yes, the cloth is stained and it looks ugly. Yet, if you really wanted to get the stain completely out you would have to do a lot of damage to some perfectly good cloth in the process.

God allows bad things to happen because He loves people very much and doesn't want to destroy good people in the process of punishing bad people. So, in everything that people do, there will be a mixture of good and bad. Your parents, your teachers, your coaches — they are all people. They are mostly good, but there may be some weeds in their lives, just like there are some less-than-perfect things in your life. Don't get discouraged by that. Remember that the only One who is perfect is God Himself. He is the One in whom we should put all our trust. In the end He will weed out the good from the bad. For right now, we just need to give people some space to make mistakes and not beat them up for it. Together we can all lovingly work together to get better, and leave the judging to God.

61

Introduction

This week we reach the climax of the first phase of Jesus' ministry. Up to this point He has been presenting the Kingdom of God to the people of Israel and inviting them to enter into His Kingdom and fulfill the promise the God made to Abraham so many centuries earlier.

Jesus had a two-pronged approach to His mission: He preached the message and then He backed up His words with the power of His healing touch. Preaching and healing; that was His way. This week we see Jesus send the 12 disciples to do the same thing. He told them to go to the cities of Israel to preach the message of the Kingdom and to heal the sick. He had modeled it for them; now He was sending them to follow in His footsteps.

The disciples knocked on Israel's door and were received with a resounding "NO!" The symbol of the nation's rejection was in the frivolous execution of John the Baptist that Herod had ordered in order to save face at a party. Just like the wicked kings of the Old Testament, Herod resisted the Word of God spoken through the prophet, followed his own desires, and killed the messenger.

In Matthew, Mark, and Luke this phase of Jesus' ministry takes place completely in Galilee. These authors intentionally kept Jesus away from Jerusalem in their story in order to create a more dramatic theme when He finally moved toward Jerusalem in his final days. In John's Gospel, on the other hand, Jesus bounced back and forth between Galilee and Jerusalem. Remember, it was acceptable practice, in those days, to organize history around themes rather than to follow a rigid chronological sequence. In both models (the synoptics and John) there is a contrast drawn between Jerusalem and Galilee. Jerusalem represented the center of power and the corruption of the status quo. Galilee represented the marginalized and the edge of the world. Whenever Jesus dips into Jerusalem in John's Gospel, it was for the purpose of speaking directly to the leadership and exposing their deficiencies. This week we see Jesus go to Jerusalem and tell the leaders that Moses himself testifies to the identity of Jesus.

With Herod's execution of John and the rejection of the mission work by the 12, Jesus brings a close to His Invitation to the Kingdom extended to Israel. He speaks the harsh and sad words, "Woe to you, cities who have rejected me. I'm going to go to the Gentiles now." Next week we will see a shifting of gears in Jesus' ministry as a result of Israel's rejection.

Lesson 1

- Matthew 9:18-26
- Mark 5:21-43
- Luke 8:40-56

Study Questions

What are the miracles that Jesus performed in these stories?

What obstacle stood between the bleeding woman and Jesus?

What kind of attitude do you think she needed to have to get close enough to Jesus to touch Him?

What reason did Jesus attribute for her being healed?

Food for Thought

The story of the dead girl and the bleeding woman is a transitional story. In many ways it belongs grouped with the stories from two weeks ago that demonstrated Jesus' healing power. He delivered people from sickness, sin, storms, and traditions. In today's reading we see more of the same. Jesus delivered a girl from death and a woman from a lifetime of incessant feminine bleeding.

In all three of the synoptic Gospels (Matthew, Mark, and Luke) this story is used as a summary and closing statement to the first leg of Jesus' ministry. In fact, Mark uses it as the one and only story to represent all the miracles that Jesus did in his early ministry of the Invitation to Israel. Matthew and Luke use it as the final, and summarizing, story that transitions into the sending out of the 12 to the eventual rejection of His invitation.

There are two ways that we can look at this story:

1. **Symbolic/Literary meaning**. When I say symbolic I do not mean untrue. This story really happened, of course, but there is a specific reason that all three Gospel writers placed it at this point of the story. The two women in the story represent the nation of Israel. The old woman had been bleeding for her whole life. It is most likely that her bleeding was some form of menstrual dysfunction. In Jewish law a woman was considered unclean during her menstrual cycle. Just imagine; this poor woman had been unclean her entire life and was not allowed into the circle of mainstream society. Her perpetual uncleanness was symbolic of the state of Israel. In Jesus' eyes, His intended bride, Israel, was unclean and unfit for union with Him. The girl (ironically the daughter of a synagogue ruler) was dead. So was Israel. She (Israel) was dead spiritually and seemingly beyond hope. By closing this chapter of the story with Jesus raising the dead girl to life and cleansing the bleeding woman, Jesus by was demonstrating what could have happened to Israel had they simply believed His message. That is the repeated theme of the story...believe. Reach out and touch Him and you will be restored, Israel; that is all it takes. Unfortunately, they did not listen and remained unfit for marriage and dead to the new life of the Kingdom.

2. **The Personal Level**. In the same way that these stories are symbolic for Israel, they are also symbolic for each one of us. The

Invitation that Jesus extended to enter His Kingdom is extended to you each day. There are two kinds of people: those who are dead and not in the Kingdom, and those who are in the Kingdom but riddled with disease and uncleanness. Where are you today? If you have not yet said, "Yes" to Jesus' invitation to follow Him and live in His Kingdom, then you are spiritually dead, unable to bring yourself back to life. Jesus can breathe His life into you and set you on your feet. Or, perhaps you do love Jesus but have allowed yourself to slip into some sort of sinful pattern. Whether it is bitterness, unforgiveness, sexual addiction, pride, envy, or self-indulgence; it doesn't matter. All of these things lead to the same place. They lead you to pain, sickness, depression, and uncleanness. Whether you are dead or bleeding, the remedy is the same; believe. Look at the bleeding woman. She knew the power that Jesus had to heal her. She fought her way through the crowd, reached out her hand, and, in faith, believed that Jesus could restore her. Would you have had that kind of courage and conviction?

I'm going to make a bold statement. I believe that a great deal of the pain and suffering that Christians experience — both emotionally and physically — is due to a lack of trust in the power of God. Now, don't get me wrong. I'm not ascribing to the name-it-and-claim-it theology that says that if you just have enough faith God can and must do whatever you ask. No way. God will do what He wants to do in His timing independent of us. That being said, there is still the reality that many of us are suffering because we don't believe the truth. Jesus said that He came to give us life and give it to the fullest. He said that our joy could be complete. He said that we could know the truth and that the truth could set us free. We can be free from worry, stress, bitterness, and unforgiveness. When we are free from these things we will become free from a great deal of the things that destroy us from the inside out. Jesus provided the way for us to dump our garbage and be made new in Him. We can focus our hearts on His Kingdom and all the worries of life will, indeed, disappear... because they just don't matter in the light of eternity and the Kingdom.

He did it for us, and He extends the gift to us. All we need to do is believe it. But we don't. Oh yes, we may believe that He died for our sins and that we will go to Heaven when we die, but we don't really believe that He can handle the day-to-day hassles of our lives. OK, maybe we think He CAN handle them; but what we don't believe...where we lack trust...is that He actually CARES about handling our stuff. We believe we are so small and insignificant in the grand scheme of things that He can't possibly want to deal with us.

Did the bleeding woman think, "Look at Him, He's mobbed by a crowd of people, I couldn't get near to him. Even if I did get close to Him, He wouldn't notice me. After all, I'm just an unclean woman" ? No. She knew that Jesus could cleanse her and she persistently got herself to a place where she was near enough to Him to touch His clothes. Her persistence and her belief in what Jesus had to offer is what brought the cleansing she needed. When there is faith like that, Jesus notices. Notice what happened. In the middle of a huge crowd that was pressing in on Him, Jesus stopped and asked, "Who touched me?" "What?" His disciples replied, "Hundreds of people have touched you." "No. Hundreds of people have put their hands on me for a myriad of reasons, but one person actually touched me. She touched me with humility, purity of heart, and unrelenting belief." Now that is touching.

Today, ask yourself, do you believe in the power of Jesus, or do you just want to believe in the power of Jesus? Perhaps today could be the day that you reach out your hand and touch Him in a way that you've never done before.

Kid's Questions

Try to imagine the big crowd that was swarming around Jesus. Do you think it would have been hard to get through the crowd and get close enough to touch Him?

Do you think you would have had the courage to push your way through all those people to be able to touch Jesus?

Have you ever had a time when you were with a group of kids and an adult was leading the group, and you wanted something but were afraid to ask for it? Let's pretend that you are in school with about 30 other kids and you need to go to the restroom. You raise your hand, but the teacher doesn't notice you because she is busy with some other kids. You can't leave the room without permission. What do you do?

What are some reasons that might cause you to be scared to get the teacher's attention?

Many times we don't get good things from God because we are simply too scared to believe that He will give them to us. In the Sermon on the Mount Jesus said that all we have to do is ask, and God is ready and willing to give us the things we need.

Lesson 2

- Matthew 9:35-38
- Matthew 10:1-42
- Mark 6:7-13
- Luke 9:1-9

Study Questions

What was the purpose of Jesus' mission?

What did He instruct the disciples to do when He sent them out two by two?

Try to summarize Matthew 10:1-42 in just two or three sentences. What was the main thrust of the mission?

Food for Thought

Today we see a model the way the church should be built. Notice in Matthew 9:35 how Jesus' mission is summarized. Matthew says that He went through all the towns and villages, teaching in their synagogues, preaching the Good News of the kingdom and healing every disease and sickness. There are three aspects to Jesus' ministry:

1. **Penetrating culture.** Jesus moved throughout the countryside and went into the synagogues. Jesus met people where they were. He *went* to the synagogue, the well, the seashore, the temple courts, and the leper colony. He did not build a ministry center and launch a marketing campaign that would draw people in to hear His message. He took the message to the people.

2. **Proclamation of the Good News.** Jesus' mission was a teaching mission. He spoke the words of truth in compelling ways in order to convince people that He was speaking the Words of God. Notice what His teaching was like. He spoke in metaphors and pictures that were relevant to the audience He was addressing. He spoke of farmers and fishermen, kings and shepherds. All of life was fair game for Jesus to draw analogies that would communicate the deep truths of the Kingdom of God. The point is that He was able to clearly articulate the truth in a compelling, relational, culturally relevant manner.

3. **A Ministry of Healing.** The biggest problem that people had was that they had inherited centuries of sin-ridden systems and patterns of behavior that had divided the races and classes, had oppressed the poor, and had allowed the spread of disease. There was an epidemic of those who were bound in the grip of sin and oppressed by demonic influence. There was an epidemic of disease, depression, and fear. There was the pain of racial prejudice and socio-economic class stratification where the rich got richer and the poor got poorer. When people are in such a hurting state they are not necessarily ready to hear the proclamation of truth verbally. What they need is to see the power of God that can deliver them from their demons and debilitations. Then their eyes can be opened and they may be ready to receive the truth of the Kingdom.

Notice what happens in Matthew 10. As Jesus is closing His exclusive mission to Israel, He gathers His 12 disciples and says, "Alright, boys, you've seen me in action. Now it's your turn. Go take the mission to Israel." In verses 6-7 we see Him send them on the same mission He had been doing. His directions were to:

1. Go to the lost sheep of Israel.

2. Preach this message: "the Kingdom of heaven is at hand."

3. Heal the sick, raise the dead, cleanse those who have leprosy, and drive out demons.

That is the model that Jesus established for the church. The leader has a mission. He calls people to follow Him and watch Him perform His mission. Then He empowers them to go and do the same mission. Where there was one, now there are 12. Those men then each take on disciples, model for them, then send them out. Where there were 12, now there are 144. This type of process is one of exponential growth within the leadership of the church.

There are two implications for the church from this.

1. For 1500 years, the local church has been primarily focused on being a geographically localized institution; for example, the church is the little white building with a steeple on the corner of the street. The pastor's job is to craft his sermons well enough and choose a target market that will draw people inside the building. That is not what Jesus modeled, nor is it what the apostles modeled in the book of Acts, nor is it what the early church fathers modeled for the first 300 years of church history. They modeled that the church is a body of believers who penetrate culture. We take the message of the Kingdom into our neighborhoods and workplaces, and even around the world. Perhaps it is time that we stop asking how we can get people to come to our church and start taking the church to people in their own homes.

2. People need healing. The best place to meet people with the message of the Kingdom of God is in their place of pain. Last week we discussed that the "good soil" is a person's heart that has been tilled by life's pain to the point that it is open and receptive to receive the message of hope, and is willing to do whatever it takes to nurture the seed in his or her life. The truth is that the vast majority of people in our world are living in the prison of the consequences of sin, both of their own sinful choices and the sinful choices of others. They need to know that Jesus has the power to release them from that prison. Some are in the prison of habitual sin and addiction. Jesus can set them free. Some are in the prison of shame from the abuse that they received. Jesus can lift them out. Some are in the prison of false teaching that is keeping them blind to the truth. Jesus can give them sight. Some are suffering physical ailment that is the result of harbored bitterness and unforgiveness. Jesus can heal their bodies.

The question we must ask is twofold: 1) Do we actually know the healing power of Jesus in our own lives, or are we running on centuries-old doctrine that has been fed to us through disembodied instruction. 2) Are we being the Good News of Jesus in the lives of those around us with our attitudes and actions, or are we just speaking words that do not match our lifestyles. In other words, are we speaking about the joy of the Lord with frowns on our faces? Are we speaking about the healing power of Jesus when we still carry around huge burdens of sin and unforgiveness in our lives? I'm not saying that we should put on an act for people so that they will believe the message. Of course not. The church has been doing that forever. I'm also not saying that you have to be perfect before you can start sharing your faith. If that were the case, no words would ever be uttered. What I'm saying is that, perhaps, many of us (myself included) have forgotten about the power of Jesus in our lives. The Good News of the Kingdom is that hearts can, indeed, be set free and made to walk in a thriving, victorious life of joy that comes through knowing and living in the truth. If we authentically took that message, through a life where words and deeds were in sync with each other, then the Kingdom of God would become an unstoppable force in the world.

Kid's Questions

Let's pretend that there is a neighborhood where everyone in the neighborhood had a disease that paralyzed their legs and left them unable to walk. One person in that neighborhood found a cure for the disease and was able to walk. What do you think that person should do with that medicine?

What would you think if that person kept the cure in his or her house and set up a sign in the front yard that read, "I have the cure, come and see me on Sunday morning from 9-10am and I'll tell you about it."

Would that be the best method to get the cure to the people? Why or why not?

As Christians we have the cure to sin. Sometimes we can be like the man who put the sign in his yard. We get together every Sunday with other Christians and talk about how great it is that we have been cured and how we wish people would come to our church service so they can hear about the cure too.

That is silly. We need to take the cure to the people who can't walk. This week, think about ways that you could talk to people in your neighborhood about Jesus.

Lesson 3

- Matthew 11:20-30

Study Questions

What was Jesus' attitude toward those who rejected His message?

What was Jesus' attitude toward those who did receive His message?

Food for Thought

Today we see the other side of the coin from last teaching. Before we observed that Jesus' mission was to bring both the Word and the healing power of the Kingdom of God to people in their place of prison and pain. I emphasized the need for the church to meet people in their place of pain and touch them there. If the teaching stopped there it could be very easy for two things to happen to Christians everywhere. First, they could feel guilted into spending time with the down-and-out and think that all their time needs to be spent trying to heal hurting people. They may even feel guilty for having fun and surrounding themselves with "healthy" or "safe" people. Secondly, they may interpret yesterday's teaching to mean that Christians need to wade in people's muck and wallow with them there for as long as it takes for them to repent.

Here's the truth. That is not what Jesus modeled. First of all, Jesus surrounded Himself with men and women who were eager to follow Him, obey His words, and do whatever it took to grow stronger in His Kingdom. These people were His community and His inner core. That inner core was not centrally located in the local church building; it was a bond of brotherhood that was held together by relationship and commitment. It could meet anywhere, anytime. Having this inner core of church-on-the-go was vital to His ministry. He was not alone in trying to change the world and deliver people all by Himself. The church is first and foremost a Jesus-centered community that, together, penetrates culture and meets people where they are.

Also, notice what happens in today's reading. At the end of Jesus' campaign to bring the message and the healing power of the Kingdom to Israel, He sits back and evaluates the fruit of His labor. It didn't look good. The people did not respond to His message. Even though He had brought physical healing to them and had demonstrated His power, they rejected His invitation. So, what does He do? He "denounces" them. This is a harsh word. It is the same Greek word that Jesus Himself uses in Matthew 5 when He says that you are blessed when men insult you for His sake. Because of the hardness of their heart and their unwillingness to repent, Jesus said, "Woe to you." In other words, He said, "I'm done wasting My seed on your hard soil. Great pain will come to you as a result of your rejection. I'm moving on." Remember how He instructed His disciples? When they encountered a home that was not receptive to their message, they were to "shake the dust" off their feet and move on. Shaking the dust was like saying, "Hey man, no skin off my teeth. You are responsible for your own stuff. I offered. You rejected. I don't have time for this."

Here's the point. Many times, as Christians we can encounter really needy people in our lives. If the love of Jesus is flowing through us then we authentically want to help them and guide them to the power of Jesus' deliverance. So, we invest time in them. We listen to their tales of woe, pain, and abuse. Our hearts bleed for them. We extend to them the help and the instruction that they need. And so we should. At that point you reach a crossroad. After you have demonstrated Christ's love and have opened the door that exposes their path of healing, you have done your part and the choice is now theirs. They can either repent (meaning to move away from their previous way of life and pain) and walk through the door that you have opened, or they can decline your help and remain in their place of pain.

Many times people are married to their own pain and they don't actually want to leave it. That may seem hard to believe, but it is very, very true. People have become so comfortable with their pain that they can't imagine life without it and they are afraid that the process of being delivered from it may actually be more painful than their current situation. They don't really want to get better; what they want is for people to pay attention to them and coddle them in their pain. Think about it. If Jesus does have the power to heal, and if they truly believe that and do the things that He has instructed, then they will be healed, transformed, reborn, and will be able to move into the community of healthy believers who are working in unity to continually grow in the grace of God. I'm afraid that we have taken the compassion of Jesus and distorted it into a sort of enabling hospice for the spiritually dying.

The bottom line is that people are either good soil or not good soil. They either want to be free or they don't. Jesus said that you are either for Him or against Him; there is no middle ground. If you are penetrating the culture and meeting people in their pain, and the seed is being authentically planted, then...guess what... you won't be living with wallowing, pain-ridden people for very long. If you plant a church with those people then they will become transformed into powerful testimonies of the power of God and the Kingdom message will be turbo-charged for deeper penetration into culture.

Let's follow Jesus' lead and have the courage to know when we have expended enough energy on hard, rocky, and thorny soil. We don't have time to mess around with people who reject our offering of peace and healing. You've planted the

seed. When they are ready to receive it, they will find you. Until then, spend your energy finding good soil, planting the seed, and then watching it grow and bringing about transformation. After all, it is not your job to make the seed grow. It is simply your job to cultivate the Kingdom in your own heart and courageously take the seed to the culture and plant it. The process of growing and producing fruit is up to God.

Caution: Don't read this as permission to stay hidden in your safe inner circle, completely isolated from the culture and rationalize that behavior by saying, "Oh, they are just hard soil anyway." You have to actually try before you can shake off the dust!

Kid's Questions

Have you ever heard the expression, "You can lead a horse to water but you can't make it drink?" What does that mean?

If you found really thirsty people and offered them nice glasses of water, but they refused it; what would you do? Would you grab the back of their heads and try to pour the water down their throats? Why? Eventually all you could do is leave the water with them and hope they drink it before it's too late.

Yesterday you were encouraged to try to tell people in your neighborhood about the love of Jesus. Today we see that sometimes people just don't want to hear about it. Don't get discouraged by that. Don't spend too much time trying to cram it down people's throats. They either want to hear or they don't; the choice is theirs.

Lesson 4

- John 5:1-47

Study Questions

How did the Jews react to Jesus' miracle of healing?

What did Jesus say was needed for eternal life?

Who were the different witnesses that testified to the truth of Jesus' message? Why was this significant when dealing with the Jewish leaders?

Food for Thought

As I mentioned in the introduction, the synoptic Gospels (Matthew, Mark, and Luke) are organized in a very different manner than John's version of the story. In the synoptics, Jesus stays in Galilee and the pagan regions for His entire ministry until the big climax in the end. They did this to show that Jesus was concerned with the whole world and only focused on Jerusalem when it was time to bring the final blow to the institutions of Israel. John has the same intention but organizes it differently. Throughout Jesus' life He travels back and forth from Jerusalem to the outlying region. Each trip to Jerusalem marks the end of one phase of His ministry and the beginning of another.

In today's reading, in Jesus' first phase of ministry, John concludes with a group of stories where Jesus is in Jerusalem. These stories parallel the intent of the stories that the synoptics were trying to accomplish. We see Jesus healing people and then being rejected by the institution of Israel. He extended to the people His invitation to the Kingdom and it was rejected.

What we read in John 5 is Jesus' two-part response to the rejection.

1. "You've missed out on life itself." In verses 19-30, Jesus clearly explains to them what it was they were rejecting. He said that the keys to eternal life were found in Him. Anyone who believes in Him will have eternal life. Anyone who does not believe in Him will not have eternal life and will be eternally separated from the Father. It doesn't get much clearer than that.

The word "believe" is a key term for John's Gospel. It really is the center of John's theology. But, what does it mean? In the English language the term "believe" can easily be relegated to the category of cognitive agreement. Sometimes we can even use it as a synonym for "think" or "guess." When we are asked, "Where is Billy?" we respond, "Hmmm....I believe he is in the backyard." That is not at all the meaning of the Greek word that we translate "believe." The Greek word is "pisteuo" which is also translated "to have faith." When Jesus says you must believe in Him, He is referring to an action as much as a mental agreement.

I love the illustration of the man who crossed Niagara Falls on a tightrope. In front of thousands of people he pushed a wheelbarrel across the Niagara Falls on a tightrope. He went back and forth a few times. Then he asked the crowd, "How many of you believe

I can push this wheelbarrel across the Falls?" Everyone in the crowd raised their hands because they had seen him do it. "OK," he continued, "who'd like to get in the wheelbarrel and let me push you across?" That is the difference between our understanding of belief and the real meaning of pisteuo.

It is one thing to agree that Jesus can save us; it is another thing to yield yourself to Him and allow Him to actually do it. That is when to believe, put our trust in, submit ourselves, and have faith in Him. Jesus said if we do that, then we will have eternal life. He will take us there.

2. "You just aren't listening." According to Jewish Law something was considered true if there was a minimum of two testimonies. In verses 31-47, speaking to the teachers of Jewish Law, Jesus points out to them He has ample testimony regarding the validity of His claims: "The Father testifies, John the Baptist testifies, the Prophets testify, and...oh yes... the guy who actually wrote the Law that you love so much, Moses he testifies about me as well." You see, when we become so enamored with our own theology and the comfort and control that it brings to our society, we become blind to the truth, even when it is as plain as the nose on our face.

By using this language of testimonies in dealing with the Pharisees, Jesus was essentially saying the case was closed and it was now time to shake the dust off His feet in regard to restoring the nation of Israel. Judgment had been passed and it was time to expand His horizons and bring the Kingdom of God to the entire world, not through the nation of Israel, as was originally intended, but through the new community of God called the Church.

Kid's Questions

Once there was a man who crossed Niagara Falls on a tightrope. In front of thousands of people he pushed a wheelbarrel across Niagara Falls on a tightrope. He went back and forth a few times. Then he asked the crowd, "How many of you believe that I can push this wheelbarrel across the Falls?" Everyone in the crowd raised their hands because they had seen him do it. "OK," he continued, "who'd like to get in the wheel barrel and let me push you across?"

In that story we can see there are two ways that people can believe something. The first way is to agree that something is true; the other way is to trust in something enough that you would put yourself into it completely.

In today's reading Jesus said that if we believe in Him then we will have eternal life. He meant the kind of belief where we actually get in the wheelbarrel. That is when to believe, put our trust in, hand ourselves over, and have faith in Him. Jesus said that if we do that, then we will have eternal life. He will take us there.

Do you believe in Jesus? Do you believe that He can take away your sins and lead you into a meaningful life now and for eternity?

Lesson 5

- Matthew 14:1-12
- Mark 6:14-29

Study Questions

What happened to John the Baptist?

Why did this happen?

Based on this story alone, how would you describe Herod's character?

Food for Thought

Today we read a sick and twisted story.

Herod is a telling personification of the spiritual state of Israel. Herod was corrupt philosophically, religiously, politically, and morally. He was on the throne, but had no biblical claim to it. He had been placed there by the Romans so that they could keep that raucous nation in line. Herod adopted every whim and philosophy around and spent much of his energy feeding his own desires. This love of self and pagan culture was demonstrated by the fact that he built theatres, bath houses, and chariot stadiums throughout Israel.

In many ways these icons of Greco-Roman culture Herod had erected were equivalent to the high places that Ahab had built when he was married to the Phoenician Queen Jezebel during Elijah's ministry in 1 Kings. As God did in the Old Testament days with Ahab, He sent the prophet to Herod to expose his sins and to prepare him for the coming judgment if he would not repent. John the Baptist was that prophet. Like Elijah to Ahab, John pointed his finger in the face of Herod and proclaimed the wrath of God. Neither Ahab nor Herod cared much for the frantic raving of those over-zealous, self-righteous, desert-dwelling, loud-mouths. They were bad for PR and were like flies that perpetually disturbed the peace.

In today's story we see the truth of Herod's heart. In a moment of passion and self-indulgence, Herod decides that it would be better to decapitate the prophet of God than it would be to lose face in the eyes of his royal constituency.

There are three points for us today:

1. **The Narrative Symbol.** This story is used in the Gospels to symbolize the nation's response to the invitation Jesus extended to them. As the ax slams down on the neck of John the Baptist, a resounding echo of "No thanks, not interested," rings in Jesus' ear.

2. **Avoiding Herod's dilemma.** Herod demonstrates the tangled web that sin can weave in our lives. When we live according to the rules of every whim that passes through our lives, when we are trying to please everyone around us, and also try to gratify every craving of our own desires, we will eventually find ourselves in a lose/lose situation. One bad decision leads to another bad decision. That bad decision can lead to a deception to cover-up the other bad decision. The deception must then be perpetuated, and then, due to our pride, we end up hurting the people we care about in order to protect

our own skin. That is the way of sin and self-gratification.

3. **Embracing the way of John.** As we see John's head sitting on the silver platter, it is a very natural response to think, "What a waste. Is this really what the Kingdom of God is all about? Is this really why John spent his whole life devoted to fulfilling God's call? Was he really supposed to end up as a party favor for a stripper? I don't get it."

In our culture we have become intoxicated with fairy tales. We like to believe that good guys always win. We like to believe that there must always be a big happy ending where everybody gets to be the hero and everybody wins in the end. Think about that for a moment. *Everybody* gets to be the hero? *Everybody* wins? When we read a story, or watch a movie, we, the audience, are identifying with the hero. We forget that in almost every story, some good guys get killed along the way. In the end, the hero wins and we feel justice has been served. So it has, but only one person is the hero. Now here's the problem. In life, we think that we are the heroes in the story. That is the message our culture feeds us everyday. It is especially dominant in the messages the media is presenting to children today. They hear, "Be true to yourself. You have the power to do whatever you want. You are the hero." In a sense, they are being told that "it's all about you."

Reality check. We aren't the heroes of the story. All of history is one big story, and there is only one Hero. Jesus is the Hero. Jesus wins in the end. The rest of us are supporting characters. Sometimes the supporting characters get killed by wicked kings for seemingly meaningless purposes.

I know that is harsh. I know that concept flies in the face of all that America stands for today. But I think it is a piece of truth that, when fully understood, will actually help us understand some of the bondage that we live under.

Throughout the New Testament there is a running theme. The church is the body of Christ. There is one head and many parts. We are the parts, not the head. We all work together, but we are not the main point. Can you imagine how much more effective our communities would be if we all realized that life isn't about us. We aren't the Hero of the story. We are all, equally, supporting characters who are serving the greater purpose of the Hero and the head.

What does this have to do with John, and with us? John was a martyr. That means that he was killed for his faith. It would be good for us to remember that today, in this day and time, there are people who are risking their lives for the truth of Jesus. For people in countries all over the world, to proclaim the truth means to invite prison, torture, and even execution. Right now, in the 21st century, this is happening in a third of the world. Sometimes bad things happen to good people, but for the right reasons.

I would rather have my head on a plate and be in the truth, than to be living "free" in the palace of Herod. As followers of Jesus it would do us well to remember that we aren't the heroes of the story, and that there may come a day when we are asked to lay down our lives for the Hero.

Let's spend some time today praying for our brothers and sisters in Christ who are putting their necks on the line, literally, for the truth of Jesus today. Pray that they will have courage and keep their eyes fixed on the hero.

Kid's Questions

How did it make you feel when you heard that John the Baptist had been killed by Herod? Why?

Did you know that there are people in the world today that are being killed because they are Christians? How does that make you feel?

Do you think that you would be courageous enough to go to prison, or even be killed for the sake of Jesus?

These situations are very real, and they can seem really scary to talk about, but they are real. Just remember, when you are with Jesus nothing can truly harm you. When we live, we live with Him. When we die we see Him in His full glory.

Spend some time thanking God right now that you live in a country that gives you the freedom to worship God. Pray for the children in countries where it is against the law to be a Christian. Pray that they will be safe, and more importantly, pray that they will have courage no matter what happens.

Introduction

In our reading this session we begin a three-part series in the middle of Jesus' story that marks a major transition in His ministry. In the previous sessions we have seen that Jesus was extending His invitation to the nation of Israel for them to enter into the Kingdom of God. In our last readings, Israel rejected His invitation. Now we will see that Jesus is expanding the scope of His invitation to encompass the entire world, both Jews and Gentiles alike. After all, that was the original intention of the promise that God made to Abraham back at the beginning of things. God said, "Abraham, I will make you a great nation, and through that nation all nations will be blessed."

The major theme of the week is bread. Jesus begins the week by feeding 5,000 people and ends the week by feeding another 4,000. Notice that there are 12 baskets collected after the 5,000 are fed and 7 baskets collected after the 4,000. These numbers clearly symbolize that Jesus is the bread of life for both the Jews — 5,000 and 12 — and the Gentiles — 4,000 and 7. While the people came to feed their bellies with physical bread, Jesus warned them that the bread He is offering is far more real than baked flour and water. His bread meant His very essence. To eat the bread of Jesus was to accept the fact that His body and His blood would be broken and spilled out as a sacrifice for their sins. To believe in Him and follow His ways — even to the point of giving up your own life — defined what would be involved in eating His bread.

At this point many of His disciples abandoned Him. There are a couple of reasons why they may have walked away. Some may have not understood His graphic metaphors that referred to eating His flesh and drinking His blood. Perhaps they thought He had snapped and was resorting to cannibalism. (Don't laugh; there are documents that indicate that this misconception of the message of Jesus was one of the reasons why the Romans persecuted the early church.) Of course Jesus didn't mean it literally, but they were not ready to see the deeper meaning behind His teaching. Another reason they may have left was that they were disappointed in His role as Messiah. Jesus' talk of His body and His blood was the beginning of His preparation for the coming death He would experience on the cross. The people of Israel were looking for a mighty warrior to lead them into battle against the Romans. They didn't want any part of a Messiah who would hand over Himself to the Romans to be executed. So, many may have left to find a Messiah that better fit their profile.

At the bottom of the drawing you see the scene of Jesus walking on the water while Peter steps out to meet Him. The key to this story was, in order to walk on water, Peter had to keep his eyes on Jesus. This is perfectly sandwiched between the two mass-feeding stories. Here we see Jesus as the center of the world. On His right is Israel, on His left are the Gentile nations, and swarming all around them are the storms of change; the only way they can move into the new era of God's Kingdom is to keep their eyes firmly fixed on Jesus, the one who can walk on top of any stormy sea.

Lesson 1

- Matthew 14:13-21
- Mark 6:30-43
- Luke 9:10-17
- John 6:1-15

Study Questions

What terrible event had just happened before this story?

What was Jesus trying to do at the beginning of the story before the people arrived? Why?

What attitude did Jesus have toward the crowd?

What miracle did Jesus perform for the crowd?

Food for Thought

If you haven't already noticed, the stories we read in these studies have taken us back and forth in the pages of all four Gospels. You may, at times, have wondered why I have mixed up things so drastically. The answer to that question will actually shed light on the story we read today.

As we have discussed earlier, there are two important things to keep in mind when studying the Gospels. 1) The authors were not as concerned with keeping a literal chronology in Jesus' life as they were with presenting a cohesive theme. 2) The synoptic Gospels (Matthew, Mark, and Luke) are very different from John, sharing only 10% of John's stories.

With that in mind, whenever you do a comparative study of all four Gospels and try to synthesize them into one fluid story, you need to watch out for some key markers. One of the most significant markers is when all four Gospels contain the same story, in approximately the same way, and in roughly the same time period.

The story of the feeding of the 5,000 is the first, and one of the most prominent, of such markers. While the order of events in the four Gospels up to this point in our study has been quite jumbled, all four Gospels agree that there is a correlation between the execution of John the Baptist and the feeding of the 5,000. These events marked the ending of Jesus' invitation to Israel and the beginning of His focus on the world.

Here are some observations to consider.

1. Jesus was deeply affected by John's murder. Matthew 14:13 says that Jesus withdrew privately to a solitary place. He didn't even take His disciples with Him. He wanted to be alone. There were two reasons why this event impacted Him so deeply. The first, and most obvious, is that John was His family. Unless you have experienced the pain of having a close relative murdered, you cannot imagine the emotional pain that Jesus must have experienced as a result of this pointless act of violence. Secondly, Jesus was filled with sorrow over the rejection by His people. He had come to remind them that God had chosen Israel centuries before. Even as they prostituted themselves with every neighboring religion that came along, God had persevered with them over and over again. He had sent them prophet after prophet to proclaim the truth of His Kingdom. After so many rejections the Father finally sent His Son to proclaim the Kingdom once and for all. And still, even when the Son Himself had come, the people didn't even recognize Him. That had

to have hurt Jesus deeply. Not only was He hurt by the rejection itself, He also knew that because of their rejection the path ahead of Him would lead to the cross where He would have to sacrifice His life for the people. This deep sorrow that came from both emotional places helps us understand more clearly the intense humanity of Jesus. He knows pain, hurt, and rejection. Because of this He can empathize with us.

2. Jesus is a man of grace and compassion. Right after the nation rejects Him Jesus is thronged with thousands of people who wanted to receive His healing. (The Bible says there were 5,000 men. It did not mention women and children, so there could have been two or even three times as many people present.) Do you remember what Jesus was trying to do in this moment? He was trying to get away and have a little downtime so that He could recoup from His deep pain and disappointment. Put yourself in His shoes in that moment. Just as you are about to head for solitude on the mountaintop you turn around to see a massive crowd clamoring for you. My first reaction would have been, "Oh nice. You don't want Me as your Messiah, but you'll use Me for my healing. It's always about you isn't it? Well, not today! I'm taking the day off. You can go heal yourself for all I care." In many ways He would have been justified if He had taken that stance. Yet, He did not. When He looked at that crowd all He could see was a mass of helpless sheep that had no one to guide them. He knew that the average people were not even aware of the cosmic significance that was unfolding before them. They were simply following their bellies and following the whims of their leaders. It was the establishment of Israel that had rejected him, not these poor people. He turned to them and said, "Come on up. I've always got time for you."

The crowd of 5,000 men represents the nation of Israel. Jesus is demonstrating to His disciples, and saying to the world, "I will feed my nation, Israel." On Friday we will see a similar event where He performs the same miracle for the Gentiles as well.

Kid's Questions

Let's say there was a kid at school or in the neighborhood that always picked on you. Everyday he would call you names and try to take things from you. How would you feel about that kid?

Now let's say that one day you saw that kid on the side of the road and he had just fallen off his bike and really hurt himself. His foot was stuck in the wheel, he was bleeding, and he couldn't help himself. What would you do? Would you laugh at him and tell him that he got what he deserved? Or, would you help him get unstuck and then get an adult to help him out? Why?

Today we say that Jesus had compassion on the crowd, even after they had rejected him as the Messiah. Jesus taught us to love people and help them, even when they don't love us. That is hard to do, but it is the Jesus' way.

Lesson 2

- John 6:25-71

Study Questions

What accusation did Jesus bring against the crowd? Why?

What did Jesus claim about Himself?

Why did some of Jesus' disciples desert Him?

In what ways could Jesus' vivid metaphor be misunderstood? What do you think His real meaning was when He said to eat His flesh and drink His blood?

Food for Thought

Life and death. When it's all boiled down, that is the sum of things. We live and we die. The question is whether we will live well and die well.

There are two ways you can look at this. On the one side you can strive to live and deny the death part how most of the world lives. We scramble through life fighting hard to live and to stay alive. We try to suck the most out of life we can and prolong the inevitability of death as long as possible. In this struggle to live we fall into various categories of success and degrees of quality of life. Some people feast at great banquets and drink from flowing goblets of fine wine. Others lie in tortured pain and scrape for scraps of bread and droplets of mucky water. Yet, there is a common element that permeates all life experience. The most basic common denominator of this human struggle is the drive to find food and water. That is the essence of life. If we can simply find bread and water then we can live. (Unless it's processed white bread. Then it's questionable whether we would live for long...but that's a topic for another study!)

In our previous study we saw that Jesus touched the people at this most basic level of their existence. He gave them bread. He filled their physical bellies with real bread. They left that place physically satisfied. That is how the people saw Jesus. They were using this perspective on life to evaluate Him. What the people wanted was a real king who gave them real bread and led a real army to defeat the very real Roman Empire. "Feed us and save us!" they cried out to Jesus.

Today we see that Jesus offered a different perspective on life and death. He revealed to the people that life was not a matter of living large and eating as much bread as you can before you die. No. Jesus came to offer a different kind of bread altogether. His bread was the bread that feeds the eternal soul. His water is the water that quenches the eternal thirst.

His bread brings new light to the issue of life and death. Jesus taught us the secret to understanding life and death is to see they are intertwined. From the first perspective they are separate and opposed issues. You live, and then you die. When you are living you fight for physical bread; baking it, selling it, and killing to keep it. Then you die. Jesus said things were different. Jesus said that the key to life is...death. Our focus cannot be on filling our bellies; our bellies will just be empty in a few hours and we'll have to fill them again. The key to real life is to focus on the life that happens after the physical death. Eternity is our real home and our true lives. The Kingdom of God is all about real life. When you eat the bread of Jesus, then you will know real life eternally.

But what is the bread of Jesus? He said it was His body and His blood. Eat it. Drink it. What? Is Jesus inviting us to be cannibals? Of course not. Jesus is saying He was about to demonstrate to the world the key to real life. He was about to give up everything He had and give up every rightful claim He had to be the King of Israel, and allow Himself to be executed by the Roman Empire. This was His bread to give up everything and die. Only then could He be raised to new life and open the gates of the Kingdom of God to the whole world.

Many people were not satisfied with this proposal. When Jesus told them of His plan, they said, "Uh, thanks, but no thanks. We need to find a real king who will give us real bread." From their perspective Jesus was a failure. He ate meager bread while alive (meaning He was not very fiscally successful) and He died prematurely. However, Jesus offered an alternative perspective. In dying, Jesus demonstrated that the physical pursuit of happiness and belly-filling was pointless and vain in light of eternity. If we would just eat the bread of His self-sacrificing attitude and drink the blood of His passion for eternity, we too would know life as it was intended to be lived. We would know that it isn't life followed by death; rather it is death being swallowed up by LIFE.

Tommy Tenney wrote a wonderful book titled *The God Chasers*. In that book he borrowed Jesus' analogy of bread and said that the Kingdom of God is like bread and the church is like a bakery. The church's job is to bake the bread of Life. That means we are to be experiencing the freedom and power Jesus promised to give us. In the experience of the bread of the Kingdom we will know true joy, regardless of the trials we face. When the church bakes the bread, then the aroma of freshly baked bread will fill the streets and draw people to it. Unfortunately many of us have forgotten about the bread of life and our ovens have grown cold. We talk about bread of Jesus but we spend most of our time clambering for physical bread to fill our bellies. We try to convince people we have the bread of life, but there is no evidence of the power and joy that is the bread...the aroma is gone.

Here's today's question: Are you eating Jesus' bread and blood of life each day, or are you simply munching on stale matza and sipping grape juice once a week?

Kid's Questions

What is a bakery? A bakery is a place that bakes and sells bread. All day long it has that wonderful smell coming out of the ovens.

Have you ever smelled bread baking in the oven? How does that smell make you feel?

Imagine if there were people in a bakery that spent a lot of money making some fake loaves of bread to put on display on their shelves. Then they stopped baking bread and spent all their time trying to convince people to come to their bakery and buy their delicious bread. Do you think that bakery would stay in business very long? Why?

Jesus said He is the bread of life and that if you want to be His follower you need to eat His bread. What did He mean? Jesus' bread was the fact that He loved us so much that He was willing to sacrifice his own life — He let people kill Him — in order to save the world. That is love, isn't it? To eat Jesus' bread is to be willing to love Him that much and love each other that much. In the church we are supposed to have that kind of love and bake that bread for the whole world.

When you look at your family and your church, how much of Jesus' bread is being baked in your oven? Do you love each other with Jesus' kind of love, or are you still fighting and being selfish.

See if you can bake some good bread this week.

Lesson 3

- Matthew 14:22-36
- Mark 6:44-56
- John 6:14-24

Study Questions

Where was Jesus when the storm started?

How did the disciples react to the storm? How did they react when they saw Jesus on the water?

Why did Peter sink?

Food for Thought

"Keep your eye on the ball!" That's what the coach tells the batter to do in order to hit the ball better.

"Don't look down, and breathe deeply and steadily." Those are the keys to conquering the challenge of rock climbing.

"Set your priorities and learn how to say 'no.' Keep your eye on the goal." Those are the success tips for the up-and-coming executive.

Focus.

It's all a matter of focus. Today we see that truth pop into...well...focus.

Here's the scene. Jesus was recoiling from the painful news of John's beheading. His retreat to the mountain was interrupted by the demanding crowd. He had compassion on them and fed 5,000 men plus women and children with the miraculous multiplication of bread and fish. Then, finally, He makes the retreat to the mountain and sends the disciples on ahead without Him. The disciples are out in the boat, at night, alone.

As was common in the Sea of Galilee, a huge storm descended the cliffs and whipped the waters into a frenzy. This had happened to them before, but Jesus had been on the boat with them and calmed the storm. Now, Jesus was up on the mountain having a little alone time with the Father. What were they going to do? Perhaps they were going to die.

Now, I believe this event actually happened, so don't misinterpret me, please. While this story is real, it is also being used by the Gospel writers (especially Matthew) as a strategic narrative device that is heavily loaded with symbolism. Jesus has just walked away from His exclusive mission to the Jews and has turned His back on that venture, leaving everyone's hopes crushed of the physical, warrior Messiah crushed. He is about to expand His mission to include the Gentiles. He is radically changing everyone's perspective. A paradigm shift of this magnitude is nothing less than a chaotic storm on the open sea in a little fishing boat. The sky is dark, the stars are hidden, the wind is howling, and the waves are crashing. And...Jesus is not there. Will they be lost? Is Jesus really who He says He is? Is He the Messiah who will bring the Kingdom of God to the entire world? As the storm raged, it didn't look good.

Then, looking rather ghost-like as He emerges through the mist-filled wind, somehow walking on top of the water as if it were solid ground, Jesus appears. Instantly the answers flooded in with a resounding, "Yes! He is the Messiah!" In the previous storm Jesus was in the boat with the disciples and calmed the storm around Him. This time Jesus comes walking on the storm, as if it doesn't even affect Him. They knew at that moment that He was all he said He was, and more. The Gospel writers were demonstrating that Jesus was able to guide the disciples through the chaotic paradigm shift that they were experiencing.

Then an amazing thing happens. Peter wants to come to Him on the water. Peter wants to experience what it is like to rise above the storms of chaos and walk in the power of Jesus. At this point we can join the Gospel writers and expand the analogy of this story to our own lives.

Here are some things we can learn from Peter's brief, but heroic walk on the water.

1. **Following Jesus is a stormy venture.** Jesus was all about shaking things up. The Jews had become myopic in their vision of the Kingdom and had settled into the comfortable place of thinking and excluding the Gentiles from the Kingdom and the table of God. Jesus was not good with that and was willing to do whatever it took to rattle everyone's theological and sociological cages to bring about change. Change is scary. Change is chaotic. If you are in Jesus' boat, expect the storm.

2. **Jesus is bigger than the storm.** While change is scary, it is not the end of the world. From Jesus' perspective He rides above the waves, rides out the chaos, and gets to the other side. He invites each of us to join Him in that place of security. Notice the place of security in this storm scene was not one of calming the storm as He did before. This time He is standing in the storm, but is not affected by it at all. Rather than calm the storm, He was inviting the disciples to come to a place where their hearts would be calmed in spite of the storm.

3. **If you want to walk on the water you have to get out of the boat.** (Credit for wording John Ortberg; I liked the title of his book.) Many times Peter was really beat up in the telling of this story. The focus of many messages has been on his lack of faith and his sinking. Here's an observation. *He actually got out of the boat!* What were the other disciples doing? They were still cowering in fear and wondering if Jesus was a ghost. Peter had the vision and the courage to see that Jesus was offering him an opportunity to live life on a different plane of existence where the storms of life become insignificant in view of the eternal Kingdom and purpose of God. He actually stepped out in faith and took a

few steps on the water. Way to go, Pete! This was a foreshadowing of the great things that he and the others (and maybe you!) would do when they did actually bring the storms of change to the world.

4. **If you want to walk on the water you have to keep your focus.** Here we are at the beginning of the study. Focus. Notice the text. It said that when Peter *saw the wind and the waves* he began to sink. Before that he was intently focused on Jesus and nothing else.

In the movie *The Legend of Bagger Vance* there is a scene where Bagger Vance is instructing a man on how to golf. The man is at the tee, ready to make his first drive. Bagger is whispering to him to focus on the ball and the fairway and to block out everything else. The cinematography is awesome as, piece by piece, each component of the scene disappears. The crowd disappears, the officials disappear, and the sounds disappear. The field of vision collapses and the golfer sees himself closer to the goal. In that moment he connects to the ball in a way he never has before. While that is just a movie and golf is just a game, the point remains true. Life is a matter of focus. Where we focus our attentions and our energies will determine the outcome of the "game."

In our lives, the cares and worries that we encounter every day are like the wind and the waves of Peter's storm. They swirl around us with raging fury and threaten to kill us. Then Jesus shows up, unaffected by them. He invites us to join Him in the Kingdom... to walk on the water. If we focus on Him, then we can do it. But, as soon as we focus on the wind and the waves we will begin to sink. When our focus is on Jesus then the other stuff is pushed aside to the blurriness of peripheral vision. It doesn't cease to exist; it just assumes its proper position of being incidental.

Where's your focus?

Pressure at work? *Wind and waves.*

The responsibility of parenting? *Wind and waves.*

Financial stress? *Wind and waves.*

Relational tension? *Wind and waves.*

Threat of terrorism and world war? *Wind and waves.*

Persecution for the sake of Jesus? *Wind and waves.*

Are these things not real and merely an illusion like the pantheists say? No. They are very real. Does Jesus not care about them? Of course He does, because He cares for you. The point is that when our focus is on Him, then He gives us the power to rise above the storm and see it from a different perspective. In the light of the eternal Kingdom of God, all these things are tiny blips on the radar, if noticeable at all.

Will you get out of the boat today? Will you trust Jesus can give you power and victory beyond your comprehension to deal with whatever adversity you may be facing?

Kid's Questions

Let's say you were playing baseball in a big stadium with lots of people watching you. You are up to bat. What is the pitcher trying to do to you? What do you have to do in order to get on base?

The key to hitting a pitch in baseball, or making a goal in soccer, or finishing your math assignment is to focus on the job at hand and not get distracted. If you start letting your mind wander or focus on the cheers and boos from the crowd then you will not hit the pitch or make the goal.

One of the most important things to learn in life is the discipline of focus.

Try this experiment. Take a piece of paper that has writing on it. Hold it about a foot in front of your face, or the closest distance where you can comfortably read what is on the paper. Now, slowly move the paper away from in front of your face, but try to keep your eyes focused at the same distnace that they were for when the paper was close up. It will feel weird, and you may have to try it a few times. What do the far away things look like?

If you did this correctly then you would notice that there was two of everything that was far away when you moved the paper. When you relaxed your eyes and let them focus everything snapped together and became one clear picture.

In the story today we saw that when Peter lost his focus on Jesus and started focusing on the wind and the waves, he began to sink. When his eyes were focused on Jesus he was able to walk on water. Pretty cool.

Remember that Jesus wants to give you the strength to handle any difficulty that comes into your life. If you keep your eyes focused on Him and not worry about things, He will give you the strength to make it.

Lesson 4

- Matthew 15:1-28
- Mark 7:1-37

Study Questions

What did the Pharisees think would make a person unclean?

What did Jesus think would make a person unclean?

t

What was Jesus' attitude toward the Pharisees?

Food for Thought

If you have been tracking with the sequence of events during the story of Jesus' life and paying attention to the imagery and flow, then today's reading may have thrown you a little.

Here's the flow:

> Jesus feeds the 5,000 with bread
>
> He walks on the water
>
> He talks to teachers about clean and unclean things
>
> He heals gentile people
>
> He feeds bread and fish to 4,000 people

What does this showdown with the Pharisees over clean and unclean things have to do with mass feedings and water-walking? Is this a hodge-podge of neat stories or is there a message being delivered with the arrangement?

I believe there is a definite message being communicated by the Gospel writers. Today's reading is the final plank in the bridge over which Jesus walks as He travels from His ministry to the Jews on one side to His ministry to the Gentiles on the other.

> The feeding of the 5,000 represents His mission to Israel.
>
> The walking on the water represents the chaos of the paradigm shift He is bringing to Israel.
>
> The feeding of the 4,000 represents His ministry to the Gentiles.

Today's story summarizes the reason the bridge had to be built. In order to understand it we must understand the language of "clean" and "unclean." Way back in the days of Moses, just after the Israelites had been set free from slavery in Egypt, God gave them a collection of Laws. These laws created lists of things that were considered clean and unclean. If you touched unclean things you were to be taken outside the camp until you were made clean again. The point of these lists was for the health of the people. God loved His people and did not want them to become sick, so He said, "don't touch things that will make you sick." The Law was given by a protective Father out of love for His children.

The Law was more of a practical issue that had to do with daily living than a theological issue that had to do with salvation. Obedience was a response to God's gracious gift of the covenant, not a system by which one could earn God's favor. The Law was for life. AND, most importantly, the purpose of the nation of Israel was to bring the blessing of God to the WHOLE WORLD. God's intention from the beginning was to draw all people to Himself to be restored to fellowship with Him in His Kingdom.

After 1,400 years of human interpretation and political corruption, the Pharisees had distorted the Law. They had taken God's gracious gift and said that it was all theirs. They said that God would only bless the clean, and since the Gentiles handle things on the "unclean" list, then God couldn't possible love them. In fact, they said God hated them and wanted nothing to do with them. In other words, the Kingdom of God is a Jewish, "clean" thing and all Gentiles and "unclean" things need not apply.

In light of this distortion we can understand why this clean/unclean discussion was placed here in the story. Allow me to paraphrase Jesus' words:

> "Guys, I'm telling you for the last time, the idea of 'clean' as you see it is not the issue. You are using the law — which was given to you for your own health benefits — as a tool to keep people away from the Kingdom of God. God doesn't care about what touches your hands or what goes in your mouth. That's just crud anyway. He cares about your HEART. You could follow every dietary law that Moses wrote down, but if you have hatred toward the Gentiles then you are the most unclean ones in the bunch. That is why I have to go to the Gentiles and finish the job that Abraham started. I'm going to heal Phoenician women, and cast out demons of Gadarene men, and bring sight and hearing (both physical and spiritual) to the people of Decapolis. You just watch Me. And if you don't like it, then you can kill Me for all I care. The Kingdom of God is for everyone!"

I'm afraid to say that there are great parallels in our culture today. When Jesus came, He had to expose the people's own gross misrepresentation and misunderstanding of Moses. They had taken the teaching of the Kingdom and turned it upside-down. They had taken a living and dynamic, cloud-following, tent-traveling relationship with the Living God and turned it into a gold-covered, dug-in-the-mud, temple-centered, power-hungry death pit. Today we may be in the same place. Our Moses is Jesus. He gave us the true law again and wrapped it in the cloud-following, Spirit-filled, meet-in-the-home-and-go-where-He-leads body called the church. After 2,000 years of human interpretation, politicizing, and corruption, we have taken what was supposed to be a dynamic relationship with Jesus and turned it into a faction-splintered, building-centered, politically driven, hair-splitting, power-hungry,

death pit. I know that sounds harsh and may be an exaggeration. The truth is there are plenty of really strong, healthy, Christ-centered churches. There were also plenty of God-fearing, Messiah-hoping Jews in Jesus' day. They followed Him when He exposed the truth to them. Today we have a mixed bag, just like then. All I'm saying is that we need to be careful that we are not more in love with our big, beautiful buildings, our clout in the community, our reputation among the denominational or associational circles, our doctrinally correct stance, and our well-managed programs than we are with the dynamic, living, on-the-move God who calls us into action and transformation. It is not the outside appearances that make us clean. It is the motive of the heart and the inner thoughts that make a person clean and that produce the real fruit by which our lives will be evaluated.

Kid's Questions

If you have a cracker, and a piece of bread, get them out and look at them. List some differences between them.

What makes bread light and fluffy?

Do you know how yeast works? Yeast is a little bacteria that is put in the dough of bread. When it gets wet and warm it begins to multiply. As it multiplies it gives off a gas. This gas forms air bubbles in the dough. Those bubbles spread throughout the dough and make it puff up. The bubbles from yeast spread evenly throughout the entire piece of dough, making it grow in size.

Jesus said that sin and wrong-thinking are like yeast. When you put a little bit in your heart it will begin to multiply and spread through every part of your life.

As Christians we need to make sure that we do not allow ourselves to become bitter or angry or afraid of things because these kinds of feelings can be like yeast that will blow holes in our heart. When these kinds of feelings pop up, we need to ask Jesus to take them away and replace them with love, courage, and hope.

Lesson 5

- Matthew 15:29-39
- Mark 8:1-21
- Matthew 16:1-12

Study Questions

How many baskets of leftover food were gathered after the feeding of the 5,000? How many were gathered after the 4,000?

What did Jesus warn His disciples to watch for?

Food for Thought

Good bread, bad yeast.

Today we have the privilege of listening in on one of Jesus' intimate teaching moments with the disciples. It's like we are sitting down on Monday afternoon and going over each play of the game film with the coach after the big weekend. This is so important for us because it is in these moments that we can begin to make sense out of Jesus' actions. If Jesus' behavior and his words don't make sense to you on your first reading, don't feel too bad, because they didn't make sense to the disciples either. These guys were nice, but sometimes it took a while for them to get on the same frequency with Jesus.

Let's look at the scene. They've just fed more than 9,000 people with 11 loaves of bread. Big miracle. They've just had a showdown with a storm and with the Pharisees over what "clean" really means. Now they have a little downtime with just the guys, out on the boat. So, Jesus kicks into a teaching moment and says, "Guys, beware of the yeast of the Pharisees." Maybe they were just dozing off or something when He said it, but they looked at each other and ask whether He was upset because they didn't have enough bread for the boat trip. HELLO! Enough bread?!? Didn't you see Him feed 9,000 people? Do you really think He is talking about having enough bread to feed 13 men? No, Jesus was using another parable to crack open the door to some deep, eternal truth.

It is in this moment Jesus teaches us two important truths about life in the Kingdom.

1. **The Kingdom is for everyone — not just a select few**. All week we have been hinting at the significance of the feeding of the 4,000 and here it is made clear. Once again, this event was not just an encore presentation for a sold-out crowd. The feeding of the 5,000 and the feeding of 4,000 took place on opposite sides of the lake. Jesus reminded the disciples that after the feeding of the 5,000 there were 12 baskets of leftovers and after feeding the 4,000 there were 7 baskets of leftovers. The 12 baskets on the Israel side of the lake represent the nation of Israel. The 7 baskets on the Decapolis side of the lake represent the Gentile nations. Jesus is providing the bread of life for the whole world. It is available to whomever wants to eat it. The banquet is set and the doors are open; come and get it.

2. **The bread is infected.** Throughout the Old Testament yeast is used as a symbol for sin. On the night of Passover the Israelites

were supposed to make bread without yeast — "unleavened bread"— so that they would not be delayed with waiting for the dough to rise. After that the ritual of having no yeast was taken further to use yeast as a symbol for the power sin can have when it enters the body. It spreads throughout our lives like the yeast spreads throughout the whole dough. Now that we understand microbiology a little better we see how incredibly brilliant the analogy was. Yeast is a living organism, — bacteria — that when introduced into a mixture of dough and brought to the right temperature, will multiply like rabbits and take over everything. In the multiplication process the bacteria gives off gas and creates big pockets of air — nothing — in the middle of the bread, making it light and fluffy. That is what sin does in our lives. It is introduced in a small quantity, but given the proper environment, it will spread like wildfire and blow gas holes throughout our hearts.

In the context of this conversation Jesus is using the familiar symbol of yeast and applying it to the teaching of the Pharisees. As 21st century Christian readers, we miss the humorous irony in this statement. For Jesus to call the Pharisee's teaching yeast would be like calling George W. Bush an Al-Qaeda terrorist or Martin Luther King Jr. a member of the KKK.

The yeast symbolism was the Pharisees' directive. They spent all their energy trying to get rid of the yeast of the pagan influences in the culture of Israel. They were yeast inspectors. At first glance this seems right. After all, isn't that what Moses told them to do? Moses warned them to not fraternize with the pagan nations because they would become infected with their pagan beliefs and slip into idolatry. Moses told them to be clean before God because God was a holy God and only clean people can enter God's presence. So, is Jesus saying that their attempts to follow Moses were wrong? Was Jesus changing the rule book? No. The problem with the Pharisees was that they lost sight of the heart of the matter. Ultimately, God wants your heart.

At this point it is important for us to ask what the yeast of their teaching really was. We have already established that Jesus was not throwing away the people of Israel. They were God's chosen people and part of the Kingdom — the 5,000. Yet, He is identifying there is some major junk in the camp with the Pharisees' teaching. This message has been repeated a few times this week, but it is important enough to repeat again. Jesus warned the disciples to beware of this yeast because He knew that that very same yeast could easily infect the Kingdom He would establish in the church and the whole cycle could repeat itself. There are two important aspects of the "yeast" we need to understand and use to examine our own situation. Is our corner of the Kingdom infected with this kind of yeast?

1. **It's a matter of the heart.** God desires to have intimate fellowship with us. He wants us to be restored to His original design when we walked in the garden with Him. The only way that can happen is when a person has a transformed heart. Heart transformation is an inside-out process. The seed of the Kingdom is planted in the heart and it grows to take over the body. The living water pours into the empty cup of the heart, fills up, and then overflows to the outside to clean up the whole body. The Pharisees thought it was the other way around. They thought if they obeyed the external behaviors as described in the Law then they would be demonstrating a heart for God. That is what we call religion. Religion is all about rules, rituals, and external behavior. God did not call us to religion. God calls us to relationship. An authentic relationship with God will demonstrate authentic life-change that will be evident in external behaviors. Hearts walking with God will love others and consider others more highly than themselves. Heart's walking with God do not have to worry about whether they washed their hands the correct number of times or if they said the words of the prayer in the right order or if they spent time with the wrong people. A heart that is right with God knows the mind of God and naturally obeys the will of God...as a natural flow.

We need to ask ourselves if we are more into religion than we are into relationship.

2. **It's bread for the world.** The Pharisees stood inside the covenant that God made with Abraham, looked out on the evil, corrupted world and considered themselves blessed and safe. As they looked out the window at the lost and dark world, they looked with contempt and repulsion, thanking God that they were not depraved and hell-bound like those rotten sinners. Jesus said that an attitude like that was infectious yeast that blows holes in the Kingdom of God. When Jesus stood in the Kingdom and looked out on the masses of people lost in the darkness, His heart wept for them and He opened the doors to shine light on them. He took the light of the Kingdom, placed it on a torch, put the torch into the hands of His disciples and sent them into the darkness in order to light the path so that people could find their ways

home. This darkness-penetrating attitude was repulsive to the Pharisees. After all, according to them, as soon as you walk into the darkness you will become contaminated by the muck and mire of sin, you'll no longer be "clean" and will be unable to enter back into the Kingdom. It would be better to let them die in the darkness than to risk contamination. Later on in the story, the Apostle Paul describes Jesus' attitude about this when he said that "God made him who had no sin to be sin for us, so that in him we might become the righteousness of God." (2 Corinthians 5:21)

In the church today, we stand inside the Kingdom and count our blessed assurances. We look out on the darkness and hear the cries of the dying and respond with varying sentiments. Some say, "Serves them right. After all, they are sinners." Others say, "Whew, I'm glad God chose me. Too bad He didn't choose them. Oh well." Still others say, "Quick, bar the doors; we can't let the darkness near us or we will be corrupted!" What is Jesus saying to the 21st century church? I think He is telling us to think hard about what we love and what we cling to as our righteousness. Are we slipping into the same mode as the Pharisees and being more concerned with doing church a certain way and keeping the darkness at bay? Are we with taking the light of the Kingdom of God into the darkness, risking the mess and the muck, and lighting a path home for people that desperately need to know the Love of God?

How can we do that? How can we bring bread to the world? Ask God to expose opportunities in your life to overflow the light of His Kingdom into a dark place this week.

Kid's Questions

Imagine if you had a bakery that baked wonderful bread all the time. Across the street from your bakery was an open field where many homeless people lived. They had no money and they slept under the bushes in the cold every night. They were dirty, missing teeth, and their clothes were torn and smelly. Most of all, they were very hungry. What would you do? Why?

We've been talking about bread all week. On Monday's study, Jesus fed 5,000 people with just a few loaves of bread and some little fish. That was a huge miracle. In today's study He fed 4,000 people.

The reason Jesus did these two miracles was to teach Israel a lesson. You see the Kingdom of God is like that bakery we talked about and the world is like the empty lot full of homeless people. The Pharisees were a group of people who were inside the bakery and when they looked out the window at those homeless people, they thought, "Those filthy people deserve to be hungry. We're glad we're not like them. Good thing we have bread. If we went out there we might get dirty and lose our own bread."

Jesus said that those thoughts were wrong and not what the bakery is supposed to be like. Jesus fed the 4,000 people because they represented the world — the — homeless people across the street. Jesus was telling us that we, being bakers of His bread, need to open the doors to the bakery and take the bread over to the hungry people. Then, maybe, they will eat and get healthy and they can start baking their own bread.

Let's find ways that we can feed hungry people, both with real bread, and more importantly, with the bread of Jesus' love.

Introduction

Welcome to part 2 of our three part mini-series right in the middle of the Life of Jesus. Last session we saw that Jesus was expanding his ministry to the entire world. That expansion was going to cause a great deal of storms for the disciples because Jesus was asking them to reevaluate everything that they had considered truth before. This week we see this transition continue.

There are really two parts to the lessons this week and two halves to the illustration.

Part 1: A Sweet Glimpse of Glory

On the left side of the illustration you see a road sign cautioning the traveler that the path ahead will be rough. At this point in the story Jesus began very clearly preparing Himself and His disciples for the brutal death that would be His destiny. The disciples did not yet understand what He was telling them, nor did they like the sounds of it. Nevertheless, Jesus was getting them ready for a very difficult and painful journey that would ultimately lead them into the deathtrap of Jerusalem.

To contrast the stark prediction of His death, Jesus invites His closest friends – Peter, James, and John – to witness a very special vision. On top of Mt. Horeb, Jesus shows His true colors. He is transfigured into His glorious form and is visited by both Moses and Elijah. In this one vision Jesus is fulfilling many Old Testament prophecies. In Isaiah 53 the Messiah was predicted to be both a suffering servant and a glorious lord. In this picture we see Jesus in both roles.

Moses and Elijah were both the strongest and

most dynamic spiritual leaders of Israel. Both of them had mysterious departures as well. Moses was buried by God himself, and Elijah was taken up in a chariot of fire. The key element of this vision was when Moses and Elijah disappeared, leaving Jesus all alone. Then the voice spoke from the cloud and said that this was the Son who is most blessed. In that moment, all authority was officially handed to Jesus to be the one and only leader of the Kingdom of God. The era of Moses and Elijah was now over and the age of the Messiah had begun.

Part 2: The Sour Taste of Reality

As is almost always the case with mountain top experiences, Jesus and the disciples had a harsh wake up call to the reality of their situation. On the mountain Jesus was revealing the glory that would be the Kingdom. It was in this Kingdom and for this Kingdom that the disciples would live and work. Peter, James, and John must have been pumped after something like that, especially knowing that they were in on the ground floor of something that big. Then it happened. They were faced with an evil spirit that they could not handle. The demon had a child in its grip and nothing they did could free him from his torment. The disciples fell flat on their face. One minute they were standing in the presence of glory itself, and the next they were flat on their faces in a powerless heap. Jesus realized that He had his work cut out for Him if he was going to train these guys to lead the charge for his Kingdom. They lacked faith, they lacked vision, and they lacked discipline.

To top it all off, they were arguing amongst themselves who would be the greatest in the Kingdom of God. Still they were thinking of gold, power, and politics. Jesus had to shake His head and say, "You guys still don't get it do you. Here, bring Me that child. Until you become like this little one, you will be nothing in my Kingdom. I'm heading to Jerusalem and I'm willing to train you in how to unlearn all the things you've learned your whole life. If you're willing to follow Me, then let's start some real training."

Lesson 1

- Matthew 16:13-28
- Mark 8:22-9:1
- Luke 9:18-27

Study Questions

Who did the people think Jesus was?

Who did the disciples think Jesus was?

Why did Jesus rebuke Peter so harshly?

What did Jesus say was required to be able to follow Hhim? What does that mean?

Food for Thought

From Superman to Satan

Poor Peter. He's like the Babe Ruth of the Kingdom of God. Babe Ruth was the world record holder for home runs, but he was also the leader in strike outs. Peter is the same. He did some amazing things. He was the only one to step out on the water, after all. But then, he said and did some lame things as well. Today we see him do both kinds of things in one chapter. One minute he is superman, the next minute he is Satan.

Superman

After a couple of years of miracles and strong preaching Jesus had whipped up quite a commotion among the people of Israel. People were talking about Him and debating about who He really was. Today, in the reading, we see Jesus walking along with his disciples like He had done so many days before. I'm sure they had discussed all the buzz about Him many times before during these long walks, but today was different. Today the conversation took a different turn. Jesus stopped, dead in his tracks, and looked at this group of men and asked them the most critical question a person could ever be asked. "Who do YOU say that I am?"

You see, this was a critical time in Jesus' life as He was coming to the crossroads of His ministry and, as we saw last week, was headed toward a worldwide mission. The road would get rough in the days and weeks ahead and He needed to know if His disciples were with Him and were seeing Him for who He truly was. After all, a bunch of them had just ran away fromHim after the whole "eat my flesh" speech. Were these guys with Him or not?

Peter piped up and said that Jesus was the Christ, the Son of God. Yeah, Peter!! Good answer. Jesus praised him for this and predicted that Peter would become the rock upon which the church would be built and the gates of Hell would not prevail against it. Wow! He's like a superman. He must have felt pretty good about himself after that.

Satan

So, there's Peter walking along, thinking he's pretty great since he's been chosen to be the CEO of the new Kingdom of God. It doesn't get much better than that. He's walking next to Jesus, just imagining his friend with the crown on His head and Him, the Rock, standing at his right hand to rule the world.

Then Jesus stops and says, "Oh, by the way guys, you do realize that the only way that my Kingdom will be established is if I am crucified at the hands of the Romans." Peter spits the water out of his mouth in shocked disbelief. You can just hear the gears going in his head as he is trying to reconcile Jesus' words with the glorious picture he has just painted for himself and his own exalted position. Going to die? That doesn't make any sense. What is Jesus talking about? How can the Kingdom be established if He is executed?

Peter says, "Say again, Jesus. You are going to die? Not on my watch. They will have to get to You over my dead body."

Then Jesus pulls him aside and looks into the exact same eyes that he had just praised as the foundation of Yis church and says, "Get behind Me Satan!"

Ouch. That had to have seemed like a cheap shot from left field from Peter's perspective. How could Jesus call him Satan when all he was doing was trying to defend his friend and protect the Kingdom?

So what was the real problem with Peter? His problem was that he had not yet caught onto the reality of Jesus' Kingdom. Peter was still operating under the physical/political kingdom agenda. When he heard Jesus say "Kingdom" he heard thrones and trumpets and power. To be the leader of that would be awesome, indeed.

Jesus knew that they were getting too close to game time for his key players to be reading from the wrong playbook, so He drew a line in the sand right there for the disciples. He told them very clearly that to be His disciples and to live in His Kingdom would mean certain death. He was going to the cross and if they wanted to follow Him they would have to be willing to put aside all their prideful delusions of grandeur and pick up a cross right along with Him. It was all or nothing from that point on.

There is a lesson for us today. In Peter's roller coaster ride from Superman to Satan we can see a trap that each of us can easily fall into. It was easy for Peter to proclaim with his mouth that Jesus was the Christ, the Son of God. It was especially easy to say it when he thought that there would be glory and power attached to it. Many times we can fall into a trap of creating a Jesus that we like. We walk up to the buffet of spiritual ideas and say, "I'll have two helpings of grace, a side of freedom, and hold the pain or commitment." When we paint a picture of Jesus that is pleasing to us and brings about our best interest, then we are all fired up and ready to make him King.

Jesus looks into each of our eyes today and asks, "Do you really know who I am? Would you be willing to follow Me to the cross? Would you be willing to give up your job, your house, your reputation, and climb down into the pit with Me as they mock Me, beat Me, and kill Me like a criminal?" That is the road that leads to the Kingdom.

The question for us is whether we have created a Jesus that makes us feel good, or if we have committed ourselves to obey the real Jesus, no matter where He may lead us.

Kid's Questions

Jesus asked the disciples a very important question. He asked, "Who do you say that I am?"

That is a question that is important for each of us to answer today. Take turns answering the question, "Who do you say Jesus is?"

Why do you think that? Why is it important to believe that?

Lesson 2

- Matthew 17:1-13
- Mark 9:2-13
- Luke 9:28-36

Study Questions

What happened to Jesus body on the mountain?

Who appeared with Jesus? What is the significance of their appearance?

What was Peter's response to this vision? Why?

What was the Father's attitude toward Jesus?

What did Jesus discuss with His two visitors?

Food for Thought

Last time, Jesus laid a pretty heavy truth on His disciples. He clearly told them that He was going to be killed and that if they want to follow Him they need to be willing to be killed as well. Today we see the other side of the story. Jesus knew that if the grim reality of His death was the only future that the disciples could see, it would be very difficult to press on. So, He invited His closest friends, Peter, James, and John, to peek behind the curtain into the reality of Jesus' identity.

In this glorious transfiguration scene we can learn some important lessons:

1. **The physical is just the beginning.** Jesus was transfigured to where His face shown like the sun and His clothes were white like light. What does all this mean? To be sure this was a demonstration that Jesus was not just the flesh and blood son of a carpenter from Nazareth. He was also the second person of the Trinity dwelling within this human form. He was and is the glorious Lord of all creation. The disciples needed to be reminded of that at this point in the story. Even though Jesus was going to die, it was only through His death that He could be raised from the dead, defeat death itself, and be exalted as the rightful ruler of the Kingdom of God. His death would not be in vain.

   There is, perhaps, another purpose for this revelation that has to do with our own existence. It is difficult to know for sure what our existence will be like after death and in eternity, but it is possible that the transfiguration is a glimpse into that reality. The apostle Paul talks about this in 1 Corinthians 15 and in 2 Corinthians 5 where he speaks of the glorification of our bodies into something beyond our physical comprehension. Perhaps this is how we were created to be in the first place and Jesus' plan was to bring us back to our original place in the presence of the glory of God.

2. **Jesus is the fulfillment of the Law and the Prophets.** The appearance of Moses and Elijah has huge significance for Jesus' relationship to the Old Testament. For the Jew, to say "the Law and the Prophets" was to refer to the entire Old Testament. Moses represented the Law and Elijah represented the Prophets. Moses and Elijah appeared to give testimony to the fact that Jesus was the Messiah that had been promised by them and all the others. More important than their appearing was their disappearing. Jesus was

left alone, the only true leader of the Kingdom of God.

3. **The disciples almost missed the point.** Notice Peter's initial response to this mind-blowing vision. "Could we just pitch some tents and live here?" That makes sense when you stop and think about it. A little while earlier Jesus had told them that He was going to die and that they might die too. Now Peter is standing in the presence of the most amazing thing he's ever seen. Why would he want to walk away from this, go back down the mountain, and reengage with the nastiness of everyday life? No, he'd rather stay on the mountain.

Here's the lesson for us today. Many times our Christian life can be about seeking mountain top experiences. We want to see the glory of Jesus; we want to feel the power and the presence of God flowing through us. We want the spiritual high that we get from attending Christian camps and conferences, or going to a well-done worship service, or being part of a bigger-than-life rally where 100's of people come to Jesus. While these kinds of mountain top experiences are good and real, we need to keep in mind one important thing; typically, in the life of the follower of Jesus, the mountain tops are few and far between. This was the first mountain top experience the disciples had had. It came at a time when they were probably discouraged and perhaps losing their focus. So, God gave them a glimpse of glory to energize them and keep them going in the battle. The truth is that the life of mission and the Kingdom of God in this present age is a life that is lived in the valleys. We are called, not to camp out on the mountain top, but to go back down the mountain, in the power of the mountain top, and shine the light of glory into the dark valley. That is not an easy road, but it is the road that we must travel and the one that leads to ultimate glory. Yes, there will be more mountain tops along the journey, but be careful that you are not living from mountain top to mountain top without engaging in the very real ministry in the valley.

Kid's Questions

Today is a great opportunity to draw a picture. Listen to the description of how Jesus was transfigured. Who appeared with Him? What was spoken? How did the disciples feel when they saw this?

Draw a picture that describes this scene.

How do you feel about Jesus knowing that this event happened?

Lesson 3

- Matthew 17:14-23
- Mark 9:14-32
- Luke 9:37-43

Study Questions

What problem did the disciples face?

What reasons did Jesus give for their failure?

What terrible event did Jesus predict would happen to Him?

Food for Thought

Post-Mountaintop Syndrome

Life seems to run in cycles. We can have really good days, and then we can run smack into a brick wall and have some really bad days. Then, just when we think it is all falling apart, we cycle back up again. While some of us may experience higher peaks and valleys than others, everyone experiences some level of this cycle.

We see this cycle repeated throughout the Bible as well. When Moses went up to the mountain to receive the Law from God, he was caught in the cloud of God's glory. He was so impacted by that mountain top experience that his face shined with God's glory. Then, when he came down the mountain he found that the people had slipped into idolatry and were actually worshipping a golden calf that his own brother, Aaron, had made. He went from the peak of glory to the pit of idolatry in one short hike.

Another great man of God experienced a similar swing. Elijah had a powerful mountain top experience when he defeated the 400 prophets of Baal in a sacrifice showdown. He challenged them to a duel of the gods and Jehovah showed up in a powerful way to demonstrate his greatness and to defeat the false prophets. Yet, when Elijah came down the mountain he was greeted, not with praise and accolades from the nation, but with death threats from the queen. He felt defeated and deflated and ran into a cave of depression.

Today, in our readings we see that Jesus had a similar experience. Perhaps that is one of the many reasons that Moses and Elijah appeared with Him. They knew what was going to happen to Him and they were comforting Him in advance. Jesus had just revealed his glory to Peter, James, and John in order to encourage them to be strong and press on in the Kingdom venture. The team must have been pumped beyond description as they descended from the mountain top. Then it happened. The disciples met a child who had been tormented by an evil spirit, and they had no power to get rid of it. You can just hear the air hissing out of their inflated egos. Right after their moment of glory they were hit with defeat.

What can we learn from this?

1. **Jesus had to go alone.** Notice that the story ends with Jesus' affirmation that He will be betrayed and handed over for execution. This moment of weakness displayed by His disciples after the mountain top was important for Jesus to remember that only He alone could be the one who would take the painful journey to the cross. His followers were weak and needed His courage and

victory before they could be empowered to fulfill their calling.

2. There was much training to be done. As you compare all three gospel accounts of this story you see that Jesus told the disciples that they lacked three things. They lacked faith, vision, and discipline. After spending two years with Jesus they still did not get it completely. Jesus knew that the next several months would have to be focused on the hard core training of His disciples to be ready to take on the task of building the Kingdom. We will see, beginning in Chapter 3, that Jesus' teaching takes a sharp turn and becomes very intense and focused on sharpening the disciples.

We can take comfort and challenge from this story. We can take comfort in the fact that even the disciples who had been hand-picked by Jesus took a long time to get their acts together. Many times we can get down on ourselves for not living the Christian Life perfectly or for making mistakes. Don't be defeated by these occasional trip-ups, even the disciples blew it sometimes. On the flip side, we should be challenged by this story as well. If we would increase our faith and the disciplines of fasting and prayer in our lives, then perhaps we would grow in our ability to be conduits of God's power in the world around us. Jesus calls us to enter into His training camp and be transformed into people who experience and distribute the power of His Kingdom in the world.

If you've made mistakes, ask for forgiveness, stop beating yourself up about it, and get back on the path. Submit yourself, and commit to the daily disciplines of study, prayer, and fasting, and allow God to do His work in you.

Kid's Questions

Have you ever tried to do something and failed at it? How did you feel? Did you want to continue doing that activity after you failed? Why?

In today's story we see that the disciples failed at something that they thought they were good at. Did they give up?

Jesus took the disciples and continued to train them so that they would become better at what they were supposed to do.

If you are struggling with something like playing an instrument, or learning to read, or being on a sports team, don't give up. It takes a long time and a lot of mistakes before you get really good at something. Can you imagine how bad it would be for the church if the disciples had given up after this failure?

Remember, there is no such thing as failure, there is only opportunities to learn and to get better.

Lesson 4

- Matthew 17:24-27
- Matthew 18:1-9
- Mark 9:33-37
- Luke 9:44-50

Study Questions

What was Jesus' attitude toward paying taxes?

How did Jesus describe greatness in the Kingdom?

What is the key to becoming first? How?

Food for Thought

Today we are reminded about the fact that everyone who was anticipating the coming of the Messiah was expecting a political leader who would come and deliver Israel from the oppression of Rome. Even His disciples had this as their default paradigm for what the Messiah would be. As Jesus moves toward the cross He needs to purge these thoughts from His disciples' minds. Today we see that He teaches them two important lessons along these lines.

1. **It's not about politics.** Jesus was challenged as to whether He should pay the temple tax. After an interesting dialogue with Peter He concludes that He will pay the tax, so not to offend. Did Jesus have to pay the tax? No. Did He have the right to stand up and fight against the tax? Yes. Why didn't He? He didn't make a big deal over it because it wasn't a deal worth fighting for. The Kingdom of God is not about politics. Politics are the human processes of people fighting for power and control over one another. Jesus didn't have time to mess around with that nonsense. He paid the tax, which was miraculously provided by God through the fish, and kept the peace. Perhaps, we, as Christians should take some cues from this. Too many times we can get wrapped up in the political agendas and think that it will make a drastic difference in the Kingdom of God. The truth is that politics is a human struggle that has little room for the truth of God. As citizens of our country we should vote and pay taxes, because that is right. But we should be careful not to get too wrapped up in the political agendas and use them to replace the simple mission of the Kingdom.

2. **It's not about power.** The disciples were arguing with each other about who would be greatest in the Kingdom of God. Can't you just hear them, "Jesus likes me best, I'm the greatest." "Hold on now, didn't you hear Him say that I would be the rock on which it would be built? I'm the greatest." Jesus must have shaken His head in discouraged disbelief when He heard this going on. He said, "So you think you are great, do you? Bring that little child to Me. Do see the innocence in his eyes? Do you see how he trusts Me openly without second-guessing and over analyzing My intentions? Do you see how he grabs each moment and finds joy, laughter, and play in it, not worrying about tomorrow? That is what it will take in order to be great in My Kingdom. You need to let go of the power-trip that you are currently on. Power

means nothing. There is only one power in the Kingdom and that is the Father. All else draws power from Him and wields it over no one. We are children of God, not lords over subjects. Until you get this concept you will not be able to enter in."

When was the last time you just played in the presence of God, like a child? Too many times we get so serious about our Christian life and about the church and how to run things that we lose sight of the joy that comes from knowing Jesus. We can easily slip into the trap of creating power structures within the church and think we need to control everything. When we do this we start setting ourselves up for playing the "Who's the Greatest" game that the disciples were playing. We need to remember that no one is greater than anyone else in the Kingdom. We are all little children, brothers and sisters, under the care of our loving Heavenly Father. We each have a role to fill in the body. Let's each do our part with joy and with a playful spirit today, realizing that it's all for God's glory and not our own anyway.

Kid's Questions

Do you want to grow up? Why?

Make a list of all the reasons it is fun to be a kid.

Today Jesus told us that we have to be like a child if we are going to enter into the Kingdom of God. How does it make you feel to know that Jesus has a special place in his heart for children?

Lesson 5

- Matthew 18:10-35
- Mark 9:38-50
- John 7:1-9

Study Questions

How did Jesus feel about a person who would harm a child?

What is the proper procedure for dealing with a person who has sinned against you?

How often should we forgive someone?

What was the meaning of Jesus' parable in the context of this chapter?

Food for Thought

Today begins Jesus' lessons for His disciples about being leaders in the Kingdom of God. The main passage for today is Matthew 18. This passage springboards off our previous reading when we talked about power. Jesus contrasts the attitude that a leader in the Kingdom who had "power" would have against the way the world behaves when they gain places of power.

1. **Kingdom Power looks out for the underdog.** Jesus taught His disciples that they needed to become like a little child if they were going to be able to enter the Kingdom. He takes it further and says that if anyone looks down on these little children or hurts them or leads them astray in any way, then there will be severe consequences to pay. In those days, children, widows, and the sick were considered lower class citizens. They were not to be bothered with, or even noticed. The political powers of the day did little to nothing to watch out for their well-being and considered them a nuisance. Jesus tells us that Kingdom Power is just the opposite. We have been given power so that we can help the powerless. People who can help themselves don't need assistance. They are like the 99 sheep. We have been give power so that we can leave the 99 sheep and go after the helpless sheep that has lost its way. Leaders in the church need to make sure that they do not get seduced by the rich and powerful in the culture. Our calling is to watch out for the down-and-outers, and to empower them to come to the Kingdom banquet.

2. **Kingdom Power seeks reconciliation, not vindication.** In the world system, when a person wrongs you, the first thing you do is fight back. You either hit them back physically or you drag them to court and make them pay for everything they have done to you, and then some. That's not how it is in the Kingdom. If someone wrongs you, you have the "power" or the "right" to seek vindication, but Jesus told us that following that path will not lead to the Kingdom. First, He said, go to the person and see if you can work things out through mutual understanding and come to an honorable agreement. If that doesn't work then bring another person in on it... for the purpose of reconciliation. If that doesn't work, then bring in the elders...for the purpose of reconciliation. If, in the end, the person is not willing to repent, then you can send them outside the community where they can think things through. Yet, even in this

last resort tactic, it is still with the purpose of reconciliation in mind. We do not use our power to push people down, even if they deserve it. We use our power to build people up and to get them on a Kingdom path.

3. **Kingdom Power forgives...always.** This point goes hand in hand with the previous one. Peter heard Jesus' words about seeking reconciliation and, being the outspoken one that he was, verbalized what the rest of us would have wanted to ask. "Yes, Jesus, that sounds nice, but how many times should we forgive someone before it just becomes pointless?" The standard Jewish answer was 7 times. This seemed very reasonable and over and above the call of duty. Jesus replied that it was not 7 times that we are to forgive, it is 70 times 7. Did He mean literally 490 times, so that you can keep a tally on each annoying person and when they cross the 491 mark you cut them off? I don't think so. Jesus was saying, "How often should you forgive? Always. There really isn't any other option." Did you hear that? As a Christian there is no room for unforgiveness in our hearts. We are called to forgive everyone, no matter what they've done. Jesus emphasized the point with the parable of the servants who had been forgiven a debt. When the one who had been forgiven didn't forgive another, he was condemned for it.

Let's make this crystal clear. The Power of the Kingdom is the power to forgive everyone, no matter what. Jesus forgave us when we didn't deserve it, we can forgive others when they don't deserve it. Why is this so important? Unforgiveness is one of the biggest gateways for the enemy to take root in your heart. When you harbor bitterness and unforgiveness towards another person it's like a cancer in your soul. It shuts down major arteries through which the presence of God flows to your soul. It allows gaps in your armor where the enemy can come in and start sowing seeds of his weeds in your garden. Think about it this way, unforgiveness does not hurt the other person, it only hurts you. It becomes a burden you have to carry with you always. Eventually it will cause you to become stressed and even physically ill. Jesus says, let it go. He has given you the power to forgive, always, under all circumstances. Remember that God is the judge. If someone deserves punishment for the wrongs they've done against you, then that is up to God and the government, not you. Let it go and let the joy of the Lord flood in and take its place.

Kid's Questions

Let's say your sister came into your room and took one of your favorite toys and ruined it. Would you:

a. Find her and hit her repeatedly on the head.

b. Run screaming to your parents, "she took my toy, you need to punish her."

c. Ruin one of her toys

d. Go to your sister and ask why she did it, then try to work out a way that she can repay you.

Jesus gave us a pretty clear method to handle situations when someone does something bad towards you.

1. First try to work it out with the person in a kind, loving manner. (No body likes a tattle tale).

2. If the person doesn't want to work it out, then get someone else to come with you to try to work it out nicely.(maybe another sibling)

3. If that doesn't work, then you can bring it to your parents and tell them that you've tried to work things out between you but the person isn't willing to do what is right.

4. At that point you let your parents handle it and feel good that you tried your best to work it out and you aren't a tattletale.

Introduction

Over the past two sessions we have observed that Jesus was rejected by Israel and thus expanded His ministry and scope of His mission to include the entire world. This session we conclude the 3 part mini-series that we could title "The time between times." Before this middle series Jesus was ministering to Israel in the region of Galilee. Starting next session we will see that Jesus sets his face toward Jerusalem for the final showdown with the power structures of Israel.

For now we will be reading exclusively from John's gospel (ch. 7-10) and see how he, in his usual unique perspective, presents Jesus' teachings and themes during this transitional period. As you can see in the illustration, this is the great I AM week where Jesus makes bold claims about His true identity. Jesus proclaimed to the citizens of

Jerusalem that He was
- From the Father, merely obeying the Father's instructions
- One with the Father
- The Eternal, Living Water
- The Light of the World
- Sight for the Blind
- The Good Shepherd
- The only source of Eternal Life

These were pretty bold claims coming from the son of a carpenter in Nazareth. The crowd was in quite an uproar. Being the time of a regular feast celebration, the city of Jerusalem was already bustling with people and bursting at the seams with travelers. Jesus' wild and crazy words in the temple courts only furthered the commotion and caused a big stir among the people to the point that the Sanhedrin sent out the temple guards to arrest Him and calm everyone down.

103

Unfortunately for the Sanhedrin, Jesus was so convincing that the guards were not willing to arrest Him.

In the end the crowd was divided about Jesus. Many people believed Him and claimed that He was, indeed, the long awaited Messiah that would save Israel and lead them into the glorious Kingdom. Others claimed that He was demon-possessed and out of His mind. Hmmm...sounds kind of like today, doesn't it? No matter where you stand on the issue, the one thing you can't deny after this week is that Jesus definitely laid it on the line about who He was. There is no ambiguity about Jesus' self-identity. He claimed to be God and claimed to be the only hope for the world. Take it or leave it.

Lesson 1

- John 7:10-52

Study Questions

Where is Jesus in this passage? What is the feast?

Why were the people not able to lay a hand on Jesus?

What was the general opinion of the crowd toward Jesus?

What did Jesus say would happen if people drank His water? How did John explain what Jesus meant by that?3

Food for Thought

Living Water

Every once in a while as we read through the gospels we come across one of those glorious moments when the author actually tells us plainly what is going on. Today we find one of those moments. In John 7:39 the voice of John, the author, breaks into the story line and he says, "Oh, by the way, when Jesus talks about Living Water, He's referring to the Holy Spirit. At this point in the story, the people he was talking to didn't have a clue what he meant because the Spirit hadn't been given yet. But, just for you, the reader's sake, that's what he's talking about. OK, back to the story."

Thank you, John. Now we now that whenever Jesus is talking about the streams of living water we can insert "Holy Spirit" there and have some insight into this most important aspect of what it means to live in the Kingdom of God.

Let's look at this topic in two ways:

1. First of all, in order to make sense out of why Jesus popped off with a seemingly unrelated topic of water in the context of chapter 7, we need to understand where and when He was. (By the way, did you notice how strange vv. 37-39 seemed at first glance? When I first read it, I was confused. With a little digging, I get it now) Jesus was in Jerusalem for the Feast of Tabernacles. In Jewish life there were three major feasts throughout the year – the Passover, the Feast of Weeks (Pentecost), and the Feast of Tabernacles (or Feast of Booths, or, just, The Feast). For each of these feasts Jews from around the world would travel to Jerusalem and party for a whole week. During the feast of Tabernacles, in particular, they would pitch tents right in the middle of the city – making sort of a tent village – and live in them for the whole week. This was to commemorate the fact that the Israelites lived in tents and were mobile during their time in the wilderness when God led them around with a pillar of cloud and a pillar of fire. During the feast there was a section when the priests would pour out water over the sacrifices. They would read three passages of scripture. It would be worth while to read them right now. I think after you read them things will start making sense.

> *Isaiah   55:1   (NIV)*
> *¹ "Come, all you who are thirsty, come to the waters; and you who have no money, come, buy and eat! Come, buy*

wine and milk without money and without cost.

Zechariah   14:8   (NIV)
⁸ On that day living water will flow out from Jerusalem, half to the eastern sea and half to the western sea, in summer and in winter.

Ezekiel   47:1-12   (NIV)
¹ The man brought me back to the entrance of the temple, and I saw water coming out from under the threshold of the temple toward the east (for the temple faced east). The water was coming down from under the south side of the temple, south of the altar. ² He then brought me out through the north gate and led me around the outside to the outer gate facing east, and the water was flowing from the south side. ³ As the man went eastward with a measuring line in his hand, he measured off a thousand cubits and then led me through water that was ankle-deep. ⁴ He measured off another thousand cubits and led me through water that was knee-deep. He measured off another thousand and led me through water that was up to the waist. ⁵ He measured off another thousand, but now it was a river that I could not cross, because the water had risen and was deep enough to swim in—a river that no one could cross. ⁶ He asked me, "Son of man, do you see this?" Then he led me back to the bank of the river. ⁷ When I arrived there, I saw a great number of trees on each side of the river. ⁸ He said to me, "This water flows toward the eastern region and goes down into the Arabah, where it enters the Sea. When it empties into the Sea, the water there becomes fresh. ⁹ Swarms of living creatures will live wherever the river flows. There will be large numbers of fish, because this water flows there and makes the salt water fresh; so where the river flows everything will live. ¹⁰ Fishermen will stand along the shore; from En Gedi to En Eglaim there will be places for spreading nets. The fish will be of many kinds—like the fish of the Great Sea. ¹¹ But the swamps and marshes will not become fresh; they will be left for salt. ¹² Fruit trees of all kinds will grow on both banks of the river. Their leaves will not wither, nor will their fruit fail. Every month they will bear, because

the water from the sanctuary flows to them. Their fruit will serve for food and their leaves for healing."

All three of these passages refer to visions that the prophets had of what it would be like when the Messiah would come and restore the glory of Israel. The temple was the symbol of the heart of Israel and the presence of God. From the temple would be flowing a river of living water, symbolic of new life. The prophets themselves, and the Jews during the 500 years since the prophecies had been made, were not really clear on what the exact meaning of the water was. They knew it represented new life, but how that new life would be manifest was still a mystery. In this moment, in vv. 37-39, when Jesus says, "If anyone is thirsty, let him come to Me and drink. If you drink from me then streams of living water will come out of you," He is actually making a commentary on these passages and on the ritual that was being performed during the feast. In essence He was saying, "The time has come to stop going through the ritual of pouring water over an animal and wondering what it all means. Now, I am the Messiah, and My Kingdom is about to be unleashed on the world. When you buy into My deal then you will be filled with the Holy Spirit and He will flood your soul with meaning and purpose, and He will overflow out of you and bring life to everything you touch. Why don't you step into the new era and drink it in."

2. Now that we have a better understanding of what Jesus said and why He said it, let's take a moment and reflect on what it means for us. If you have put your trust in Jesus, then you have the Spirit in you. As Ezekiel said, you are standing in the river of life. Notice what happened to Ezekiel in the vision. At first he was ankle deep in the river, then he was knee deep, then he was waist deep, and eventually the water was so deep that he could swim freely in it and it was so vast that no one could swim across it. That's how it is with the Spirit of God. God is infinite, awesome, and refreshing. He is water that cools the scorched soul and refreshes the parched spirit. He is deep enough to be completely immersed within Him and swim forever. However, it is also possible to be standing on the shore in ankle deep water.

It's a lot like standing on the beach at the ocean. There before you, stretching as far as the eye can see, is the mysterious deep. It is too big to comprehend, really. Right in front of you, though, at your feet, the ocean is only a quarter inch of sea foam that tickles your toes. If you take a step closer, it will splash up around your shins. At this point most people are OK. They can handle some mild splashing. Many people, however, are petrified of the steps beyond that point. If you move farther out you will start being pulled into the currents of the waves. The waves are strong and unpredictable. If you struggle against them they could hurt you. If you submit to them they may take you places you didn't necessarily want to go. It takes courage to get out there.

Some people, on the other hand, put on the wet suits, wax the boards, and start paddling, anxiously awaiting the wild ride of the untamed ocean. They have courage. They have skill. And they have respect for the power of the sea. With the combination of these things they can have an incredible experience of surfing the waves.

Here's the truth. The Kingdom of God is out there, in the middle of the waves. The shore is the safety of the dry, grainy sand of our own agendas and our own self-preservation. God invites us to drink deeply from the river of life and to paddle boldly into the adventure of the Spirit. Where are you today? Are your toes being tickled? Are you enjoying the safe, refreshing splash on your shins? Those are good, but they are just a glimpse of what it could be. Pray that God would give you the courage to throw yourself into His Spirit and allow Him to guide you each day into the things that He wants you to do.

Kid's Questions

Have you ever been to the ocean? If you haven't, you've probably at least seen it on TV.

Spend some time talking about what it is like to swim in the ocean.

Jesus said that the Holy Spirit is like a spring of living water. The Spirit is like a river that is as big as the ocean. He is water that gives us clean water to drink. He is also deep enough where we can jump in head first and swim around. But, just like a big lake, or the ocean, there is a beach where you can sit and look at the water, but never get in. A lot of times people are afraid of loving God and following Jesus because they are afraid they might get caught in the waves. The problem is that if you never get in the water, you'll eventually dry up. Jesus invites us to get into the nice, refreshing water of the Holy Spirit and go for a swim.

Have you invited Jesus into your life and allowed the waves of his Spirit to guide you along yet. Or are you still standing on the shore, afraid to get in the water?

Lesson 2

- John 8:1-30

Study Questions

Why did the men want to stone the woman to death?

How did Jesus defend her?

What reason did the Jews use to not have to listen to Jesus' words? How did Jesus respond?

What did Jesus say would be the final testimony to the truth of His statements?

Food for Thought

Light of Life

This week we are looking at a four chapter section of John's gospel; ch. 7-10. It is important that we keep the big picture and the overall flavor of this section in mind as we read, because it would be very easy to get lost and confused in the details of it if we didn't. Basically, these four chapters are one big discussion/debate between Jesus and the leaders of Israel.

Here's the basic flow of the debate

Jesus makes big claims: I am the living water, the light of life, and the true Shepherd. If you follow Me, you live; if you don't, you die.

The Israelites respond: Where's your proof? You have no testimony. How can we believe you just because you say it?

Jesus responds: I am sinless and My testimony about Me is valid because I come from a place you can't even understand. Secondly, My Father has sent Me and His testimony about Me is valid. If you knew Him, like you claim you do, then you would know Me.

The Israelites respond: You're mad and demon-possessed.

Jesus responds: You are blind, and your father is the devil. After you've killed Me, you'll see all the "evidence" you need. Until then, you just have to take My word for it.

With this basic outline in mind, we can make better sense out of the individual parts. Today we encounter two pieces of the debate; the woman caught in adultery and the controversy over his testimonies.

Let's begin with the second. Jesus made the bold claim, "I am the light of the world. If you follow Me you will have the light of life." The Jews responded, "Prove it." Well, the truth is that, in that moment, Jesus couldn't "prove it." All He could say was, "I am what I am. You've seen My healing power. I know where I come from. I know what My Father told Me to do. If you don't believe Me it's because your heart is so dark that you won't receive the light. In fact, you are so dark that you will eventually kill me. I'm not happy about it, but I know it has to happen. When it does happen, and when I am hanging up on that cross, you will see that My total self-sacrifice will put to rest any notion that I am in it for My own human glory, and the light of my truth will shine like a beacon of hope for the whole world. Maybe then you'll figure it out."

In our lives we are faced with this situation all the time. We know we love Jesus. We know the difference that Jesus has made in our lives. We know we have the power of the Holy Spirit in our lives. We may have even experienced miracles in our lives. Yet, when we sit across the table at the Starbucks with our skeptical friend, we hit a brick wall in the discussion. They read the gospels. They hear your testimony. They may even see the changes and miracles in your life. Yet, they are unconvinced. What do you do? The answer is in a simple question...What can you do? What did Jesus do? He laid it out as clearly as He could, then He put the ball in their court. You need to love that person, and continue to authentically follow Jesus, but you need to not allow their hardness to drag you down.

Now, the second piece of the story is the scene with the adulterous woman. She was caught in the act of adultery, so she's probably half dressed at best as they drag her into the middle of the street. Remember, it's a feast week so this probably became quite a spectator event as the crowds of men are looking for a diversion as they hang out in their tent village. The woman is lying in the dust in total disgrace.

There are two lenses looking at her. The first lens is that which is attached to the hand that holds the big rock, ready to throw at her. This lens sees her for the act she has just performed. She's had sex with a man that is not her husband. Maybe she's a prostitute. Maybe she's the desperate housewife of a "good" Pharisee. Who knows. Nonetheless, when this lens looks at her all they can see is the disgrace that she brings to the nation. They think to themselves, "You are the reason we are in bondage to the Romans. It is because of your sin and the sin of those like you that God has withdrawn His blessing from us and we are suffering. If we could just eradicate the wretched sinners like you who are messing up the dream that we call Israel, then God's blessings would flow on us once again and we would be free. You, and all like you, must die."

Does that sentiment sound familiar to you? Who are the people that are lying half naked in the dust in our culture today? Who are the people that the "righteous" of our society have dragged from their acts of sin and thrown into the street to publicly humiliate and eradicate? The "righteous" say, "If only we could rid our country of the sexually immoral, the homosexuals, the abortionists, and the secular humanists that are polluting our children and destroying the moral fabric of our society, then God would smile on us once again like he did in the days of our founding fathers." Hmmm.....

What was Jesus' lens? When He looked down at this woman, do you know what He saw? He saw a woman. He saw a child who was stuck in the muck, scared to death. He looked through the eyes of love. Then He looked into the eyes of her accusers and said, "Which sin is worse, your hypocrisy or her sexual immorality? Did you ever stop to think that it may be your own sin of pompous self-righteousness that is what is clogging the arteries of God's blessing to the nation? Are some sins more sinful than others, or does yours not stink? If one of you is without sin, then by all means, you have the right to judge the sin of this woman. Throw the stone."

Thud. Thud. Thud. One by one, the stones drop and they walk away. Once again, they could not trap Jesus, or find fault in Him.

Now, let's not leave the story there. Notice what Jesus is NOT saying. He is not saying, "Hey leave this woman alone. After all, she has the right to live however she wants because she is a child of God. If she wants to mess around and get a little on the side, that's her business and no one else's." No way! Jesus is not saying that at all. What He does is he kneels down, puts His finger under the woman's chin and raises it, looks her in the eye and says, "I love you. Now, don't sin anymore. It's going to kill you. Drink living water now, it will wash you up and make you whole. Move away from this life and into the light of life."

Here's the deal. As Christians we have to remember that there is only one judge for the world, which is God Himself. We need to be careful that we don't forget that. As the church we are called to shine the light of hope in the world through the language of love. Jesus Himself said that He did not come into the world to condemn the world, but to save the world. If Christians would spend less time condemning sinners for being sinners, (duh, that's what they are) and spend more time loving people in spite of their sin, then perhaps more light would shine into the darkness and eyes would be opened to the Kingdom of God.

Kid's Questions

Let's pretend that you have a little sister. Now let's say that you and your little sister have just been playing a game and its time to clean it up, but she doesn't want to clean it up. She doesn't mind if the room is messy and her part of the game is lying all around.

How do you feel? What do you do?

Now, let's be honest. Have you ever had a time when you got something out and your parents wanted you to clean it up, but you didn't want to and you complained about it? Did you make the mess? Yes. Did your parents have the right to ask you to clean it up? Yes. Yet, you whined and complained about it, right?

Do you think it is fair for you to get mad at your little sister for treating you the same way you have treated your parents?

In the story we see that the Pharisees wanted to kill a woman because she had done something wrong. Jesus reminded them that they were not perfect either. Jesus reminds us that we should treat people with love and compassion first before we point a finger at what they are doing wrong. Perhaps, if you showed kindness to your little sister instead of yelling at her, she would have been more interested in doing what was right.

Lesson 3

- John 8:31-59

Study Questions

What bold claim did Jesus make in 8:31?

What argument broke out as a result of that claim?

What did Jesus mean by the phrase, "Before Abraham was born, I am?"

Food for Thought

At first glance today's section of the debate between Jesus and Israel seems to be a bantering about Fathers. It almost seems like a child's fight on the playground with a lot of "oh, yeahs" thrown in the mix. Something like this:

Jews: Abraham is our father.

Jesus: Oh yeah, well if Abraham was your father then you would believe Me because God is my Father.

Jews: Oh yeah, well God is our Father, too.

Jesus: Oh yeah, well if God were your Father, then you would know Me. Instead, your father is Satan.

Jews: Oh yeah, well we think you are Satan, so there.

Jesus: Oh yeah, well I honor My Father, and if you believed Me you'd never see death.

Jews: There, now we know you're crazy. Abraham died, are you greater than our Father?

Jesus: Oh yeah, well Abraham "your father" saw Me and believed Me.

Jews: Are you nuts? He died centuries ago, how could he see you?

Jesus: Before "your Father" lived, I AM.

Jews: Kill him.

There is a lot of great truth in that dialogue, not the least of which is Jesus' radical statement that He is eternal. Yes, that's what He said. He said, "Before Abraham was" – This is past tense. Abraham lived in time, and then he died. – "I am" – present and continual...eternal. He didn't say, "Before Abraham was, I was." That would have been impressive, of course, because that would have made Jesus older than any living human in history. But, he said, "I am." He is always in the present tense. Why am I emphasizing this? There is a common misunderstanding about Jesus that has been around since the 4th century. There is a belief that Jesus was created by the Father way back in the earliest moments of creation. They say that from our perspective Jesus seems essentially timeless, but there was a time when He did not exist. This is a false teaching. Jesus, like the Father, eternally exists in the present tense. When the Father appeared to Moses at the burning bush He said to Moses, "Tell the people that 'I AM' sent you." Now Jesus says, "I AM."

Jesus claims later on to be one with the Father. Jesus is eternal and co-equal with the Father... "He is."

Now, while all that is wonderful and good, it is not really the point of the passage. The point is found in the opening statement that Jesus makes. He says that he is the truth and that his truth would set the people free. What was their reaction to that statement? "Free? Free from what? We are not slaves." They went on to say that, they are children of Abraham and therefore are not slaves to anyone. That is what sparked the bunny-trail argument about Fathers. But the real issue is that they were unaware of the fact that they were slaves to sin.

They were so unaware that they were slaves that they didn't even understand their own reason for not being slaves. It was actually very silly to say that the fact that they were Abraham's children was proof that they were not slaves. Hello? Did they forget the whole 400 year slavery thing in Egypt? Did they forget that throughout their history they slipped in and out of bondage with neighboring countries? Did they forget that they were currently under the thumb of the Roman Empire and not truly free? They were blind to the fact that they were imprisoned in their own sin.

This is a problem that we run into all the time today. We run into it as we witness to others and as we look at our own lives. The truth is that sin is like a prison cell. It is like a slave master. When we give into it, it takes over our lives and keeps us bound up in the prison of shame, blame, self-absorption, and other-consumption. Yet, the greatest deception of sin is that it cloaks itself and tries to get us to believe that it is not around us. We mask it and hide it and try to pretend that it doesn't exist.

Jesus said that He was the light of truth and that His truth is like a spot light. It shines into the dark corners of our hearts and exposes the sin task-masters that are hiding out and controlling our minds from behind veiled curtains. His truth is like an x-ray that penetrates the "happy Christian" surface and exposes the malignant masses attached to our heart.

Jesus' truth will indeed set you free. The first step toward that freedom is to admit that you are in bondage. Pride and the fear of being exposed is really the glue that holds sin tightly fixed to our heart. If we would swallow our pride, then the teeth of sin and the roots that hold it fast would be dissolved and the Holy Spirit would be able to easily remove it and wash us clean.

Is there something in your life today about which you have been living in denial? Let the truth beam of Jesus shine in today, expose it, and eradicate it for you. Then you will be truly free to live and to love without fear.

Kid's Questions

What are the three tenses in the English language? Past, present, and future.

Say the following verbs in all three tenses.
Run: ran, run, will run
Play: played, play, will play
Be: was, am, will be

How would you say that you played a game before someone else was born? How about this; before my little brother was born, I played soccer. Does that make sense? What if you said it like this; before my little brother was born, I play. Does that make sense? Why?

What about this sentence that Jesus said, "Before Abraham was born, I am." Does that make sense? Do you think that Jesus made a grammatical error? What do you think he meant by using the present tense of "be" to refer to a time that was centuries earlier?

Do you remember when God appeared to Moses at the burning bush? God said that his name was "I Am." That means that God is eternal. He has no beginning and no end. He is not in the past or in the future, he is always right now. When Jesus said "I am" he was claiming to be God.

How does it make you feel to know that Jesus is eternal, the great "I AM?"

Lesson 4

- John 9:1-41

Study Questions

What did the disciples think was the cause of the man's blindness? What was Jesus' reaction to their ideas?

What attitude did the Pharisees have about the miraculous healing of the man's eyes? Why?

To what did they attribute the miracle?

What was Jesus' accusation toward the Pharisees? Try to put this into your own words.

Food for Thought

Light for the blind (Who's really blind here?)

Today we see John's wonderful storytelling skills shining through. For the past two lessons we have been entrenched in the verbal battle between Jesus and the leaders of Israel. In chapter 9 John takes a break from the dialogue and inserts a story that will demonstrate that the same points of the argument about the identity of Jesus and the spiritual condition of the leaders.

Jesus heals a man that has been born blind. A little spit, a little dirt, a quick wash in the pool, and, poof, the man can see. The Pharisees catch wind of this miracle and they drag the man and his parents into court and grill them about it. After much brow beating, the man throws his hands up in exasperation and says, "Look, fellas. Here's the deal. I don't understand how it happened. All I know is that one minute I'm blind as a bat and the next minute I'm seeing as clear as you do. If that ain't God stuff, I don't know what is. If you want to understand it, why don't you ask Jesus yourself?" The Pharisees get frustrated, insult the man, and throw him out.

In this story John deals with two very important issues:

1. Don't be too quick to associate sin with sickness. In Jesus' day there was a pervasive belief that sickness was the direct result of sin. If you were sick then it was obvious that there was sin in your life and that you were unclean. This attitude is demonstrated in the way the disciples reacted when they encountered the man who had been born blind. Their prejudice was exposed as they asked Jesus who had sinned, the man or his parents. This pervasive attitude is further exposed in the words of the Pharisees in v. 39 when, in exasperation, they attack the man and say, "you were steeped in sin at birth." In other words, "because you were born blind, you were obviously the spawn of sin and you got what you and your parents deserved." Notice that his parents were afraid of the Jews. Of course they were. They had been told their whole life that the reason they had a blind child was because they were sinners. Their sin kept them perpetually shunned from society and in the "outcast" department. All because of a genetic defect. Sad.

Jesus demonstrated that this theology of sickness was not correct. The man was not blind because of sin. He was blind so that Jesus could demonstrate His power. He demonstrated His power not only to heal the blindness, but also to love the outcast.

We need to be careful to not be too quick to see a demon behind every sickness or behind every circumstance that seems disappointing or "wrong." The truth is that God is not as concerned with our "comforts" and our "wellness" as He is with the state of our heart. Sometimes God may even use sickness or harsh circumstances as a tool to bring us into a deeper relationship with Him. Let's make sure that when we encounter sick people that we do not pull out the Bible and beat them on the head with it too quickly or in a spirit of condemnation. Let's love people and try to discern what God is really doing in the situation before we jump to any conclusions.

2. The second truth has to do with blindness. There is actually a great deal of wonderfully sarcastic humor laced throughout this story. You can just hear John's muffled giggles as he recalls these events and weaves them into his attack against the stubbornness of the leaders of Israel. He uses the brush of irony as he paints a picture where a seeing blind man is surrounded by "seeing" men who are actually stone blind.

This story parallels the story of the adulterous woman in that both stories expose the truth about the real nature of sin and its effects on people. In both stories the "righteous" men who supposedly had great insight into truth formed a circle of superior self-righteousness around people they considered "sinners." In the case of the woman, she was a sinner, but they had forgotten that they were also sinners. In the case of the man born blind, his condition was misunderstood and was accused of sin based upon his external conditions when he had not even committed any sin to deserve his situation. While their external circumstances seemed "righteous" their heart was actually darkened by the blindness of sin. So much so that when they were confronted with an act that could have only come from the power of God, they could only see it through distorted lenses and call it an act of Satan.

Jesus' words in v. 41 summarize it, "if you were blind, you would not be guilty of sin; but now that you claim you can see, your guilt remains."

These stories colorfully illustrate Jesus' teaching in Matthew 7 when He warns us not to judge one another. We need to be careful to take the plank out of our own eye before we start pointing the finger at specks that are in another person's eye. As followers of Christ it is our job to love all people, regardless of their circumstances or their sin. If we are walking in the light of Jesus' truth and being perpetually cleaned by the flowing water of the Holy Spirit then we will be able to love the unlovely and the sinner. Through that love they will see the light of the Kingdom. May we never be blinded by self-righteousness and lose sight of Jesus' work in the world around us.

Kid's Questions

Have one person stand in the middle of the room. Blindfold that person. Put an object somewhere in the room and have another person in the room give instructions to the blindfolded person that will guide them to find the object. How did it go?

Now, blindfold two people and place an object in the room. Have one of the blindfolded people tell the other blindfolded person how to find the object. Did it work? Why?

In today's story we see that Jesus healed a blind man so that he could see. The Pharisees did not like the fact that Jesus had done this and they were not willing to admit that Jesus had done something good and from God. The Pharisees were supposed to be guides for the people of Israel, but they were so blind because of their own pride that they were like blind guides. It doesn't work very well, does it?

We need to make sure that we don't start feeling so good about the good things we do that we forget to love the people around us who are really struggling to do what is right and become like blind guides.

Lesson 5

- John 10:1-39

Study Questions

What did Jesus accuse the Pharisees of being?

What metaphors did Jesus use to describe Himself in this passage? What was the point of each metaphor?

What was the final conclusion of the crowd about Jesus?

Food for Thought

The Good Shepherd

When you are reading the Bible it is important to remember that the chapter and verse divisions were not part of the original document. After the story of the blind man and the Pharisees John did not stop and say, "Now I will conclude chapter 9 and begin ch 10." No, those artificial divisions were added centuries later as a way to better reference the books.

Why do I bring that up right now? Glad you asked. Please look at John 9:41. Read from that verse and ignore the chapter division of 10:1. You will notice that there is not even a paragraph break between the end of chapter 9 and the beginning of chapter 10. Jesus moves, in one breath, from telling the Pharisees that they are blind and are guilty of sin into the phrase "I tell you the truth the man who does not enter the sheep pen by the gate, but climbs in by some other way, is a thief and a robber." In other words, Jesus is pointing His finger in the Pharisees face and saying, "You guys are supposed to be the shepherds of Israel, the spiritual leaders of God's flock. Yet you guys are blind. You are so blind that you can't even see the gate (Me) that leads into the pen where the sheep live. Instead, you jump over the fence. Well, guess what. Anybody who jumps over the fence is not a true shepherd, but a thief. You guys are hereby removed from duty. I am the real shepherd and leader of Israel. Be gone with you now."

Wow! Can you imagine how the Pharisees must have felt when Jesus said this? This upstart, country-bumpkin teacher from Galilee now had the gaul to assume that He could take their role as leaders of the nation.

At this point I could spend a lot of time explaining the intricacies of Jesus' metaphor of being a Shepherd. He is not only the Shepherd; He is the gate and lays down His life for the sheep. While I could spend a lot of time on that, and it would be good, I'm not going to. The message is simple. Jesus loves us, He is our leader, and He will always protect us. Got it?

Instead, I want to present to you a passage of scripture that may help you understand why Jesus chose this metaphor at this particular place in time. The Shepherd monologue concludes the debate between Jesus and the leaders of Israel that we have looked at this week. By using the metaphor Jesus was actually fulfilling a prophecy that Jeremiah wrote over 500 years earlier. This scripture would have been very familiar to the Pharisees and as Jesus told them that He was the

Shepherd, the words of Jeremiah must have been running in the back of all their minds.

Jeremiah 23:1-8 (NIV)
¹ "Woe to the shepherds who are destroying and scattering the sheep of my pasture!" declares the LORD. ² Therefore this is what the LORD, the God of Israel, says to the shepherds who tend my people: "Because you have scattered my flock and driven them away and have not bestowed care on them, I will bestow punishment on you for the evil you have done," declares the LORD. ³ "I myself will gather the remnant of my flock out of all the countries where I have driven them and will bring them back to their pasture, where they will be fruitful and increase in number. ⁴ I will place shepherds over them who will tend them, and they will no longer be afraid or terrified, nor will any be missing," declares the LORD. ⁵ "The days are coming," declares the LORD, "when I will raise up to David a righteous Branch, a King who will reign wisely and do what is just and right in the land. ⁶ In his days Judah will be saved and Israel will live in safety. This is the name by which he will be called: The LORD Our Righteousness. ⁷ "So then, the days are coming," declares the LORD, "when people will no longer say, 'As surely as the LORD lives, who brought the Israelites up out of Egypt,' ⁸ but they will say, 'As surely as the LORD lives, who brought the descendants of Israel up out of the land of the north and out of all the countries where he had banished them.' Then they will live in their own land."

The Jews in Jesus' day looked back to Moses as their great Shepherd who delivered them from the bondage of Egypt. Now Jesus is the Moses, He is the great Shepherd who delivers God's people out of the bondage of distorted truth, racism, and self-righteousness and opens the gates of the kingdom of Heaven to the whole world. Moses was the Shepherd who defined the Jews. Jesus is the Good Shepherd who defines the church.

As we end our week, let's take some time to thank God that He loves us so much, that, even when we mess things up, He comes back and starts things new again. Like a loving shepherd, Jesus takes care of us, His sheep. When we are sick, He heals us. When we are hungry He feeds us. When we stray He redirects us. He helps us grow and be productive. Rest in the promise of that wonderful truth.

Kid's Questions

When you have a pet, how do you get your pet to come to you? Generally you call out and say something like, whistle "Lassie, come here girl," whistle, whistle.

What happens when you call the animal? Why?

If you were a stranger, do you think the animal would come to you as easily? Why?

Did you know that Shepherds call their sheep like you would call a dog? When the shepherd calls for the Sheep, the sheep recognize his voice and come running. Jesus said that he is the Shepherd and we are like sheep.

In the world there are a lot of religions and false teachers who claim to have the truth. They call to you and pretend to be the Shepherd. Only when you really know the true Shepherd will you be able to know his voice when he calls. Do you know Jesus? Do you know the truth well enough to tell when something that is said to you is not right?

Make sure you spend time every day reading the Bible and talking to God in prayer. That way you will make sure to know the sound of the true Shepherd's voice and stay away from wolves and thieves that may try to trick you.

Introduction

A New Series

This session we begin a two-part study of Jesus' final journey toward Jerusalem. On the master illustration (from the introduction to the whole Life of Jesus Study) we see that He has come down from the mountain top experience of the transfiguration and has emerged from His time of retooling. The transition time is over. Jesus has jumped off the cliff, has set His face toward Jerusalem, and is speeding toward His destiny.

As He travels toward Jerusalem, beginning His trek in Perea and moving through Samaria and into Judea, He recasts the vision of the Kingdom. With each step His words become more intense and his eyes become more focused on the coming

pain, suffering, and ultimate victory that He will accomplish.

This session we get to hear solely from Luke as we look at Luke 9-16. In the same way that Matthew presented the message of the Kingdom early on in his gospel through the Sermon on the Mount and the Parables of Jesus, Luke chooses to wait until this moment in Jesus' life to lay out the master plan for the coming Kingdom. This makes sense when we realize that Matthew's focus was on the Jewish reader, while Luke's focus was on the Gentile reader. In Luke's presentation we see that the Kingdom of God is being directed toward the Gentile, the lower class, and the outcast.

The Illustration

Let's walk through the illustration. Overall you see that Jesus is moving toward Jerusalem. Along

117

the way He is teaching about the Kingdom. In the lower left the number 72 represents the army of disciples that Jesus sent out, two-by-two, to bring the good news of the Kingdom to all the cities in the region. The simple message they carried was that the Law of the King was to 1) Love God and 2) Love Neighbor. Seeking to find loopholes and justification for their own lack of love, the teachers asked Jesus to define the term "neighbor." He confirmed their worst nightmare when He defined neighbor as the man lying beaten and bleeding on the side of the road.

Moving down the path, Jesus was met with resistance and confusion by the crowd and the leaders of Israel. The leaders thought He was demon-possessed. The crowd only wanted Him for His miracles and healing power. Jesus told the crowd that they were either blind or completely distracted by the "stuff" of life. Then He turned to the leaders and blamed them for the ignorance of the masses. Because of their lack of leadership, Jesus declared that the leaders would be removed from the office that God had given them and replaced by His authority and leadership. This enraged the leaders and they began to plot His demise. Aware of the traps that would await Him in Jerusalem, Jesus warned His disciples that it would cost them everything to follow Him.

Off on the horizon are the metaphors that Jesus used to teach the principles of His Kingdom. The Kingdom was about finding the lost – the lost sheep, the lost coin, and the lost son – not about protecting your holy assets. Because the leaders had lost sight of this fundamental truth that had always been present in God's plan since the days of Abraham, and since they had led the crowds into distorted perspectives, the leaders would not be present at the banquet table of the Father. In fact, the leaders would be standing outside in the cold looking on in astonishment at the rag-tag group of people that the Father actually allowed to join Him in the end.

Warning

There are some things that will be important to understand from the outset of this sessions's study in order to get the most out of it:

1. We will be covering more material than we have in the past.

2. At first glance it may seem that this section in Luke is just a hodge-podge of stories that Luke threw into a "miscellaneous" category. That couldn't be further from the truth.

3. The fact is that Luke 9-19 is a brilliant piece of story telling. We must remember that the gospel writers were not simply telling the

story of Jesus in a detached, reporter-like manner. The Gospel writers were preaching a very intentional message to the readers. In these ten chapters Luke pulls out all the stops and preaches what he believes is the heart of the gospel message. As you read it, think of it like a sermon. Luke uses each individual story as if it were a heading in his outline. Each story carries one piece of the message to progress his specific idea.

4. The best way to think of this section is like a conversation that is taking place between Jesus and the Jews (sometimes the leaders, sometimes the crowd). In order to help you see the big, sweeping flow of thought, and not get caught up in the details of each individual story, I will begin each daily "Food for Thought" with a section that looks like a script from a play. What I'm doing here is trying to climb into the mind of Jesus, and, more specifically into the mind of Luke, and write the dialogue between Jesus and the Jews in the meaning that Luke was trying to portray by telling the stories that he told. In other words, I am interpreting the meaning of the story and writing my interpretation in the words of a dialogue between Jesus and the Jews.

Let me pause for a moment and speak directly to you. I'm struggling a little bit with this sessions's writing. My struggle comes from the fact that 1) I love this section of the gospels so much that I want to write on and on about it, 2) If I wrote on and on about it there would be hundreds of pages to read and it would cease to be effective as a daily Bible study tool, and 3) you don't have time or desire to read hundreds of pages of my commentary on these 10 chapters. That being said, I'm actually going to shoot for a "less is more" approach to the writing and pray that you will get the point of this section by reading the dialogues. I will control myself and pick only one or two nuggets from each section to elaborate upon each day, knowing that I am turning my head away from some precious gems. Hopefully the Holy Spirit will point them out to you as you journey through the pages with Him.

Lesson 1

- John 10:40-42
- Luke 9:51-11:13

Study Questions

Where is Jesus when He sets out for Jerusalem?

What does it take to follow Jesus?

What were Jesus' instructions to the 72 when they came into a town?

What are the two basic commands that Jesus' followers are supposed to obey?

What attitude does the Father have toward the requests of his children?

Food for Thought

Big picture dialogue

9:51-56

    Jesus: I'm going to Jerusalem.

9:57-62

    Jews: Can I follow, please? It sounds fun.

    Jesus: No free-loaders or half-hearted followers allowed.

10:1-24

    Jesus: My true disciples take the Kingdom to the Gentiles.

    Disciples: It works!

    Jesus: Cool, My plan works. This is going to be worth the suffering.

10:25- 28

    Jesus: The rules of the Kingdom are simple: Love God and love your neighbor.

10:29-37

    Jews: Who is my neighbor?

    Jesus: "Love neighbor" means to love the unlovely, not just the "safe" person.

10:38-42

    Martha: Can I just wash the dishes first?

    Jesus: "Love God" means to not be distracted by stuff.

11:1-13

    Jesus: The Kingdom is available, all you have to do is ask.

A closer look

9:51-56 I'm going to Jerusalem.

v. 51 is actually one of the key verses in the gospel of Luke. It is the hinge verse on which Jesus' ministry swings in focus and tone. Before v. 51 Jesus ministered in Galilee and had a more positive tone. After v. 51 Jesus became a laser focused man on a deadly mission. His teaching became intense. The key phrase that turns the story is, "Jesus resolutely set out for Jerusalem." The Greek phrase is literally translated, "Jesus strengthened [or strongly set] His face for the journey He would make to Jerusalem." If this were an action hero movie this would be the scene when Arnold would start off hunched over the body of his just-killed partner, then, as he stood up the camera would zoom in tight on his face. Just as the camera locks in on his face, we see the muscle in the side of his jaw bulge as his teeth clench, right in sync with the "dun-dun-dun-dunnnnn" chords of the orchestra. Everyone in the theater sits up and prepares themselves because they know that Arnie is gonna kick some butt.

In v. 51 we have a similar moment. Jesus is ready. Israel has rejected Him. He's played their game long enough. Now it is time to face His destiny and make the journey to Jerusalem, which, He knew full well, would end with an agonizing day of torture and execution. He was ready. Let's go.

9:57-62 No free-loaders or half-hearted followers allowed.

As He sets out and begins His heroic march to the city, a series of happy-go-lucky, Kingdom glory seekers run up to Him and say, "Can I come? Can I come? I'd really like to be part of Your Kingdom party!" Jesus, without even looking to the side says, "Yeah, right. You have no idea what you are asking." And keeps pressing toward the goal.

10:1-24 Take the Kingdom to the Gentiles...cool; this is going to be worth the suffering.

Jesus sent His disciples ahead of Him with the message of the Kingdom. His mission hadn't changed, but the scope of His field had broadened. Back in chapter 9, at the front end of the story, Jesus had sent the 12 out, two-by-two, to proclaim the message of the Kingdom. Now, as He was in the Gentile region of Perea, and was passing through Samaria, He took 72 of His followers (after weeding out the happy-go-lucky bunch) and sent them out on the same mission as the 12 had done, only this time to everyone. This time, the disciples came back with wonderful tales of victory and power. This moment must have been a gift from the Father to Jesus to serve as an encouragement for Him, for Jesus was flooded with hope as He saw a glimpse of the fact that His mission of taking the Kingdom of God to the Gentiles would actually be effective. Yet, He knew that the reality of this foreshadowing would only be realized after the painful suffering that He was going to endure. This glimpse of victory filled Him with the courage He needed to step into the snake pit that awaited Him.

10:25- 28 The rules are simple: Love God and love your neighbor.

In the previous section He sent them on a mission to take the message. But what was the message?

Here we see the clear, simple message of the Kingdom of God. If you want to be a citizen of the Kingdom then you are to simply 1) Love God and 2) Love your neighbor. Of course, this message is couched in language that was directly targeted at the Jewish leaders who believed that the citizens of the Kingdom were not only to follow the 10 commandments, and the 261 laws that Moses wrote in Leviticus, but they were to also follow the hundreds of commands, regulations, rituals, and ceremonies – traditions – that the Jewish leaders had established as well. Jesus said, "No! It's really simple. If you love God and love your neighbor, then the Law of God will be completely fulfilled as the authentic overflow of your heart."

10:29-37 Love neighbor means to love the unlovely, not just the "safe" person.

The leaders knew where He was going with this simplified Law and tried to justify their extreme prejudice and superiority complex by pulling a typical politician's move. They said, "Define 'neighbor'." In other words, they wanted to see if there were loop holes in the system (after all, that was their game. They created so many laws that it was impossible to understand them, so they, as the creators and perpetuators of the laws and traditions, could use them and break them as it fit their agenda and no one would be the wiser). Jesus would not stand for that kind of deception, distortion, and manipulation... not on His watch. He saw right through their scheming and cut to the chase with the parable of the "Good Samaritan." Of all the "righteous" men who passed the hurting man on the road, only the Samaritan demonstrated the true spirit and law of the Kingdom of God. Of course, this example rattled the cages of the leaders to the core of their identity. How dare he say that a Samaritan (you know, those half-breed dogs that are sub-human and not deserving of a crust of bread from God's banquet table) would be considered more righteous than they are in the eyes of God!

10:38-42 Love God means to not be distracted by stuff.

Luke uses the simple story of Mary and Martha to define what Jesus meant by loving God. Mary was focused on Jesus while Martha was distracted by the stuff around her. Please note that this is not an indictment against people with the spiritual gift of service whose spiritual pathway is acts of service to others. Nor is it an endorsement for laziness that is couched in "spirituality." This story was placed here in the flow of Luke's presentation to be an analogy and a foreshadowing of Jesus' subsequent teaching about being distracted by the things of the world, and in being so distracted, being unable to authentically know and love God.

11:1-13 The Kingdom is available, all you have to do is ask.

The Pharisees had complicated the simple truths of God's Kingdom and had distorted the message. They believed that they had to go through rigorous ceremony in order to be considered clean before God and worthy to be heard. They believed that their commitment to this strict religious system made them better than everyone else and the only people who had God's ear. Jesus set the record straight in this section. He said, "God is your Father, He loves you, He knows what you need better than you do, and He wants to be in relationship with you. All you have to do is ask and trust Him. No pomp, no circumstance, just authenticity...it's that simple. So come on."

Kid's Questions

Look at the illustration for this week. Do you see the man lying by the side of the road? What do you think happened to him? How does it make you feel to look at him? If you really saw someone like that by the side of the road, what would be your reaction? Why?

Read Luke 10:25-37, if you haven't already.

What position in society did the first three by passers hold in society?

Who was the good neighbor? Why?

How did the Jews feel about the Samaritans? Why?

In this parable Jesus taught the people that it doesn't matter how important you may be in the church, or how much people respect you. God doesn't care about those things. What God wants is for his people to love everyone, no matter how much it hurts or how much it costs. Even a Samaritan was a better neighbor than the spiritual leaders of Israel.

Let's make sure that we never look down on someone and always try to help people who are in need.

121

Lesson 2

- Luke 11:14-12:12

Study Questions

What accusation is made against Jesus? What is His reply?

Why are the people not able to correctly interpret the signs that Jesus gives them?

What is Jesus' attitude and accusation against the Pharisees?

What promise does Jesus make to the disciples regarding their coming trials and persecutions?

Food for Thought

On this, the second day in our study of Jesus' journey toward Jerusalem we see that Jesus meets opposition from the teachers and leaders of the Jews.

Big picture dialogue

11:14-28

> Jews: You are possessed and in league with Satan!
>
> Jesus: Just the opposite, I drive out Satan by the power of God. If you don't change your ways, the demons I drive out may come back and get you.

11:29-32

> Jesus: Israel is so blind it can't even see that the signs and miracles I am performing prove that I'm from God.

11:33-36

> Jesus: If they had the light of truth in their eyes, they would be able to see who I am...but they don't.

11:37-54

> Jews: Jesus, why do you eat with unclean hands and yet claim to be with God.
>
> Jesus: You guys are so mixed up. It's not about the outside stuff, it's about the inside stuff. You are in big trouble for having misrepresented God's law leading the nation into false teaching.
>
> Jews: That's it, let's kill him.

12:1-12

> Jesus: I know what you are whispering about. You want to kill Me. That's fine. Just remember, you can kill My body, but I can kill your soul.

A closer look

From 11:33-36

We talked about this a little last session, but it is worth revisiting. The point of this analogy may be somewhat lost to the 21ˢᵗ century reader, because the analogy is based upon the "scientific knowledge" of the ancient world. In Jesus' day they didn't know anything about photons and the behavior of light in the way that we do today. (I'm not saying that Jesus didn't understand it. He understands it better than we do, because He created it...duh. We have to remember that

Jesus had to communicate eternal truth to people within the cultural and linguistic framework in which they lived. Otherwise they would have no idea what He was talking about). So, the point Jesus was making was based upon a common understanding that light actually emanated from the eyeball. It's not that they didn't think the sun had something to do with it, since we can't see at night, but they believed that there was something inside the eyeball that was necessary for the person to see the world. That is what Jesus meant when He said the eye is the lamp of the body. If you have "good light" in your eyes, then you can see. If you have "darkness" in your eyes then you can't see; you are blind. Knowing that the people understood this to be true about the physical process of seeing, He was able to make a spiritual analogy. If you have the light of truth in your eye (or heart, or spiritual understanding) then you will be able to see the truth and be transformed by it in your whole self. If you have the darkness of false teaching in your eye, then you will be blind and unable to receive the truth. The eye (your heart or your spiritual understanding) is like the lampstand for your whole life. If you put the truth there, then your whole life will be full of light.

Jesus spoke these words as a commentary on the fact that the Jews were blind. They had snuffed out the light of truth and their lives were full of darkness. They ask for a sign, but are not spiritually able to see the truth when it is plainly set before them.

We need to be careful that we are lighting the light of truth in our "eyes" each day and not allowing ourselves to slowly move into the world's systems and let the darkness snuff out the light.

From 12:1-12

I'd like to zone in on v. 11. Jesus knows that He is going to be cruelly beaten and killed. He also knows that His disciples will be treated no less harshly as they fight against the darkness and try to bring the light of his kingdom to the world. In v. 11 He stops and speaks directly to the disciples with words of comfort. I believe He is also stopping and looking directly into your eyes across the millennium and saying to you, "If you are brave enough to simply follow Me, you don't need to worry. I will be with you. I will give you the Holy Spirit and He will always be present. If you will just surrender your need for control and trust that I've got you covered, then you will be amazed at the things I can do through you in just the right moment. You just be surrendered and open, I'll take it from there."

Many times we think we can't be effective for Jesus because we haven't gone to Bible school, or because we can't craft our words well or speak eloquently. Stop thinking like that. The disciples were just a bunch of guys. They weren't the refined intelligentsia; they were fishermen and tax collectors. Yet, God used them to change the world because they were submitted to following Him and be open to being used by Him. You have the same Holy Spirit that they had. Let Him work through you today.

Kid's Questions

How would you feel if your thoughts were broadcast over a loud speaker so that everyone around you heard them, or were projected like a movie over your head so that everyone around you could see them?

Are there things that you have thought in your mind that you would never want your parents to know? You don't have to tell them, but you do have to know that God knows them.

Today Jesus said, "What you have said in the dark will be heard in the daylight, and what you have whispered in the ear in the inner rooms will be proclaimed from the roofs." He said this because the Pharisees were secretly plotting to kill him, but I think the principle is true for everyone. God knows what we think. We can't hide anything from him.

This week, if you ever find yourself grumbling about your silly sister or complaining about your parents, remember that God is right there hearing everything you think and seeing everything you imagine. Ask him if he is pleased with your thoughts and ask him to help you turn them into something positive.

123

Lesson 3

- Luke 12:13-13:9

Study Questions

Where should our focus be? Why?

What will get the manager in trouble with the master?

Why should the lamps be kept burning? What would happen if the lamps went out?

What affect can the truth of Jesus potentially have on family systems?

What were the people not able to do that Jesus thought they should be able to do? Why?

Food for Thought

Big picture dialogue

12:13-34

Jesus: Your eyes are focused on the wrong thing and you are asking the wrong questions. Don't worry about "stuff," instead be concerned about the Kingdom. God will take care of you.

12:35-48

Jesus: Instead of wasting your time micromanaging junk that is just going to burn anyway, you should be focusing on the matters that last for eternity. Keep watch because there will be a day of reckoning when all accounts will be settled in an eternal perspective.

12:49-53

Jesus: I know My words are harsh and challenge the status quo. They are so "out there" that it will get Me killed. I know that my teaching will rip families apart, but, as sad as that is, the truth is more important than false peace.

12:54-13:9

Jesus: If you weren't blind you would see that I am bringing in the new age of the Kingdom and that everything will be different. Stop misinterpreting the "signs" around you and wake up to the fact that I'm the only sign you need.

A Closer Look

From 12:35-48

In v. 41 Peter asked Jesus whether He was speaking the parable to them specifically or to everyone. Did you notice that Jesus did not answer him directly, but launched into another story? That leaves us still asking the question that Peter asked.

I believe that Jesus is really talking to leaders in this section. He's speaking both to the leaders of Israel who are being reprimanded by God for being bad manager's of God's estate, and to the disciples to whom Jesus is about to appoint as the new managers of God's estate.

Before we can fully grasp the impact of this parable we must remember the context from which it flows. Jesus is talking about a society that is built upon a type of feudal system. There were two classes of people in Jesus day; the rich who owned land, and the poor who were owned by the rich. Every wealthy person who owned land also owned servants. To use this analogy does not mean that Jesus condoned slavery; He was simply using a system that everyone was very aware of. With that in mind we can get to the point.

Leaders, please listen.

As leaders in the Kingdom of God it is easy to forget that God is the only owner and master of the Kingdom. He is the only one who holds authority and reserves the right for judgment. He has appointed and established certain people to be managers, or stewards, of his estate. Their job is to look after it and make sure things run well and maintain productivity while he is away. The problem is that, if the master stays away too long, the managers start getting really comfortable in their position of authority. They start thinking that they are somehow better than the rest of the servants and are privy to the luxuries of the aristocracy. They have forgotten one important thing...they are slaves too. When the master returns, according to the rules of the system to which Jesus is using as an analogy, the manager/slave deserves nothing because he was simply doing the task to which he was assigned.

Jesus was telling Peter that the Pharisees had violated this basic principle. They had elevated themselves above their position and used their false power to abuse the people. While Peter was probably in wholehearted agreement, shaking his head up and down in indignant affirmation of Jesus' assertion, Jesus stuck his finger on Peter's chest and said, in a stern tone, "Watch yourself! You could fall into that same trap. Never forget that you are being put in your position as a steward, a servant of God for the service of his people. Don't become like the Pharisees, because I'd hate to have to come back in 2,000 years and spank your butt like I'm having to spank theirs."

Did you hear that leaders? We must be careful to never think too highly of ourselves than we ought. Never forget that the leadership gifts – apostles, prophets, evangelists, pastors, and teachers – are foundation stones, half buried in the mud, upon which the people of the Kingdom will be built up and ascend into maturity in the body of Christ.

From 12:57-59

This is one of those little passages that, on first reading, makes you stop and go, "huh? What does this have to do with the rest of the passage?"

Step back from it and remember that Luke is riding a train of thought. He would not have

arbitrarily thrown in some incidental piece of Jesus speak for no reason. I believe this has to do with the theme of light in the eyes, distraction, and distorted perspectives, and misinterpreting the times.

Let's cast it in this light. At 8:00am on September 11th, in the World Trade Center, there were thousands of people who were starting another typical work day. I'm sure that many of them were entrenched in petty arguments with fellow cubicle dwellers. One guy was probably fooling around with his secretary while his wife slaved at home with the kids. The company on the 12th floor was using the attorney on the 32nd floor to sue the company in the penthouse suite. Just another day in a distorted, distracted society.

Imagine how different their attitudes and behaviors would have been if they had known that as they were driving to work that day a group of terrorists were sliding their way past airport security, boarding commercial airliners, and setting their sites on the window in front of their desk?

Jesus is telling us that our focus is wrong. We are concerned about petty things to the point that we will drag each other to court over nothing. Stop allowing petty things to eat up your time and energy. Stop bickering, start forgiving, and get on with the business of bringing the love of God to the world.

Kid's Questions

Let's pretend that it is Saturday and your Dad said that he wanted to take you to the movies that night. However, the only way you could go to the movies was if your bedroom was cleaned up by the time he got home from running his errands. He left in the morning and didn't know exactly when he'd be back. If you're not done when gets home, you won't go to the movie.

What do you do? Do you:

a. Say, I've got plenty of time; I'll just read a comic book or play with my toys for a while?

b. Force your little sister to clean your room and threaten to break her toys if she doesn't do it?

c. Get mad at your Dad for making you do anything in the first place and pout.

d. Figure that you should work hard right away and get the job done so that you'll be prepared when he returns home?

Hopefully you chose d.

Jesus said that his Kingdom was kind of like this story. Jesus left and said that he would be back soon. He left us with a job to do. We are supposed to be salt and light in the world and shine the truth of Jesus to everyone around us. Too many times people choose option a, b, or c instead of keeping watch, and keeping oil in their lamps (or batteries in their flashlights in our century).

Make sure you wake up each day and realize, Jesus could return today. Will I be doing something that will make him proud when he gets back, or will I just be goofing off and wasting time?

Lesson 4

- Luke 13:10-14:35

Study Questions

Why were the Pharisees upset about the healing of the woman?

What do the parables of the mustard seed and they yeast have in common?

Who will be in the Kingdom and who will not?

In what way were the Pharisees misusing their feast?

Who will be at the banquet of God?

What does it cost to follow Jesus?

Food for Thought

Big picture dialogue

13:10-17

> Jews: Jesus, you just healed a person on the Sabbath. How could a man of God work on the Sabbath?
>
> Jesus: Ugh! You hypocrites! You'd save an ox on the Sabbath and think nothing of it, yet you condemn Me for bringing new life to this dear woman?

13:18-21

> Jesus: The sin of the leaders is so widespread that it seems unchangeable, but don't worry, the true kingdom is like a tiny seed and like a little bit of yeast. Over time it will grow and overpower this sinful status quo.

13:22-30

> Jesus: The door to the Kingdom is very narrow and only a few will make it. Oh, by the way, the few who make it aren't the ones you would expect.

13:31-35

> Jews: Herod wants to kill you.
>
> Jesus: I know. (Actually, I know it's you who want to keep Me out of Jerusalem) I'm prepared to do whatever it takes to save My people, Israel.

14:1-24

> Setting: Jesus is eating at a feast with the leaders of the Jews.
>
> Jews: I want to sit at the head of the table.
>
> Jesus: Don't exalt yourself like that and be so full of pride. Stop schmoozing each other and politicizing. Start inviting the lower class to eat with you for a change.
>
> Jews: Yeah right. What really matters is that we will be at the feast of God in his Kingdom, right?
>
> Jesus: Oh right, that reminds me...about the Father's banquet. You were invited, but you never showed up, so He changed the guest list and you're not on it. He's invited all the poor people and Gentiles that you've snubbed in his name. K?

14:25-35

> Jesus: As for the rest of you onlookers; don't get too smug as I lambaste your leaders. You are all responsible for yourselves. I'm not messing around. Yes, the Kingdom is for everyone and is freely given, but it is not cheap. If you want to follow Me into the

Kingdom then you need to be willing to do as I do and give up everything – all your creature comforts, material safety nets, and self-image props. When you do that, then you will be like salt in a tasteless and rotting world.

A Closer Look

From 14:1-14

Who are the heroes in our society? We tend to idolize people who can put a ball through a metal hoop, or sing and dance, or tell stories really well. We also idolize the people who wield power both in politics and in economics. If they can climb their way to the top of the political rat race, then they deserve special treatment. If they can lead a company that makes billions of dollars, then we will build them a shrine. We even idolize people who aren't real, but are simply characters of fiction that are depicted by an actor. For these "heroes" we are willing to pay millions of dollars and sacrifice hours of time. We applaud them because they entertain us; we cater to them because they have power over us. We spend time and energy wondering how we can either become like them or get close enough to them to ride the wave of their success and eat the crumbs of luxury that fall from their tables.

It was no different in the days of Jesus. That is how every society works. Every society, that is, except the Kingdom of God. Jesus told the leaders and his disciples very plainly to not elevate themselves to places of honor. When we get sucked into the upward mobility cyclone there is only one thing that can happen. We get so focused on moving toward the next carrot and covering our assets, that we can no longer see the truth of the people around us. Jesus reminds us that what really matters in the Kingdom of God is not how we treat people who already have all that they need, but how we treat people who have nothing.

God created the world to be able to sustain life. If every person in the world were completely unselfish, and we took only what we needed, gave the rest to those who could not provide for themselves, and then mutually empowered everyone to live in harmony, under the authority and leadership of God, then there would be no war and no famine. Instead, we hoard wealth and keep people down. As members of the Kingdom of God we must never forget that God does not play that game and will not tolerate those who do. He especially has little patience with those that He has placed as leaders in his Kingdom that introduce and perpetuate that kind of hero worship within the space of the Kingdom.

Let's take our eyes off of the superstars and start focusing on those in need. If we did that, perhaps the Kingdom of God might actually grow around us.

From 14:15-35

What does it mean to feast at God's banquet? Throughout the Bible the image of sitting at a person's table to share in a meal symbolized being in good relationship with someone and being of the same mindset. This was called table fellowship. To feast at God's banquet means to be in step with God's plan for the world, to be in good relationship with Him, and to be included in His family.

Would you like to sit at that table someday? Would you like to be seated in the place of honor at that table? What will it take to ensure your place in that most glorious position? The Pharisees thought they had the answer to that question wrapped up. They were children of Abraham, living under the promise of God. They were the defenders and protectors of God's most holy manner of living. They had kept the unclean out and the nation free of infection. Surely God would have a special seat for them at the banquet. Guess again guys. You were so busy keeping people out of the banquet that you forgot to go in yourself.

OK, we know that the Pharisees aren't going to be there (at least the ones who continued to reject Jesus' new order), but what does it take for us to be there? Should we work really hard at being "good?" Should we make sure that we read our Bibles everyday and do our lessons before we meet on Sundays? Should we take our spiritual gift inventories and figure out our fruitful and fulfilling place in the body of Christ and serve each day? Should we start a homeless ministry and make 300 lunches every Saturday and deliver them to the guys lying under the bushes? Should we give everything we own away and live under the bushes with those guys? What should we do? The answer...stop wanting it.

Jesus said that we must give up everything we have to be able to follow Him. He didn't say that we need to work really hard at doing the right things to get a good seat at the table. He didn't say give away your possessions to the poor to get a good seat at the table. He said give up everything you have. I believe the true heart of Jesus' message, in light of the context of this whole message from Luke, is that we need to give up our need to have a seat at the table. We are servants. All glory goes to God. There is nothing that we can do that will elevate us one bit in the banquet guest list. If we would figure out that we are servants and that what we are called to do is simply obey, then all the struggle and turmoil would be removed. If God says, "Go wash that toilet," we do it with a thankful heart. If God says, "give all your money away and live with the homeless," we say, "No problem. Right away, sir." If God says, "Invent something, make a lot of money, and use it to fund ministry," we say, "Yes sir, where would you like me to make the check?" If he says, "Use your artistic skills to infuse the world with beauty, joy, and hope so that they remember that I love them," we say, "What size canvas would you like?"

You see, the point is not about sitting at the banquet table. That is so selfish and self-exalting. The point is that we are to enjoy the fact that God is our Master and we have nothing to worry about but to simply obey.

Many people spend their whole lives doing really "good" things and appear very self-sacrificing and "take-up-your-crossish" to the people around them, but inside they are keeping tally marks and stockpiling eternal rewards and a seat at the banquet table. True love and true discipleship gives it all away, even a seat at the Father's table, all for the glory of God.

Kid's Questions

When you share your toys with someone, do you expect that that would share their toys with you? Of course you do, that's only fair.

Have you ever found yourself wanting to be someone's friend, or sharing your stuff with someone because you wanted to be able to play with something that they have? When you really stop to think about that, is sharing with that person, for that reason, really a way of showing love for that person?

Many times we make decisions based on our own selfish desires. We can use people to get what we want. Jesus told us that we should learn how to give things away and show love to people and not want anything in return. The people who need what we have the most are the people who can't pay us back. Let's figure out ways that we can give to people who are truly in need and can't give back to us. That is a better demonstration of the kind of love that God has for us.

Lesson 5

- Luke 15:1-16:18

Study Questions

What do the three "lost" parables have in common?

Why is the older brother upset?

Why was the manager fired? What did the manager do in order to protect himself once he was fired?

What was the Pharisees' attitude toward money?

What was Jesus' attitude toward the Law?

Food for Thought

Big picture dialogue

15:1-32

> Jews: You eat with "sinners." How could you be a man of God?
>
> Jesus: You have forgotten what the Kingdom of God is all about. People are lost out there and they need to be found, not condemned. If you lost a sheep or a coin, you'd look for it. God lost his children because of rebellion. He wants them back, and He will accept them when they return, whether you think they are "sinners" and "unclean" or not.

16:1-15

> Jesus: You were put in charge of leading the Kingdom and seeking the lost, but you blew it. So, you're fired. Once there was a manager who was fired, like you are getting fired, but at least he was smart enough to start forgiving people on his way out in order to soften the blow of his demise. You aren't even that smart. You are hard-hearted to the very end. All you are concerned about is money and power.

16:14-18

> Jews: Oh yeah? How do you know what we value?
>
> Jesus: You think you are fooling people, but you're not fooling God. You accuse Me of distorting the Law, but actually you are the ones who have been distorting the law. I'm simply following the Law the way God intended for it to be followed. You accuse Me of claiming that God is divorcing Israel and running off with a new wife. Never. If He did that He would be an adulterer. God is not divorcing Israel. You are the ones who have been in bed with a prostitute and God is simply reclaiming His bride and cleaning her up after you made her dirty. So there.

This fascinating dialogue with the leaders of the Jews will be continued next session as Jesus travels closer to Jerusalem.

A Closer Look

From Luke 15:11-32

The story of the Lost Son or the Prodigal Son is one of the best known stories of the Bible. Even if people have never cracked open the Bible in their lives, they know about the Prodigal Son returning home. While many people know this story, most people don't realize that story really isn't about the Prodigal Son. The story is really about the older son. Remember, this parable is told in the context of a 10-chapter long dialogue between Jesus and the Jewish leaders. In the process of the dialogue Jesus has fired the leaders for being poor stewards of God's Kingdom and misunderstanding their job description. In the two parables preceding this one Jesus tells the leaders what the focus should be like. They should be looking for lost things like you would look for a lost sheep and a lost coin. In this parable He is holding a mirror up to them to reveal their current attitude in light of the truth that Jesus is teaching about the Kingdom of God. According to Jesus' teaching the Father is welcoming home the lost son who was tramping around the countryside, squandering his inheritance, and becoming defiled with the pigs. The leaders, on the other hand are being like the older son who resents the Father for loving his child and extending grace to him. The hardness and resentment of the older son is actually keeping him from having table fellowship with the Father. If he would have put aside his self-righteous, "you-owe-me-something" attitude and simply joined in the celebration with the Father over the homecoming of the lost son, then they would have all had table fellowship over the fattened calf.

There is a lesson for us. Many times we can fall into the trap of keeping score. We tally up all the good things we do, and we keep a parallel column recording all the times we get thanked or recognized for it. Perhaps we have been a "good" Christian all our lives and then one day a guy comes into the church from off the streets and gets all the lime light for the "amazing testimony" that he has. He gets special treatment from the pastor and the next thing you know he's on staff at the church or is starting a ministry that is really successful. Deep inside we think, "Now doesn't that just figure. Here I've been cleaning toilets and working in the nursery all my life, and never has anybody even said a 'thanks' to me, and then this guy waltzes in and gets the lion's share. Well that's it. I'm outta here." At one level that reaction would be understandable. After all, everybody wants to be affirmed and acknowledged. Yet, at the core of that attitude is a selfishness that can only lead to bitterness. Bitterness then becomes a prison that robs us of joy and freedom.

In the Kingdom we are to rejoice with those who rejoice and mourn with those who mourn. We are not in competition with one another for God's love or accolades. God's love is eternal and infinitely expansive. It can envelope each of us to the depths or our soul and still have enough to overflow. We are all players on the team and need to stop keeping internal score. We serve one master, and He is all that matters.

From Luke 16:18

Once again we trip over a little verse that seems to be sticking up like a root across the path. We didn't expect it, it doesn't seem to fit in the flow of thought, and we stumble on it.

When you read in the NIV there are little headers that label the sections of the book. Sometimes those are really helpful. Other times they are tragically destructive to the study of scripture. Remember, they are not part of the original text. Luke did not stop after v. 17 and say, "now I am going to make a non sequitor remark 'regarding divorce'." I just don't think that's how Luke composed this gospel.

Let's look closer at what Luke was getting at with the inclusion of this phrase. Read vv. 14-18 again, ignoring the break between v.17 and 18.

Here's the flow:

> You're not fooling God, He knows your hearts.
>
> He does not value what you value.
>
> The Law and the prophets were preached, now the good news of the Kingdom is being preached, yet people are trying to force their way into it.
>
> The law isn't being changed here,   it can't be.
>
> Anyone who divorces his wife and marries another is an adulterer.

I believe Luke is saying that the Jews are accusing Jesus of changing the Law and saying, in essence, that God is abandoning His wife, Israel, and marrying a new woman, the "Kingdom" that Jesus is proclaiming that includes Gentiles. Jesus is responding by saying that God is not abandoning Israel because if He did that would make Him an adulterer. After all, everyone knows that if you divorce your wife and marry someone else you are an adulterer.

Let's stop and address a hot issue for a second. This verse is not Jesus' teaching regarding divorce. Jesus is using a commonly held belief regarding divorce and applying it analogously to God's relationship with Israel. Does that mean that we cannot use this verse as a proof text in our marriage and divorce discussions that are being hotly debated in the church? I'm not saying that. Nor am I saying that Jesus didn't believe this statement on divorce to be true. I think He did agree with the basic premise of it, otherwise He would not have used it to demonstrate His point regarding the nature of God. However, whenever we use scripture, we must always be sure that we are using it in its proper context. So, the bottom line of this little bunny trail is this: in Luke 16:18, Jesus did not stand up in front of the people for the purpose of teaching about divorce and remarriage. He was using an already accepted axiom from the Jewish culture to demonstrate a deep truth about God.

Now, back to the main point. Jesus' argument to the Jews, then, is this; "since God is not an adulterer, and will never abandon Israel, or revoke the Law that He gave to her, it becomes clear that you, in fact, are the ones who have distorted the Law and are sleeping around with the prostitutes of self-righteousness and pride. I'm simply getting God's bride back on track, cleaning her up from your mess, and presenting her perfect for her groom. The perfect bride is one where all people, Jew and Gentile, poor and rich alike can come to the feast without any concern for competition or condemnation from their peers. All people are equal as servants of God.

Kid's Questions

If you lost your favorite toy, or your pet ran away, how would you feel? What would you do about it? How would you feel when you found it?

Now, let's pretend that your family was planning a big vacation in six months. Your dad said that all the kids could do a specific list of chores every week in order to earn spending money on the trip.

Pretend that one of the kids in the family got really mad at your parents and ran away from home a week later. She was gone for six months. How would you feel about it? How do you think your parents would feel about it?

Now, let's say that one week before your trip

your sister shows up. She looks bad and has obviously had a very rough time living on the streets. When she shows up how would you feel?

Now let's say that, when she comes home, your parents throw a big party and they say that, since she's back and they are so happy to have the family back together that she can come on the family trip AND have some spending money. You worked hard the whole six months to earn the money, and she gets it without having to work. How do you feel?

That is just like the story Jesus told about the two brothers. The older brother was upset that the Father celebrated over the younger brother's return and didn't want to join in the celebration. By pouting about it, who really lost out?

You see, we need to be careful to not judge other people or to get upset when others get treated differently than we do. God loves everyone equally and doesn't play favorites. We need to rejoice with people when they rejoice, and cry with people when they cry, and not be the judge of everyone else's affairs. All we have to worry about is doing what we know to be right before God.

132

Introduction

The city of Jerusalem grows larger on the horizon in this sessions's picture as we continue in this, the second half of our two part mini-series that covers the final journey that Jesus made toward His destiny of the cross. Last week we heard exclusively from Luke as he presented his version of the Kingdom of God through a series of stories that tracked his dialogue with the Pharisees. This week we begin by catching the tail end of Luke's dialogue. Later we are joined by Matthew, Mark, and John as all four gospel writers track with Jesus' final journey as He crosses the Jordan River, and passes through the Judean cities of Jericho and Bethany.

The Illustration

The illustration has three basic sections, reading left to right.

Finishing in Perea

In Luke 17:11 Luke changes the focus of his dialogue a bit. The Pharisees asked Jesus to tell them when the Kingdom would come. Jesus pointed to the horizon and said that there was a terrible judgment coming and that the Pharisees would be very surprised at who would be part of the new Kingdom and who would be taken away in the storm of judgment. Just like it was in the days of Noah and the days of Lot, when God brought judgment on the world, so it would be when judgment would sweep down on Jerusalem. The Pharisees thought that, because of their position in the nation, their education,

133

their observance of the Law, and their financial and political power, they were at the front of the line for being delivered from the judgment and entering the Messiah's Kingdom. Jesus set the record straight. He told them that only the people who were willing to sacrifice their pride, power, and possessions -- people who were willing to become like a little child -- would be allowed to enter the Kingdom of God. Only the people who had been completely humbled and stripped of the external trappings of life would be able to crawl through the eye of the needle -- the narrow gate -- and enter the kingdom. The Pharisees resented Jesus' accusations towards them and resolved to kill Him when He reached Jerusalem.

In Jericho

As Jesus entered the city of Jericho, the disciples asked about who would be the greatest in the Kingdom. With two stories and a parable Jesus answers the question. The blind man who is healed and the tax collector who is redeemed, those are the great ones in the Kingdom. The ones who think they are great, like the Pharisees, are in for a big surprise when the king finally shows up. The ones who mismanaged the responsibility that had been entrusted to them (a la Pharisee) will be stripped of their position, thrown out, and the lowly servants will be given their share.

In Bethany

In the final section we see the beautiful story where Jesus raised Lazarus from the dead. Jesus' good friend had been dead for four days by the time Jesus showed up, but, in order to demonstrate the Father's power and glory, Jesus declared that He was the resurrection and the life and He brought Lazarus out of the grave and into the land of the living. The Pharisees' reaction to this event was astounding. Rather than being convinced of Jesus' power and authority, they became more rigidly set against Him. Out of fear for both invoking the wrath of Rome and losing their own power in Jerusalem, they decided that they did not only have to kill Jesus, but now they had to kill Lazarus as well. Life destroyed death and, in response, fear and greed plotted to destroy life.

Lesson 1

- Luke 16:19-31
- Luke 17:1-37
- Luke 18:1-14

Study Questions

Why did Abraham say that he would not send someone back from the dead to warn the rich man's brothers?

What expectations should the servant have toward the master's response to his work?

How did the lepers respond to Jesus' healing?

What did Jesus say society would be like when the Son of Man was revealed? What did this analogy mean?

In what way is God like the judge in the story of the persistent widow? What promised is being made in the telling of this story?

What attitude is Jesus attacking in the story of the Pharisee and the tax collector? Why?

Food for Thought

Our reading today is split into two parts. The division comes between Luke 17:10 and 17:11. 17:11 begins with the phrase, "Now, on His way to Jerusalem." If you do a careful study of Luke's writings (Luke and Acts) you'll see that there are these little "progress reports" throughout them that serve as subject and section dividers. They are the closest things to paragraph divisions that Luke had. It's as if you can hear him taking a big breath at the end of 17:10, pausing a second, then saying, "Now, let's move to the next part of my story."

16:19 – 17:10 is actually the final section of last session's study where Luke lays out his view of the Kingdom. The second section, beginning in 17:11, launches us into the second leg of His journey towards Jerusalem. It is in this second section that we find parallel passages with Matthew, Mark, and John, so we'll start jumping around in the reading once again.

16:19 -17:10 The conclusion

This concluding section consists of 3 parts; the parable of the rich man and Lazarus, a simple command, and then the bottom line.

Allow me to paraphrase what I believe the message of these three sections is saying.

Jesus: In this life we tend to lose our focus and forget what is really important. For example, the rich man thought he was pretty important, and definitely thought he was more important than that wretched homeless man lying on the street corner. He was surprised to discover that death is the great equalizer and that, on the other side of that threshold, the truth is revealed. When he died, the rich man left his riches behind discovering that all they bought him was an eternity of suffering. Lazarus, however, ran into the arms of his loving Father.

It is so sad that society lives according to these mixed up values. What is even more sad is that it was the "spiritual leaders" of society that taught these mixed up values. It will not be pretty for those leaders on the final day.

Guys, the Pharisees are caught up in keeping score, asking "Who's on top," "Who's better than whom," "Who has the latest book out," "Whose church is bigger," "Who has more clout with the masses," "Who has more money." Those kinds of standards lead a person to create mini empires. Mini empires lead to power. Power leads a person to need to control things and protect assets and image.

135

Here's the truth. Living in the Kingdom is simple. Forget all that stuff. Don't keep score. Life is a simple one-to-one process. If someone sins, call it sin. If someone repents, forgive them. Nothing more, nothing less. Don't hold grudges, don't pass judgment; just speak the truth in love, all the time, every day.

Disciples: Jesus, that sounds great, but it's just too hard. Will we ever be able to live without competition and power struggles? Increase our faith!

Jesus: Yes you can. In fact, you could have faith strong enough to do miracles. Would you like to know the secret to that kind of faith? STOP DESIRING IT!!!! Let me explain. Deep down inside you want mountain-moving faith because you want to show the Pharisees, and everybody else, that you are righteous, and that God loves you enough to give you big time gifts. If that is your motive then you are no different than the rich man. The bottom line is that it isn't about you at all. You are a servant. When the slave comes in from the fields from a hard days work, does the master say, "Great job. You must be tired. Why don't you sit down and I'll fix you a dinner." No way. The master says, "Fetch my dinner. When I'm done, you might get some." The slave does not work for accolades, the slave works out of obedience realizing that he is nothing but a tool for the master.

That may sound harsh to you and the opposite of the love of Father that I have taught, but let Me explain. The point of this parable is that true freedom in the Kingdom of God only comes when you are completely stripped of self and self-gratification and/or self-exaltation. When you realize that your job is to simply release all desire and need to be in control of your destiny and allow the Father to use you whenever and however He sees fit, then you will be able to be absolutely free to not worry about life.

17:11- 18:14 The Coming Kingdom

This next section begins yet another dialogue and demonstration regarding the Kingdom of God. The first story demonstrates the nature and irony of Kingdom ministry. Ten lepers were healed. (Remember, the first step of the kingdom is to heal the sick and set the captive free). Yet, in spite of the miraculous healing, only one is grateful. Isn't that just like people? We want Jesus for what we can get out of Him. We cry out for God when we are in need, then as soon as things are fine, we forget about him. The real irony of this story is

that the only grateful one was a Samaritan. Once again, this demonstrates that the Kingdom of God that Jesus was bringing was one in which all people would be welcomed.

The second story opens with a question from the Pharisees. They asked Jesus what He thought about the coming of the Kingdom. In order to understand this scene fully we need to keep in mind what the standard answer to this question was among the Jews. Almost everyone expected the coming kingdom to be a political movement where a mighty king would rise up among the Jews, oust the Romans, and establish an autonomous Jewish Kingdom once again. Jesus' response has three parts to it.

1. **The Kingdom is already here.** The truth about the Kingdom is that it is not a political, physical reality within the current power structures of the world. In other words, it's not just one Kingdom, or political paradigm, among many. The Kingdom is a relationship with the Father, through the saving work of the Son, and the power of the Holy Spirit. (This becomes clearer in the book of Acts.) The Pharisees were too blind to see this Kingdom that was standing right in front of their faces.

2. **There will be a coming Day of Judgment.** The big surprise and irony of this response was that Jesus was warning the Pharisees that the very judgment that they were predicting would come on the "sinners" of Israel was actually coming for them. As it was in the days of Noah and Lot when God judged them, and as it was in the days of Jeremiah when God destroyed Jerusalem through the empire of Babylon, so it would be when God brought judgment on Jerusalem. It is very likely that Jesus was referring to the coming events of A.D. 70 when the Roman armies destroyed the temple in Jerusalem, leaving the Jews very little hope for a Kingdom on Earth.

3. **Jesus will return some day.** Part of this response was spoken to the disciples. Jesus was encouraging them that He would in fact return some day to establish His Kingdom in eternity. In the book of Acts, after Jesus ascended into the clouds, the angels said to the bewildered disciples, "This same Jesus, who has been taken from you into heaven, will come back in the same way you have seen Him go into heaven." As disciples today, we also share this same hope. We live in the reality of two Kingdoms. We have the present Kingdom of "Christ in us, the hope of glory" (Colossians 1:27) of which the Holy Spirit is the guarantee (Ephesians 1:13-14) in which we can experience all the joy and fulfillment

of living in relationship with God. But, we also have the hope of one day being reunited with Jesus in an eternal Kingdom where our existence will be beyond our comprehension (2 Corinthians 5:1-10). It is our belief in this truth that gives us hope to press on.

It is this hope that sparks Jesus' comments in the next section. Jesus knew that times would become very difficult for His disciples in the days after His departure. He encourages them to pray and be persistent. After all, isn't God so much more willing to give them whatever they need than an evil judge?

Kid's Questions

Focus on Luke 18:9-14.

What attitude did the Pharisee have?

What attitude did the Tax collector have?

Which attitude is the kind that Jesus wants from his people? Why?

Have you ever been playing a game where you lost and the winner came up to and called you a loser? They said, "I won and you lost, so I'm better than you!" How did that make you feel?

That kind of attitude is called arrogance. God does not like arrogance. As followers of Jesus we need to always remember that God loves everyone, and no one is more important than anyone else. We need to always look at other people the way God looks at them. He loves them and wants to help them.

Lesson 2

- Matthew 19:1-30
- Mark 10:1-31
- Luke 18:15-30

Study Questions

How does Jesus feel about divorce? Why?

What attitude are we supposed to have before we can enter the Kingdom?

Why did the rich young man leave discouraged? What was keeping him from entering the Kingdom?

Food for Thought

Today it could be very tempting for us to study the tree and lose the forest. Here in the middle of a large forest of Kingdom teaching stands a tree that addresses the topic of divorce. In America, in the beginning of the 21st century, especially among "evangelical" churches, the topic of divorce and remarriage is a hotly debated one. Should divorce be allowed? Should pastors be allowed to continue in their lofty positions after being branded with the scarlet D? Should divorced and remarried people be allowed to continue in uninterrupted fellowship without dealing with the sin? How do you repent from remarriage? All of these are wonderful questions that we could spend our whole time discussing. Indeed, many books and many hours of dialogue have been spent over this very important discussion.

Yet, we must remember the forest. We must remember the rule of good Bible study. Switching metaphors, we must remember the beautiful quilt (or tapestry) that is being created by the sewing together of diverse stories from Jesus' life. In simpler, less poetic terms, we must always keep in mind the context of the passage before we dissect it for its meaning and application to our lives.

We will come back to those questions, but first... the forest...the tapestry...awaits.

In case you hadn't noticed, you had to turn to Matthew and Mark today. You haven't done that for a while. How'd it feel? At this point in the story, Matthew and Mark's stories are running in almost perfect sync. This tandem pair also runs very closely parallel to Luke. So, today, we see three stories being sewn together unanimously by the gospel writers. They must be meant to be seen together.

Here's the flow:

- The Pharisees try to trap Jesus by asking Him His opinion about the hotly debated topic of divorce.

- Jesus tells the Pharisees that they are asking the wrong question and completely misunderstand the heart of God because their hearts are hard.

- Jesus then tells them that, unless they become like little children, they will not enter into the Kingdom of God.

- Finally, Jesus encounters a rich young man who claims he wants to enter the Kingdom of God. Jesus tells him that he must obey the commands to enter the Kingdom (he's baiting the man, because, of course, this is what the man already believed). The man replies that he has obeyed the commands from the time of his Youth. (Wow! That in itself displays that he may be either blind to his own sin or so self-inflated that he's self-deluded).

- "Fine," replies Jesus, "Then go sell everything and report back for duty."

- "Huh? You want me to give up my big house on the golf course, my Cadillac SUV, my VIP pass to the arena, my membership at the spa.... Can't I just write a check, or take a mission trip or something?"

- "Nope. Give it all away."

- The man left discouraged...ya think?

So, what's the point of all this? Can a husband and wife never get divorced? Will divorced people never enter into the Kingdom of God? Should single people never marry? Do we have to give away all our material possessions and live in abject poverty in order to be considered worthy to enter the Kingdom? Is that what Jesus is saying? Maybe. But, perhaps, He is saying something even deeper. Perhaps He is saying this, "If you think that these are the real issues, then you are too blind to even see the Kingdom when the door opens up to you. You have to become like a child before you can see the Kingdom. Children don't give a rip about the stuff you guys worry about. Kids just play. There are two things that kids do. 1) They trust their parents to provide their needs, and 2) they live perpetually in the present, not remembering the petty squabbles of the past or worrying about the problems of the future. Yes, children fight all the time. But then, two minutes later they are outside jumping and skipping like lifelong buddies. Children don't hold grudges. They don't recognize race, riches, or social status. They treat the President the same way they would treat the homeless man. Children trust, and they are in the process of learning to obey. That's it. The Kingdom is that simple. Trust your Dad and love your brothers. Don't keep score about yesterday, or worry about tomorrow. If you can tap into that truth then you will no longer want to divorce your wife but will see her for the sister that she truly is. If you can grasp that childlike vision then you will not care about your riches, but will desire to give to anyone who has need, with no need for repayment."

Now back to the tree.

Do you see the point? The Pharisees were trying to trap Jesus by pulling Him into a political/ religious debate over technical loopholes in the marriage laws. Their motivation was that of selfishness, not for the love of God and the desire to do His will.

In our culture divorce is happening at epidemic proportions. Does God condone divorce? No. Is divorce part of God's perfect plan for His people? No. God's desire is that His children would love each other unconditionally and unselfishly. God's desire is that a man and woman would understand that marriage is not about romance and love and warm-fuzzies. Marriage is about covenant and the primary purpose for marriage is to be a real-life demonstration of the covenant relationship that God has with His people. God will never leave His covenant, no matter how bad the cheating, prostituting spouse gets. He will set boundaries, He will institute justice, but in the end, He will always open his arms to reconciliation. Unfortunately, our culture has forgotten about all that and has bought into the idea that the most important value in life is our own personal "happiness" and comfort. After all, we're Americans and we have the "right" to pursue life, liberty, and happiness...right? Sadly, millions of people lie bleeding and suffering, as children have been sacrificed on the altar of divorce in the worship of self fulfillment.

Don't get me wrong, I know that marriage is difficult. I've counseled enough couples to know the hellish stories that people endure. Some people are married to evil people who are bent on destroying them. Tough love is often required. Granted. We must remember that our gracious Father takes each life and each situation on a case by case basis and we need to be careful to not slip into a self-righteous, stone-casting attitude, (we talked about that last session). Yet, the vast majority of divorce in our culture has nothing to do with real "evil". The vast majority of divorce is happening because our culture has enabled people to take the easy way out of almost every difficult situation. We have forgotten that it is through the difficulties and pain that we grow the most. May God never deal with us in our covenant relationship the way that we deal with each other in ours.

Let's try to get back to a childlike faith where we can actually put all our petty nonsense aside and play together.

Kid's Questions

Read Matthew 19:16-30

What did Jesus tell the rich man he had to do before he could enter the Kingdom of God?

Why did the rich man get sad about that?

What if Jesus told you to give away everything you have – your toys, your books, your video games, everything – to the kid in the homeless shelter? Would you be willing to do it? Why or why not?

I know this seems harsh, but the truth is that if there is anything in our lives that we would consider more important than obeying Jesus, then that thing is really the God that we worship.

Does this story mean that God doesn't want you to have fun and play? Not at all. In fact, the story right before this one said that until we become like little children, we can't enter into the Kingdom. What do kids do? They play! God loves for kids to play and have fun. What he doesn't love is when his children get so attached to "stuff" that they stop loving him. So play all you want, just remember who gave you all the cool stuff you have and never let anything stand in the way of obeying him when he calls you.

Lesson 3

- Matthew 20:1-28
- Mark 10:32-44
- Luke 18:31-34

Study Questions

Why did the servants grumble against the landowner? What was his response to their grumbling?

What did Jesus say would happen to Him when He got to Jerusalem?

What request was made of Jesus? What was His response to this request?

Food for Thought

Matthew 20:1-16

"That's not fair!"

Have you ever heard that burst out of the mouth of a child? As children that was one of our favorite responses to circumstances that we didn't like. Our parents take away our TV privileges because we, once again, left the bike in the front yard. "Hey, that's not fair." We don't get desert because we didn't eat our vegetables. "Hey, that's not fair."

Then we grow up and the scenarios get a little more sophisticated.

We've worked hard for a company for years and they promote a new recruit. "Hey, that's not fair."

We've tried hard to get pregnant and the unmarried teenager is on her third child from a third boy. "Hey, that's not fair!"

Our son is called to duty and killed in a foreign country, fighting someone else's battle. "Hey, that's not fair!"

What does fair mean, anyway? When we say unfair what we are really saying is, "Hey, I don't like what you are doing to me. It is painful and I don't think I deserve to be treated this way."

What does fair mean? Is God fair?

I'd like to propose today that God is NOT fair.

In Matthew 20:1-16 Jesus tells a parable about some workers in a field. The owner of the field hires the workers. Some of them are hired in the beginning of the day, working all day in the heat, and others are hired at the end of the day, only putting in a couple of hours. At the end of the day, everyone gets the same wage. "Hey, that's not fair!" Now, from our perspective, given the propensity we have to see unfairness at every turn, it is easy to sympathize with the disgruntled worker, isn't it? After all, a workman is worth his wages, right? Doesn't the Bible say that somewhere?

So what is the point of the parable?

There are two levels at which we need to examine this story. The first level has to do with the immediate context. As Jesus has been traveling toward Jerusalem He has been informing the people that the Kingdom of God will be open to all people, not just the descendants of Abraham and those whose foreskins had been removed. Even though the Jews had been God's people for centuries and had suffered great persecution for it, Jesus was treating the Gentile (the "new" guy) as an equal. At this first level Jesus was saying that God has the right to do this because, after all, it's His field.

That statement leads us to the second, and broader, level at which we can look at this story. The bottom line is that it all comes down to ownership and rights. God is the owner of all things, not us. God is the one who established the universe and dictated his moral standard through the very essence of his goodness. He's in charge and He can call the shots, not us.

We, on the other hand, are the ones who betrayed Him, turned our backs on His loving-kindness, and attempted to usurp His authority and power in the universe and in the governance of our own lives. So, what does "fair" mean? What would fairness look like? Fairness would look like God obliterating us and making us suffer for the heinous ways in which we have betrayed Him and openly mocked His majesty and sovereignty. Fairness would be that no one would be able to even approach the Kingdom and the banquet hall of the King, let alone sit at the table. That would be fair. But, as I said at the beginning, God is not fair. God does not give us what we deserve, but, instead, in all unfairness, He took our punishment on Himself in our place. He bought us back from slavery at the cost of His own Son and now owns us. None of us "deserve" anything from God. Everything we get from Him, every breath we breathe is a gracious gift for which we are undeserving servants.

Now, in light of that, does it seem so bad that God loves people enough to allow some people to slip in under the wire and receive the same blessings as we have who have been in the Kingdom our whole lives? You bet it does. As a redeemed slave under the protection of a benevolent master who loves me and watches out for me, I should be celebrating every time another person wakes up to the unfair nature of God and enters into His gracious gift of freedom from sin, punishment, and death.

What's even less fair of God is that He not only redeemed us to become His slave, He also removed the slavery label from our hide and replaced it with adoption papers. He has loved us so much that He has elevated us to the status of child, able to access the full inheritance of His glory. How fair is that?

Yes, bad things happen to us that bring us pain and suffering. Yes they are awful, but they are not unfair. They are simply the unfortunate byproduct of a sin-struck world. God is not ignoring us by letting them happen. God is loving us enough to give us strength to work through them with the hope He has given us through His unfair love.

Matthew 20:17-19

Jesus announced to His disciples, in black and white terms, that He was about to demonstrate the full extent of His unfairness by going to Jerusalem and dying at the hands of the leaders. The disciples were not prepared to absorb this truth.

Matthew 20:20-28

In light of the previous discussion, doesn't the request of James and John's mother sound trite? We can understand that a Mom wants the best for her boys, but wow, did she (and they) miss the mark. Tomorrow we will see what greatness is all about.

Kid's Questions

When you think of a really great person, who comes to mind? Who are some of the greatest people in our country? What makes them great?

Read Matthew 20:20-28.

What did Jesus say greatness looked like? Why?

As you grow up you are going to have people tell you to work hard in school and fight hard in sports and practice hard in your music lessons so that you can get a scholarship, go to college, and be great someday. All those things are good, but if you think achieving those goals will make you great, then you are wrong. The world things those things are great, but God has a different set of standards that he uses to tell whether a person is great. God looks at a person's heart to see if that person is humble, kind, generous, patient and loving. A person like that is considered great in God's Kingdom. You could be the president of the United States, or the street sweeper downtown, it doesn't really matter to God. That means that right now, as a kid, you could be great in the Kingdom of God. You can start with how you treat your brother or sister.

Lesson 4

- Matthew 20:29-34
- Mark 10:44-52
- Luke 18:35-43
- Luke 19:1-27

Study Questions

Describe the two men that Jesus encountered in Jericho. Why do you think the stories of these two men were told at this point in the bigger story line of Jesus' life?

What did the landowner expect from his servants while he was away?

What was the landowner's response to the servant who did not handle his responsibility well?

Food for Thought

Greatness. It is the American dream. Every child fantasizes about being the star quarterback throwing the hail Mary pass at the end of the game to clench the title, or rushing into a burning building to save the little child, or receiving the Oscar for best actor, the Emmy for best singer, or the Nobel Prize for best scientist. We are taught from the moment we enter the school system that the "good" people are the ones who land on the top end of the bell curve. They are the ones who make it into the Ivy League schools or get the sports scholarships, who get elected Homecoming King and Queen, and get life handed to them on a silver platter. With that golden carrot hung before us, we strive to achieve success and, depending upon our level of drivenness, will take any measure necessary to end up on top.

Does that sound familiar? That scenario is understandable for people who are naturalists, operating under the worldview of atheism where natural selection is their religion. It only makes sense for them because, after all, might makes right...the survival of the fittest. But, what about the church? What happens when that kind of mentality creeps into the church?

If you were to do an objective study of the American church today, removing the "Jesus language," and simply observe the behavior patterns of the system itself, I believe you would be surprised. The average church in America functions much like, if not exactly like, the average corporation in America. There is a CEO who sits at the top of the heap. How did he get there? He has the best track record and the best credentials. He has either had more education, more experience in the "big chair," has more natural ability as a public communicator, has the right connections, or any combination of those traits. Bottom line, he is very successful at what he does. He produces results. Then there is a board of directors that holds the CEO accountable to fulfill the mission statement and stated "outcomes" of the organization. If the CEO is successful they cheer him and probably give him a raise. If he drops the ball, they fire him and find another CEO who can "get the job done." Under the CEO come the hired hands, the staff, who implement the plan. Each of the hired staff is an "expert" in his or her individual field. The job of the CEO is to build a machine that can produce a quality product, get the right pieces for the machine (staff members), keep the machine well oiled (have systems, strategies, and incentives in place) so that it functions without interruptions. Whenever a piece of the machine gets out of line, it is replaced and the hum of the machine continues.

What is the motivation of this machine? Well, that is where it gets tricky. On the surface, inscribed in the literature and spoken from the public platform, there are biblical mandates to reach the world with the gospel of Jesus and make disciples of all nations. That sounds great. But what does it look like? What does a fully devoted follower of Jesus really look like? That is where the American church has tripped along the way. We have tried to quantify the FDF (Fully Devoted Follower) and create the prototype of the "end product." We create a list of what the ideal FDF will look like. By setting this end goal vision, we can then establish practical and efficient systems that will, through the process of a well-oiled machine, produce the desired FDF at the end.

There are a couple of fundamental problems with this System of thinking. First of all, machines produce clones. A well-oiled machine is a static system that is rigidly programmed to do one thing and to do it incredibly well. Therefore, the end product will always look the same. Instead of developing followers of Jesus, we tend to stamp out church-going drones who step in line with the system. If they don't end up looking like our end product, then we throw them on the reject pile and move on.

The second problem is that, by using the American Corporate system, and the success-driven mentality of our culture, we are compelled to measure the results of our system, to quantify the "spiritual fruitfulness" of our end products, and to see if we are doing a good job and being successful. So, we place numbers and measuring devices on people's lives and create quality control teams and output inspectors to see if we are making the cut. Because this mentality is flowing directly from the American, success-driven cultural value system we automatically equate BIGGER, BETTER, FASTER, STRONGER as successful. If more people are coming to our church we are doing something right. If other churches are looking at what we are doing, then we are successful. If we are maintaining a steady average growth percentage, then we will be keeping the board of directors and the shareholders happy. The successful machine hums on, so we tear down a wall in the factory and build another machine right next to it, and now we can double our annual output. If we are growing and pumping out more FDFs than we did the year before, then we are successful. If our FDF factory is more successful than the one down the street, then our CEO might get to publish a book about how he did it, and how his strategic thinking and brilliant leadership skills allowed him to fine tune the machine to achieve a higher annual yield than ever thought possible. By tapping into the latest and greatest marketing strategies that technology has to offer, the annual yield could potentially grow at exponential levels.

In the church world he has thrown the winning pass, gotten the Oscar, and has the noble prize hanging around his neck.

Hail the conquering hero.

Jesus was asked, "Who is the greatest in the Kingdom of Heaven?"

Jesus responded, "First of all, if you want to be great, then you need to be willing to follow in My footsteps into Jerusalem. I am going to walk past the cheering hoards, shouting "Hosanna! We love you Jesus." I'm going to ignore the paparazzi. I am going to walk past the marble and gold and flowing robes of the religious leaders and the power and position that they hold. I am going to hand Myself over to the Romans. They will beat Me, spit on Me, insult Me, and eventually treat Me like a common criminal and hang Me out to dry like a worthless piece of leather. Unless you are willing to follow Me there, you will be nothing in the Kingdom.

Secondly, walk with Me into Jericho. I'll show you who the great ones are in the Kingdom. See that blind man there? His name is Bart. He has been begging by the side of the road his entire life. He's never been given the time of day by anyone. Yet, when I walked by him, he could see Me. Even though there was no physical light in his eyes, he could see the Kingdom of God for what it really is. He's great. Do you see that little guy in the tree? His name is Zach. Everyone hates him. He's a sell-out, they say, because he collects taxes from his own people, extorts them, and gives it to the Romans. He's been rejected by his people, and is nothing more than an entertaining rat to the Romans. He's empty inside. Today, though, he saw the Kingdom. His heart has been humbled and changed. He's great. I can work through a guy like that.

Gentlemen, let me remind you of something, once again. Greatness in the Kingdom has nothing to do with power or "success." Look at where that kind of thinking got the last group of leaders. The Pharisees are so blind and so self-absorbed in their own success press, that they have taken the things I've given them and buried them in the ground. You are going to be put in places of leadership in My Kingdom. Never forget that you are just a servant. Each of you will be given gifts to use for Me. They are not yours, they are Mine. Use them well. Put your pride in your pocket and simply listen to My instructions, do what I say, and don't buy into the value systems of this world. It is only when you are nothing that you will be anything at all."

I realize that today's commentary could be perceived as nothing more than a cheap shot against the successful and large churches of America. It could be seen as nothing more than a "sour grapes" message from a peon. Perhaps it is. Regardless of what it is, it is always true that one should never tear something down unless there is something with which to replace it. Jesus came to tear down the power structures of His day, and He offered a replacement. Every generation, I believe, is called to do the same. The Kingdom of God is a reality that flies into culture, like a flying wedge, for the purpose of transforming culture. As soon as the Church adopts the wisdom of the culture in which it exists it ceases to be a transforming agent, blends into the background of culture, and is no longer visible to the truly seeking. The Kingdom needs to stand out as an alternative to the cultural wisdom, offering love and hope that cannot be found in the culture itself. The Kingdom of God is in the business of tearing down the "wisdom of the world" and the power-wielding systems that it produces, and replacing it with the life-giving simplicity of the Kingdom. Jesus taught us, and His disciples taught us, all throughout the gospels and the epistles, that the Kingdom of God is a family, a garden, a tree, a flock, and a seed. These are organic things. The church is not supposed to be a machine that operates in a linear, end-product oriented fashion. The church is a space like a field. The space is cultivated, the seed is planted, and then, in humble submission to the forces of life itself at work in nature, the cultivator waits to see what miraculous fruit will grow. The church is a community. The community is the space where authentic relationships can be fostered and people can be known for who they really are. People are complex and it takes time to get to the heart of the person. Making disciples is an organic, messy process that required patience, time, and the humility to admit that you don't know exactly how to do it. Each person is a unique plant. Their version of the FDF will be according to the design God has for them. I believe that we, as the church in America, need to stop asking "Who's the Greatest" and implementing systems that our culture teaches that are based on success-oriented, achieve greatness values, and get really simple and honest. We need to stop thinking "bigger, better, faster, stronger" and start thinking, "smaller, more honest, patient, and humble." Maybe then, we can witness blind men who see, lame men who walk, and the Kingdom of God that flourishes among us.

Kid's Questions

Read Luke 19:11-27.

A mina is not a person who digs in the ground for precious metals. Nor is a mina a person who is under the age of 18. A mina was a form of money in Jesus' day. You could read the story and replace the word "mina" with "dollars" if you like. That might make it make more sense to you.

What did the landowner expect the servants to do with the money he gave them?

Did each servant have the same amount?

Let's pretend that you are on a soccer team. There are different positions on a soccer team, right? What are the forward and mid-fielder supposed to do? What are the defenders supposed to do? What is the goalie supposed to do? At the end of the game, will the coach evaluate how well the goalie played based upon how many goals she scored? No. She wasn't supposed to score goals; she was supposed to stop goals. Will the forward be evaluated by how well she blocked goals? No. She was supposed to make goals.

The same is true in the Kingdom of God. God has given each person a special set of gifts and abilities and a "position" to play on the team. No two people are exactly alike. Our job is to 1) figure out what our position is, and 2) play our part of the game to the best of our ability, and 3) remember that all of our efforts are to bring glory to God, because they are his gifts, not ours.

Lesson 5

- John 11:1-57
- John 12:1-11

Study Questions

What kind of a relationship does Jesus seem to have with Lazarus, Martha, and Mary?

Why did Jesus not go straight to Bethany when He heard the news of Lazarus' illness?

What bold claim did Jesus make about Himself in his discussion with Martha? What does this mean?

How did the Pharisees respond to the miracle of Lazarus' resurrection? Why?

Food for Thought

Today we witness a beautiful story. In John's gospel this story is the one that serves the same purpose as the last two week's worth of Luke's gospel. Luke chose the space of time between Jesus transfiguration and His triumphal entry to be the platform from which He would present the full-on message of the Kingdom of God. Matthew and Mark chose to highlight the Jericho experience with Bartimaeus and Zacheus as their narrative tool to show us a glimpse of the true Kingdom of God. In all three gospels, these pre-Jerusalem stories served as narrative tools to present the readers with a stark contrast between what the Kingdom of God should be – humility, love, healing, service – and what the Kingdom of God had become under the mismanagement of the Pharisees – power, corruption, blindness, and death. Today we see how John chose to accomplish the same goal. Instead of Jericho, John chooses to shoot his scene on the set of Bethany at the home and graveyard of his dear friends, Lazarus, Mary and Martha.

You've read the story. Allow me to make some observations that are, what I believe, were the key points that John wanted us to learn from this scene.

1. **Jesus was a man of deep compassion.** The shortest verse in the Bible, John 11:35, teaches us one of the deepest truths about Jesus. He wept. Why did He weep? He knew He was about to raise Lazarus from the dead. He knew there would actually be a happy ending to this particular story, so what was the problem? I think He wept for two reasons. First, I think He truly loved this family. They were His close friends. Mary was the one who had anointed His feet with oil. This was probably His regular stopping place when He would visit Jerusalem. This demonstrates to us the deep humanity of Jesus. He knows our pain when we suffer great loss and sorrow. He cries with us authentically when we hurt. The next time you are in pain, remember this scene. Imagine Jesus scooting up beside you, draping His arm over your neck and shoulders, and just sobbing right along with you. He knows your pain and longs to share it with you. Secondly, I think Jesus was crying for an even deeper reason. His dear friend was wrapped up in burial cloths and lying in a dark hole. That corpse was symbolic of Jerusalem, the nation of Israel, and humanity in general. Why had Adam and Eve made such a stupid choice? Why did humanity turn from the Father? It didn't have to be this way. Now Jesus was going to have to suffer

intensely to set things right again. As Jesus visualized His friend lying in the tomb He probably pictured himself lying there for the three days that were in His very near future. He was sad that things had gotten so bad; He was upset that He was going to experience so much pain. He wept.

2. **Jesus is the Resurrection.** Notice the dialogue that Jesus had with Martha. Jesus said, "Martha, don't worry, Laz is going to rise again." Martha agreed with Him without missing a beat. This demonstrates a significant point of theology that we must address. There was a strong debate among the Jews of Jesus' day that revolved around the end times and the final state of man. The Sadducees believed that when a person dies, they die and that's it. Your spirit and your body simply go into the pit and you are worm food. To them, the only thing that is important is to worship God properly in life and pass on the "spirit" of the nation to the next generation. The Pharisees, on the other hand, believed that when you die, your body and spirit go into the ground and your soul goes to sleep. You wait there, unconscious and "sleeping" until the final day when God would come to earth, raise everyone from the dead, weed out the good from the bad, and establish his Kingdom once and for all. Obviously Martha had a Pharisaical perspective on this point. So, when Jesus said that Lazarus would rise, she said, "Yes, I know that he will rise in the final day, but that doesn't really bring me comfort right now." In Jesus' reply is one of the most important, fundamental truths about the identity of Jesus, the role He plays in the cosmos, and the claims He made about Himself. Jesus said, "I am the resurrection and the life." In that one statement Jesus was claiming many things. He was claiming to be God, because only God could raise the dead. He was claiming to be the fulfillment of the long awaited Kingdom, because the resurrection of the dead would be part of the end times. He was claiming to be the only way to eternal life, because it was only through belief (trust) in Him that the resurrection of the dead would be realized.

3. **Being raised to life is a community event.** When Lazarus hopped out of the grave he was fully alive. Yet, there was one small problem. He was so wrapped up in his grave clothes that he was not able to get himself unwrapped. Jesus had to tell the people around him to unwrap the cloths and help him get unbound. That is how it is in the kingdom of God, the church. We all begin in the dead state of sin. It is only through the power of Jesus that we can be brought back to life and enter into the Kingdom of God, no human can do that for someone else; it's a miracle. Yet, even though the spark of life is in us, we are still bound up by the clothes of death. In other words, many of us are still plagued by the old sinful ways that we had before our new life in Jesus and we are bound up with bitterness, guilt, shame, and cherished sin. We are so bound up in these things, that we cannot get ourselves unstuck from them. That is why we live in community. That is why we need the healing touch of others around us, whether they are compassionate friends or trained counselors/healers. It is not a sign of weakness on your part or lack of concern on God's part that you can't get out of your bondage. It is part of the process of entering the Kingdom of God that you are brought to a place of humility where you admit that you need the help of others to help you get out of the stinking wraps of death.

4. **Jesus is life.** John began his gospel with the words, "in Him was life and that life was the light of men." In this story we see that truth demonstrated in living color. It is important to understand this aspect of Jesus if you want to read further in the New Testament. For Paul, the guy who Jesus hand-picked to take the Kingdom to the Gentiles, the idea of the Resurrection Life of Jesus in our present reality was a central theme. In other words, Paul believed that our current Christian experience is one of living in the power of Jesus' resurrection every day. It was the power of the Holy Spirit that raised Jesus from the dead, and that same Holy Spirit dwells in us and offers us the same power every day. Every breath you breathe and every step you take, if you are walking in step with the Spirit of God, is taken in the power of resurrection life that comes from Jesus. He is the life we live both now and forever.

5. **The blindness of sin tries to stamp out life.** Notice the reaction of the Pharisees to the miracle of Lazarus' resurrection. Here a man is standing in front of them that had been dead for four days and what did they have to say about it? Did they say, "Wow! That's amazing. Power like that can only come from God!" Nope. They said, "Oh great. Another reason to hate Him. This is not going to be good for us in the polls. When the people find out about this they are going to go wild and start a riot. Then the Romans will get upset with us and tighten the screws. They may even blame us for the trouble and

remove us from power. We can't have that, now, can we? I guess we don't have to only kill Jesus, we have to kill Lazarus, too." There were two things that blinded them from the truth. The first was fear. They were afraid of the Romans, and they were afraid of this unknown power that was being demonstrated. The second was pride. They did not want to lose their exalted positions in the political structure of Israel. When you really think about it, this is just another demonstration of fear. They were afraid of losing power. They were afraid of submitting to the power of God. Their fear blinded them so severely that they were willing to take whatever measures necessary – even deception and murder – to protect themselves. We need to pay attention to this. It is very easy for us, as followers of Jesus, 2,000 years later to pass judgment on the Pharisees and wag our heads in disbelief. Beware. I'm afraid that we, in our American churches, have become more like the Pharisees than we would care to admit. We have erected our institutions and embraced the power-structures and comforts that they bring. They feed our ego, and our need for self-worth. Our institutions have been legitimized by culture and even provide the leaders of these institutions the power and perks of public office and public popularity. These benefits of success can be interpreted as "fruitfulness" and "God's blessing" when, perhaps, they are backdoor traps that slowly lower the blindfolds over our eyes, rendering us unable to see the truth of God when it is evident before us, and unable to respond to the truth when it commands us to move. We can become like the rich young ruler who was unable to walk away from these cultural props that sustained his exalted position. Each day, we need to ask God to strip away anything that may stand in the way of our ability to obey His Spirit when he speaks. Too many times we would rather silence the voice of the prophet, and justify it as being for "a greater good" than humbly admit that we have been duped and repent before God, walk away from the artificial edifices we have constructed, and descend into the lowly regions of eternal truth and life in the radical, unpredictable Kingdom of God.

Kid's Questions

Have you ever known someone who died? How did you feel?

How do you think Martha and Mary felt when their brother, Lazarus, died? How did Jesus feel?

What wonderful miracle did Jesus do for Lazarus?

Spend some time drawing a picture of the scene where Jesus brings Lazarus out of the grave.

As you are drawing, talk about how amazing it is to know that Jesus is so powerful that he can even defeat death itself. If Jesus can bring us back to life, then we have absolutely nothing to fear in life, not even death!

Introduction

Welcome to Jerusalem – the Holiest Place on Earth!

Jesus has finally entered into the city towards which He has been traveling during our past two sessions. At the time that Jesus arrived in the capital city it was not only the holiest place; it was the hairiest, craziest place as well. It is important to keep in mind that Jesus and His little band of disciples were not the only group of travelers that had been making their way toward Jerusalem. It was the time of the Passover; that big, annual spring event when everyone made their way to the holy city of Jerusalem to celebrate the deliverance that God had given his people from the hands of the Egyptians so many centuries earlier.

It was a wild time in the big city. The hotels were booked solid. People slept on the street. As with any large crowd in a big city, the intentions of the various groups of people were varied. Some of the people came for the pure purpose of worshipping God in his temple. Others saw this over-stuffed throng of pilgrims as an opportunity to cause trouble and to progress their political, anti-Roman, agendas. Knowing that anything could happen in Jerusalem during Feast weeks, the people were charged with energy, the Romans were on high alert for trouble, and the Jewish leaders were praying that nothing stupid would happen to bring the wrath of Rome down on their heads.

Enter Jesus. By this time the word had spread across the short 2 mile distance from Bethany that Jesus had raised a man from the dead. That definitely piqued the crowd's interest. It's not that Jesus really needed any more publicity, for by this time He was quite well known in the country for His wonder-working ability and His boldness with the Jewish leaders. The crowd was waiting to see if He would show up again this year to provide the usual entertainment – you know...healing some people, stirring up debates, and going a few rounds with the Pharisees and Sadducees. So, when the crowds saw Jesus riding into town on the back of a donkey they went wild. They threw their coats down in His path – just like the crowd had done for King Jehu in 2 Kings – and started waving palm branches in the air. They filled the air with shouts of praise that came straight from the usual Feast Psalm (Psalm 118) "Hosanna! Lord Save us! Blessed is he who comes in the name of the Lord!" It is hard to say how many of the crowds were authentically worshipping Him and how many were caught up in the excitement of the moment. Yet, we can be sure that His followers knew that this vision of Jesus on a donkey was a sure sign that something big was about to happen.

At this point we need to stop and recognize that this study marks the beginning of one last two-part mini series. This session and the next we will see that Jesus has one final showdown and dialogue with the Jewish leaders in the streets of Jerusalem before the events of the "Passion Week" officially begin.

As you can see in the picture, there are three major sections to the stories of this session's reading. First, Jesus enters Jerusalem with a great deal of seemingly positive excitement from the crowd. In the study we will explore how this "Triumphal Entry" relates to some important Old Testament prophecies and foreshadowing of the Messiah. Secondly you can see that Jesus is causing some trouble on the Temple grounds. After witnessing the commercialism that revolved around the buying and selling of animals that would be used for sacrifice, Jesus blew a gasket of righteous indignation and ran the money-changers out of the temple. He threw over their tables and said that His Father's house was a house of prayer and they had made it into a den of thieves. By healing the blind and the lame on the temple grounds He reemphasized that the Kingdom of God was not about ritualistic religion, but was about bringing life and light to the lost, sick, and blind. As a follow-up to his physical act of "cleansing" He told two parables that demonstrated that He had come to take over the leadership of the Kingdom and was going to lead God's people back to truth. Finally, you can see two big, nasty bear traps that the Jewish leaders set out for Jesus. We

will discuss how Jesus brilliantly deflected and redirected these trick questions, causing the leaders' plans to backfire in their faces.

Three Entrances

Typically, when you think about these events, you think of Jesus' entry in Jerusalem as a single occurrence. However, if you look closely, you will notice that Jesus actually enters the city three times. Mark's account of the story is the one that makes this crystal clear. Remember, Jesus was staying in Bethany, just 2 miles away, at the house of his friends Martha, Mary, and the newly resurrected Lazarus. Since their house was within walking distance, and since the city was crowded with Passover pilgrims, it makes sense that Jesus would use it as His bed and breakfast spot for the Passover week.

As we map out the three entrances we will uncover a wonderful jewel of truth that tends to stay hidden to the casual reader.

Mark 11:1-11 **Saturday**. Jesus enters the city on a donkey, gets greeted with palm branches and shouts, looks around to see that nothing is really going on because it is the Sabbath, and returns to Bethany.

Mark 11:12-19 **Sunday**. On the way into the city Jesus curses a fig tree for having no fruit. He then goes to the temple and "cleanses" it by driving out the moneychangers, and then goes back to Bethany in the evening.

Mark 11:20-13:37 **Monday**. On the way into town the disciples notice that the fig tree is withered. When Jesus gets to town He enters into a big debate with the Jewish leaders and ends up preaching up a storm for two more chapters.

Here's the jewel...

Saturday He enters as a KING, riding on the king's symbol of peace; the donkey.

Sunday He enters as a PRIEST and cleanses the temple, setting the record straight on what true worship of God is supposed to look like.

Monday He enters as a PROPHET and boldly speaks the scandalous truth of God, calling the people, one last time, to repentance before it is too late.

KING, PRIEST, and PROPHET. These are the three "offices" or roles that Jesus plays in the Kingdom of God. Pretty cool, huh?[1]

Lesson 1

- Matthew 21:1-11
- Mark 11:1-11
- Luke 19:28-40
- John 12:12-19

Study Questions

How did Jesus enter the city?

How did the people respond to his entry?

What Old Testament scripture was being fulfilled in this event?

How did the Jewish leaders respond to this event? Why?

Food for Thought

Enter the King.

When you think of the triumphal entry of a king, what comes to mind? If you were a Roman, living in Jesus' day, you would probably think of that glorious day when Julius Caesar returned to Rome after his victory over the Gauls. This was a gala event that centered on a huge parade that wound its way through the main streets of the capital city. All the soldiers, the dancers, the musicians, and the dignitaries joined in the parade, going out before Caesar. Then, following in his wake, came a long train of conquered and chained barbarian hoards, coming to the market to be sold into slavery. Now that was the triumphal entry of a king who had been victorious in battle.

Is that what happened when Jesus came into town riding on the back of a donkey? Not exactly. Before we go any further, we need to get one thing very clear. In our culture, the donkey is a symbol that stands for lots of things, but none of them really positive (unless you're a democrat, then it's positive for you, but derogatory for the elephant clan). Generally if you think someone is stupid you call them a donkey (but not usually in such a polite term!) Please scrub that imagery from your mind. In Jesus' day the donkey was actually a very noble creature. Throughout the Old Testament, and in historical documents, we see that the donkey was the animal that a king rode in times of peace. If a king was at war he would ride the war machine of the day, the horse. Donkey = peace; horse = war. So, when Jesus entered the city on a donkey, He was not entering as a mighty, triumphant warlord; He was entering as a humble king who was bringing peace.

In order to truly understand this event we must become familiar with two passages of scripture. I know you've already done your Bible reading for today, but please turn, first, to Zechariah 9:9-13.

The events of Jesus' final week before His death only make sense when you have a solid understanding of Zechariah. Zechariah was a prophet (a teacher of God's people) who lived in Persia when the Jews were still in captivity. The city of Jerusalem had lain destroyed and desolate for 70 years. The people were lost and confused, wondering if God was real and if He would ever rescue His people from their captivity, forgive their sins that got them there in the first place, and restore the temple. The Lord came to Zechariah and gave him a vision of the restoration of Jerusalem. Zechariah's message had two layers of meaning. The first layer spoke about his immediate future when God would empower the current high priest,

Joshua, to return to Jerusalem, and along with Zerubbabel, rebuild the temple. That was exciting enough in itself. Yet, his message also carried a deeper meaning that had a much longer lens. His message spoke of the coming Messiah who would ultimately restore Israel to its full glory and bring the supremacy of the Kingdom of God back to earth and fulfill God's big-picture destiny for the world. If you have time, read through the whole book of Zechariah and see how clearly Jesus is presented in his message.

We don't have time to comment on the whole book, so we are going to zone in on Zechariah 9:9-11. v. 9 says, "See, your king comes to you, righteous and having salvation, gentle and riding on a donkey." He goes on to say that this king will destroy the war tools of Israel and "will proclaim peace to the nations. His rule will extend from sea to sea (i.e. the whole world)."

In light of this, we could say that Jesus' "triumphal entry" into Jerusalem wasn't "triumphal" at all. Instead, He was actually entering the city, fully claiming to be its true King, but coming in an act of peace. He was not coming to establish His physical throne in Jerusalem and defeat the Romans; He was coming to peacefully surrender His life to his enemies. He was fighting a very different battle here. He was not coming into Jerusalem; He was passing through Jerusalem, lying down His life, and then moving on into His exalted place of glory so that He could expand the Kingdom of God to the entire world. No longer would the Kingdom of God be confined within the walls of a physical city, nor the worship of God be performed by one man inside the closed off walls of a holy room. Jesus came to bust out the Kingdom to a global, cosmic level where His glory would be seen by all people and His temple would be in the hearts of the faithful. More on that tomorrow.

The second passage we need to look at is Psalm 118. This Psalm was a common song that was sung during the Feast Celebrations in Jerusalem. Now the people were singing it in reference to a specific person. They shouted, "Hosanna!" That is a Hebrew phrase "yasha anna" which means "Oh Lord, save us!" So, when you look at Psalm 118:25, it reads, "Hosanna" in the Hebrew. Now that we realize what the people were actually shouting at Jesus while He rode the donkey, let's look back a few verses to Psalm 118:22-24. "The stone the builders rejected has become the capstone." What does that mean? Look, again, at Zechariah. This time look at Zechariah 4:6-8 (NIV) *6 So he said to me, "This is the word of the LORD to Zerubbabel: 'Not by might nor by power, but by my Spirit,' says the LORD Almighty. 7 "What are you, O mighty mountain? Before Zerubbabel*

you will become level ground. Then he will bring out the capstone [cornerstone] to shouts of 'God bless it! God bless it!'"

We will explore this more later this week, but, in these songs of praise we see the fulfillment of prophecy. Jesus is the cornerstone for the new temple of God. The current temple was going to be destroyed. That would happen in A.D. 70, when the Romans would come in and completely tear down the temple, much like Nebuchadnezzar did in the Old Testament. Jesus was coming to build the new temple. To be the living temple of His people, of which He is the cornerstone. He was laying down His life, to be buried as the foundation for a new temple of God. May we cry out to this King, "Hosanna. Save us, we pray!"

Against these two scriptural backgrounds, perhaps we can see a more distinct contour of the portrait of Jesus that is being painted in this "untriumphant" entry. There is one more aspect of this that we need to look at. Throughout the Messianic prophecies there are always two, seemingly contradictory, aspects of the Messiah presented. Even in Zechariah 9 we see it. On the one hand He is portrayed as a humble, suffering servant. On the other hand He is seen as a mighty, conquering hero. How can He be both? Well, this topic is debated among Christians. Some say His victory is over sin and was wielded in the fact that He humbly died. Thus, His Kingdom was fully established after His resurrection, and we are living in it fully today. Others say that the coming of the Messiah actually happens in two phases; these two phases being separated by time. The first coming was on a donkey, in humble submission, opening the doors of grace to all who would enter in. The second coming will be very different. This coming will be a "Triumphal Entry" of epic proportions.

As we move out of today, I simply want you to meditate on this passage from John's Revelation of a very different portrait of Jesus (the Truth) on a different day.

11 I saw heaven standing open and there before me was a white horse, whose rider is called Faithful and True. With justice he judges and makes war. 12 His eyes are like blazing fire, and on his head are many crowns. He has a name written on him that no one knows but he himself. 13 He is dressed in a robe dipped in blood, and his name is the Word of God. 14 The armies of heaven were following him, riding on white horses and dressed in fine linen, white and clean. 15 Out of his mouth comes a sharp sword with which to strike down the nations. "He will rule them with an iron scepter." a He treads the winepress of the fury of the wrath of God Almighty. 16 On his robe and on his thigh he has this name written:

KING OF KINGS AND LORD OF LORDS. (Revelation 19:11-16)

Kid's Questions

When you think of a mighty king, what does he look like?

When you hear the story of Jesus riding into Jerusalem on a donkey, does that match up with your picture of a mighty king? Why?

The donkey was a symbol of peace. Jesus came to bring peace.

Today, take a piece of paper and divide it in half. On the left hand side draw a picture of Jesus as he looked riding in on the donkey.

Now, read Revelation 19:11-16 and draw a picture of how Jesus looks in this description. When Jesus comes back, he's going to be like this picture.

Jesus is both pictures. Which do you like better? Why?

Lesson 2

- Mark 11:12-26
- Luke 19:41-48
- Matthew 21:12-22

Study Questions

Why does Jesus curse the tree?

What happens to the tree as a result of the curse?

What angers Jesus at the temple? What does He do about it?

What does He say about the true nature of the temple?

What does He do at the temple after He has run out the money changers?

What lesson does Jesus teach the disciples from the experience of the withered tree?

Food for Thought

Enter the Priest

As has been the case throughout our study, it is important to note the sequence of events as they are told by the gospel writers in order to get the full impact of the message they are presenting. The events of Jesus' second entry into Jerusalem are no different. Remember, previously Jesus entered for the first time on a donkey, as a King. Then He went back to Bethany. Today Jesus enters again and presents us with a different aspect of his role in the Kingdom of God.

Let's map out the sequence of events first.

- On the way to the city gate He wants to eat a fig, and, finding that the tree was bearing no fruit, He cursed it.
- Inside the city He goes directly to the temple and runs the moneychangers out in a wild rage, and declares that this is a house of prayer, not a den for robbers.
- On the temple grounds He heals the sick and gives sight to the blind.
- The children praise Him.
- The Jewish leaders are indignant and plot to kill Him.
- He leaves the city.
- The next morning the fig tree is withered.
- He teaches the disciples about moving mountains.

Notice that the act of cleansing the temple is couched within the story of the fig tree. It is obvious that these two events are interrelated. So, we need to look at both of them and see what is going on. First, let's look at the cleansing.

The first question we have to ask is, "Why were there moneychangers in the temple in the first place?" and, "Why was Jesus so upset about it?"

The moneychangers were there as a service to the Passover pilgrims. Remember, the worship of God at the temple revolved around the sacrifice of animals. According to the laws of Moses, each family was supposed to bring the best of their flock to the altar to be sacrificed to God. If a family was poor and had no cattle, they were permitted to offer doves in place of a lamb. Also remember that many of these people traveled great distances to get to Jerusalem and it was very difficult to transport an unblemished animal and keep it unblemished. So, as a service to the pilgrims, the leaders set up a marketplace in the temple courts where people could come and purchase an animal for sacrifice. After all, it is much easier to carry a purse full of coins than to transport an animal. You have to feed it, protect it, and keep it pure all the way there. With coins you can expedite the trip and still get the desired sacrificial outcome. This streamlined system allowed Passover Pilgrims to get a bigger worship bang for their buck, so to speak.

So, why was Jesus so upset about it? After all, these people made the effort to come all the way to Jerusalem out of obedience to God, and the leaders were simply trying to service their needs. Well, at this point scholars differ in their interpretation of why exactly Jesus was upset. Some say it was because the Jews had commercialized the worship of God and made it more about buying and selling rather than worship and sacrifice. They made it too easy for the people to show up, throw some money on the table, and watch an animal they had never known be carried to the priests by a servant boy, and be slaughtered by a priest they had probably never met. Other than the money loss, where is the sacrifice in that? Others feel that the real problem was that the Jewish money changers were taking advantage of the out-of-towners and not giving them a fair exchange for their foreign currency. This would heighten Jesus' attack against the racial prejudice and the superiority complex that the Jerusalemites had toward all the other "second-class" Jews and non-Jews.

The answer is that it is probably a little of both, and something else as well. We can really see into Jesus' heart by both His words and actions. He says, "This is a house of prayer," then He immediately replaces the moneychanger's table with a moment of healing. In other words, Jesus was saying to the Jews, "You guys have completely missed the point. You think that this temple was built so that you can spill the blood of animals and have your sins washed away. Don't you remember what God said to David through the prophet Nathan? He said, 'I don't want your sacrifices, I want your heart.' The sacrifice I desire is a humble and contrite heart that comes before Me in authentic love and devotion. You guys aren't doing that. You are more concerned with 'expediting' your pilgrimage and squeezing the most value out of your sacrifice transaction. Heaven forbid that you pay top dollar for the animal you are presenting to God. You have turned this whole thing into a mockery. God simply wants you to talk to Him with a clean heart. That's called prayer. Then He wants you to take that clean heart and use it to touch the sick, the hurting, and the blind around you and bring healing to their lives. Shine the light of hope to the world. All I see here is darkness, selfishness, pompous ritual, and self-righteousness."

Notice the two things He highlighted: Prayer and Healing. Prayer is our vertical relationship with God. We are to love God with all our heart, mind, soul, and strength. Healing is a horizontal relationship. We are to love our neighbor as ourselves. You see, the Kingdom of God is that simple. Love God and then overflow that love to others. We will see later that Jesus is establishing that He, Himself, will be the cornerstone of the new and true temple of God which will be built by the stones of the people in his Kingdom. The temple is the body of Christ, the family of God, the flock, the individual stones being fit together to create a relational space in which the Spirit of God can dwell in fellowship with His people and overflow the love, grace, and truth of God into a dark and dying world. In that temple there is a holy of holies which is the very heart of God. Our high priest, Jesus, enters into that place and rips open the curtain so that we all can have access to that holy place. So Jesus, the Priest, has now cleansed the temple, and in just a few short days, will lay down His own life as the ultimate and final blood sacrifice that will once and for all pay the penalty for the sins of the world and bring reconciliation between God and man, thus rendering the stone temple in the physical space of Jerusalem obsolete.

Now back to the tree. The fig tree had no fruit, so it was cursed and it withered. The temple and the leaders who were put in charge of the temple system were not bearing the fruit of the Kingdom of God, so they were rejected. The withered and gnarled fig tree was a saddening picture of the destruction that was soon coming to the city of Jerusalem.

OK, that symbolism is easy to understand, but what's with the mountain being thrown into the sea business? Jesus explained the withered tree by saying, "I tell you the truth, if anyone says to this mountain, 'Go, throw yourself into the sea,' and does not doubt in his heart but believes that what he says will happen, it will be done for him." Most of us look at this verse and find it difficult to understand its relevance to the fig tree. So, we tend to interpret it to mean that, "Just like Jesus used His supernatural power to destroy a fig tree, so, too, can I, if I have enough faith, pick any mountain I want and move it." I'm not sure that is exactly what it means. In order to really understand Jesus' explanation of the withered tree, we must, again, turn to the pages of Zechariah. In Zechariah 4:6-9 God is encouraging Zerubbabel about building the new temple in Jerusalem. Here is a man who is being commissioned by God to rebuild the proper place of worship for God's people. Zerubbabel is afraid because he knows that he will face great opposition in Judah from the surrounding enemies when he starts the building project. So, God says to him, "not by might nor by power, but by My Spirit.' What are you, O mighty mountain? Before Zerubbabel you will become level ground. Then he will bring out the capstone to shouts of 'God bless it! God bless it!'"

Jesus was reenacting this scene for His disciples. Jesus was saying to them, "Boys, just like Joshua was commissioned to build a new temple, I'm calling you to build the new temple, the church. It's not going to be a temple of brick and mortar, but a temple built of people, held together by relationship, of which I'm the chief cornerstone. I know it will be difficult and you will encounter great opposition and you are scared, but, just like I said to Joshua, this is a mountain that I can level before you if you will just believe. I will give you My Spirit and you will be able to build the temple of God in the hearts of all people in the world, one life at a time."

May we be that kind of temple. The challenge for us today is to examine our temple. Have we made the worship of God something that is an external action that we have to do? Have we created systems to expedite our worship experience and still get the biggest bang for the buck? It doesn't matter if you attend a mega-church of thousands or a house church of 10, you can fall into this trap. If you believe that church and worship is something that you "do" on a Sunday morning, then you are standing on dangerous ground. Worship is everything we do, because it flows out of who we are. We are the temple of God, each one of us being individual bricks. The temple is not in our individual hearts, it is in our collective hearts being held together by the mortar of relationship, held fast in the bond of peace. The church is the community, and the effectiveness of our worship has nothing to do with the "stuff" we bring to offer God but has everything to do with the way that we demonstrate love, healing, and community with each other and with the people around us. Let's make sure that our local "temple" has strong mortar; that we are flowing in an attitude of continual prayer and overflowing in authentic love for one another.

Kid's Questions

Let's say it was your birthday and you were having a big party. You were really excited because all your friends and family were coming.

Now let's pretend that when everyone got there they were in really grumpy moods. They came up to the gift table and slammed it down and said, "There, I hope you like your stupid gift. My mom made me blow my whole allowance on it." Then they all started fighting with each other and arguing about who brought the better gift. No one played games and no one talked to you at all.

How would you feel? Would the gifts mean that much to you?

This is what it was like at the temple. The temple was designed to be a place where people could come and worship God and bring him their gifts. He's like the birthday kid. But, in Jesus' day, it was like everyone had forgotten about the birthday boy and they were just slamming their gifts on the altar with a grumpy attitude and arguing about how much it cost them.

That is why Jesus ran the moneychangers out. He said that his temple was to be a house of prayer. It should be a place where people can love God and demonstrate God's love to each other. Today we know that the temple that Jesus built is the community of his people that gather together for worship. When your church gathers, how well are you loving the "birthday boy" when you bring your gifts to him? Are you loving him and each other, or are you grumpy?

Lesson 3

- Matthew 21:23-32
- Mark 11:27-33
- Luke 20:1-8

Study Questions

What question did the elders ask of Jesus? Why?

How did Jesus respond? Why?

What was John' basic message?

What was the point of the parable of the two sons in Matthew 21:28-32?

Food for Thought

Enter the Prophet

Imagine what would happen if a strange man barged into a traditional church service, walked right up to the pulpit and began speaking. He says, "You guys are doing things all wrong." Then he takes out a sledge hammer and smashes the organ and the piano, rips the robes off of the choir members, and rushes the ushers out of the aisles. All the while he is screaming, "You are desecrating the Father's house!" I'm sure the biggest men in the congregation would converge on this man, jump him, and throw him in a locked room until the authorities arrived.

That is how the Pharisees and Jewish leaders must have felt when they came around the corner that day and saw Jesus throwing tables around, telling people what they can and cannot do, and running the money changers off the premises. Crawling into their perspective, it is easy to see why they would be a little disturbed by this. In reality, their response was rather subdued. They didn't want to make a scene. So, they came up to Jesus and asked, "By what authority are you doing this?" In other words, "What makes you think that you have the right to barge in here and start acting like you own the place? Who are you anyway? You are just a country bumpkin from Galilee for crying out loud."

The Pharisees were stuck, however, because they knew that a large number of people in the crowd believed that Jesus was actually from God. If they just arrested Him for no reason, then they would be the bad guys. But, if they didn't respond to His insurrectionist behavior, they could have a riot on their hands. They thought the best way to get Him would be to trap Him in his words.

"Where is your authority" they asked? Did Jesus answer them? No. In typical Jesus fashion, He did not play their game. Instead He turned the questioning back on them and used their own foibles against them. Knowing that they were politicians and lived and died by their image with the masses, He placed them between a rock and a hard place. By asking them about their opinion of John the Baptist, He was forcing them to decide between speaking the truth and saving their popular vote. Jesus knew that they would cave under the pressure of politics. They were spineless men who cared more about their positions of power than about proclaiming the truth. They believed that John was not correct, yet they were not courageous enough to speak it boldly. Jesus on the other hand, was courageous enough to speak the truth, no matter

157

the cost. He knew who He was and did not need to jump through anyone's hoops to prove it. If the Pharisees were not willing to be courageous enough to speak their mind, then He would not indulge them in answering their question.

There is more to this story than just noticing how clever Jesus was at getting out of traps. The key to this story has to do with the message of John the Baptist. John came to bring a message of repentance. As was the typical ministry of all the prophets of the Old Testament, John was sent to the nation of Israel to tell them that they were sailing far off course and, because of their distorted perspective of truth and their blatant sinfulness, they were heading straight for disaster. John called out to them to repent, to change their ways, and come back to God before it was too late. In this time before Jesus' death, He is continuing the ministry of the prophet and offering one last chance to the Jewish leaders to listen to His message and come back.

This point is especially highlighted in Matthew 21:28-32 when Jesus tells the parable of the two sons. One son says, "Yes I will obey," then doesn't. The other son says, "No, I won't obey, then does." Jesus points out to the Jewish leaders that they are like the first son. They say with their mouths that they want to obey God, but in their hearts they are full of pride, envy, hatred, and greed. The "sinners" are like the second son. They initially have rejected the Kingdom of God, but now, when it is presented authentically through the person of Jesus, they are experiencing transformation and are actually entering into the kingdom. In both cases, actions speak louder than words.

For the rest of this session we will see how Jesus fulfills the role of the prophet in the Kingdom. The prophet's job was to clearly and boldly present the truth of God to the people, and specifically to the leaders of the people. As Jesus dukes it out with the Jewish leaders He is explaining to them why the coming destruction of Jerusalem is the result of their unrepentance and hardness toward the Messiah. Just like in the story of Jonah, had the Jerusalemites repented and returned to the heart of God like the Ninevites had done, then they would be spared. But it will be better on the Day of Judgment for Nineveh than for the unrepentant, hard-hearted city of Jerusalem.

There is a lesson for us today. How often are we more like the first son than the second? It is easy to say, "Oh sure, God, I want to know You more deeply," then go for four weeks straight without taking time to open the Bible. Or we say to a person in our church, "I really want to get to know you," then never call. Which would you like better; to have someone tell you they will call you because they want to get to know you, and not call, or, have someone call you out of the blue and engage in a meaningful conversation? Obviously it is the second choice. What happens when we behave like the first choice? We lose credibility and our integrity is tarnished. No longer can people trust our words. Worse yet, we communicate to the person to whom we have made a commitment that they are not worthy of our time. We filled them with expectations and then let them come crashing down.

As the church, let's take time to weigh our words carefully. If we want to do something, let's make sure that we are totally committed to doing it before we flap our gums about it. Before we commit, let's make sure that it is something we really desire to do and not just an aspiration. We need to be careful about these things both in our relationship with God and in our relationship with each other. The only thing we really have is our integrity. If we make big promises in the name of kindness or cordiality, but don't follow through, then we have lost that one thing we had. It is very difficult to get integrity and trust back once it is lost.

Kid's Questions

Which would you like better:

A. Your parents tell you that you are going to go on a great trip, then, when the day arrives, they go shopping instead and pretend like they never promised.

B. Your parents tell you that you cannot go on a great trip and that you don't deserve to go on a trip because you are all little brats. Then, one day, they apologize for what they said and they surprise you by taking the whole family on a trip.

How would you feel if A happened? Why?

How would you feel if B happened? Why?

Jesus told the Pharisees that God would prefer if people said the wrong thing first and later repented, than to pretend to say the right thing but never follow through on it.

We need to be careful that we don't tell someone, whether it's God or a friend, that we are going to do something and then not do it.

Lesson 4

- Matthew 21:33-46
- Mark 12:1-12
- Luke 20:9-19
- Matthew 22:1-14

Study Questions

What did the landowner require of the tenants?

How did the tenants respond to the landowner?

What consequences did the tenants have to pay for their actions?

How did the King respond to the rejection of his invitation?

Why was the person thrown out of the banquet?

Food for Thought

The Prophet Preaches Parables

In today's reading Jesus continues His conversation with the Jewish leaders, explaining to them why He is doing the things He is doing. They did not listen to the message of John the Baptist and they have not listened to Jesus' message. They are not willing to repent of their ways, and so they will face the consequences of their actions. To drive these points home, Jesus uses two parables.

A Vineyard

The vineyard represents the Kingdom of God; the truth about how humans can come into authentic relationship with their creator. The elders of Israel were the "tenants" who had been put in charge of the vineyard. Here are some key points from the story:

1. **The fruit belongs to the landowner.** The key to this story is found in Matthew 21:34, "he sent his servants to the tenants to collect his fruit." You see, the fruit of the vineyard belongs to the landowner, not the tenants. The tenants had started to believe that they actually owned the land and had the rights of the owner to hoard the fruit for themselves. They became so tenaciously adhered to this distortion of truth that they were willing to murder to preserve it.

2. **Management was changing hands.** Because of the mismanagement of the former tenants, the landowner was now handing the field over to a new team. The elders of Israel were being removed and Jesus' disciples were moving into leadership of the true vineyard.

3. **The new vineyard looked different.** Jesus went on to explain to them, after the parable was finished, that He was the cornerstone upon which the new Kingdom would be built. Here He ties back into the message of Psalm 118 that the people were chanting a few days earlier. The Jewish leaders were rejecting the cornerstone upon which the Father was going to build His new temple. If you reject this cornerstone you will be crushed by it. If you ignore it you will trip on it and be dashed to pieces. Unless you are placed on it by the Father and mortared in through the Spirit of God in the bond of peace with people from all nations, you will not be a part of the new deal.

The Banquet

The parable of the second banquet teaches the same message as the vineyard, but expands it a bit. The vineyard parable told the leaders how they had missed the mark in the past. The banquet parable tells about their present and the future condition. The banquet of God is the Kingdom. The picture of a banquet is a beautiful one. The Father invites people to come in and eat with Him. In the ancient world, to eat with someone was to demonstrate fellowship and intimacy with that person. The Kingdom of God is not a power trip or a set of rituals; it is a relationship that takes place over a meal. The elders had rejected this version of the Kingdom. They were too busy doing the really important things that important people do. Because of their rejection, the Father has rejected them and opened up the dinner table to everyone. The Father was not just upset with the rejection of his invitation, He sent his army to destroy the city. That would happen in just a few short years. The Roman army would, indeed, march on the city of Jerusalem and graze it to the ground, while the real banquet was going on with sinners and gentiles all around the world.

Let's take a moment to hear a word of caution. At this point it would be easy for us, as 21st century Christians, to look smugly back on the Jewish leaders and think, "they got what they deserve. They are out and we are in. Ain't it grand to sit at the wedding feast?" Be careful of that attitude. Notice Matthew 22:11-14. Among the newly invited wedding guests there was a man who did not have on wedding clothes. He got booted and sent out into the destruction with the first round of people who rejected the invitation.

Here's the point. Just because Jesus opened the gate and invited people from every nation (good and bad) to come to the feast, it doesn't mean that anybody can just waltz on in and graze at the buffet. The Father has issued a certain attire. You have to wear what he wants you to wear if you want to sit at the table. "That's oppressive!" You might think. Perhaps. But, remember what got the vineyard tenants booted? They thought they owned the vineyard and could call their own shots. They were wrong. If we are going to come to the banquet and eat at the table, then we need to come to a place of brokenness and humility where we recognize that our own clothes are not good enough. The Father has provided the clothes for us through his Son, but we have to be willing to go through the awkward phase of taking our own clothes off, being exposed in our nakedness, and then putting on the new clothes. Through that humble act of submission and obedience, we can then come to the table with the proper attitude and enjoy the wonderful fellowship that awaits us with the Father.

I'm afraid that too many times in our culture we buy into the idea that God caters to me and that I can come to God on my terms. If I don't like a certain aspect of God's feast, then I will simply remove it from the menu. It doesn't work like that. We have to come to God on His terms, for His glory, to serve His purpose. It may sound harsh, but in all reality, it is only through this humble attitude that we can experience true joy and freedom.

Think about it this way. When you walk into a room, many times you start comparing yourself with others. That person has nicer clothes, so they must be more wealthy or better than me. I have better clothes than that person. Oh, how many times growing up did I feel that Sunday morning was a competitive fashion show among certain women in our church! We tend to compare ourselves with each other at every level, not just the clothes we wear. We think, "That person is smarter, or more holy, or funnier than me." In the Father's banquet we are not allowed to wear our own clothes. He clothes us with His glory so that we are all equal. When we can't compare ourselves with others it becomes much easier to focus on Him. Praise God that He has provided the proper clothing for us through the death and resurrection of Jesus. At the King's feast we are all equally present because of the grace of God, nothing more and nothing less.

Kid's Questions

Let's pretend that there are two teams, one team is RED and the other is BLUE. You are not a member of either team, but you have been invited to a big party that is being held by the Blue team. These people really take their colors seriously and they expect that everyone will show up to the party wearing blue.

What would happen if you showed up wearing red? What if the host of the party thought that you may have been mistaken, so he offers you some blue clothes, but you refuse? You make a big stink and shout, "I have my rights, and I can wear whatever color I want!" How would the host feel? Would everyone at the party be having a good time?

Jesus said that in the Father's Banquet (which stands for the Kingdom of God) everyone will be wearing clothes that have been provided by the Father. You don't have to do anything to get them; you just have to be willing to put them on. If someone comes to the banquet and demands that they be allowed to wear their own clothes, then the Father is going to throw them out of the party.

We need to always remember that God is in charge of everything. We need to follow his rules because he's the host.

Lesson 5

- Matthew 22:15-33
- Mark 12:13-27
- Luke 20:20-40

Study Questions

In what trap did the Herodians and Pharisees try to catch Jesus?

How did Jesus escape the trap?

In what trap did the Sadducees try to catch Jesus?

How did Jesus escape the trap?

Food for Thought

Traps for the Teacher

Adversity makes for strange bedfellows. The Pharisees were getting so desperate to catch Jesus that they were willing to fraternize with the Herodians in order to do it. The Herodians were Jews who were pro-King Herod. Remember, Herod was not a real Jewish king according to the line of David. He was a puppet king that had been established by the Roman government. Herod was more of Greco-Roman than he was a Jew. The Herodians believed that it was good for Israel to have this type of liaison between the Romans and the people. By having Herod in place it made for better peace and easier movement and trade in the Empire. The Pharisees, on the other hand, saw Herod as a disgrace and a symbol of all that was evil and corrupted in the nation. They generally snubbed their noses at the Herodians.

Now, in the shadow of the threat they perceived in Jesus of Nazareth, the Pharisee's fears grew strong enough to move them into an alliance with the Herodians in order to bring this man down. So, together, the Pharisees and the Herodians laid a verbal, political trap for Jesus.

"Should we pay taxes, or not?" That was the question. As a Roman Province, Judea was obliged to pay taxes to Caesar in exchange for the protection and benefits they gained from the technological advances the Roman Empire had brought to the region – political peace, roads for travel, aqueducts for fresh water, etc. The Herodians believed they should pay the tax in order to keep the peace. The Pharisees believed they should not since it would communicate submission to the authority of Caesar.

The Pharisees' resistance was not just a political issue, it was religious as well. The Romans believed that the emperor was a god and that he was to be worshipped as the first and foremost God. All other gods were permitted to be worshipped in the Empire as long as the Emperor got highest billing in the pantheon. Well, obviously, the Pharisees were not about to break the first commandment and worship Caesar by paying taxes to him.

So, how did Jesus handle this political pickle that the Herodians and Pharisees had him in? If He says, "Yes," then He would probably lose the popular vote of the people, since the majority of the people resented the tax. If He said "No" publicly, then He would be setting himself up to be arrested by the Romans.

How did He handle it? He demonstrated for us one of the greatest tools that a leader can use. He showed us that we should not pop off with an answer too quickly. We should always make sure that we understand the question clearly before we commit to an answer. More importantly, we should make sure that the people who are asking the question really understand what they are asking. Quite often, as was the case here, people are not really asking the question they are asking, but are either laying a trap or are asking a deeper question. Jesus deflected the decoy question by returning the question with a question of His own. By doing that He is no longer on the defensive, but has put His attackers on the defensive.

Now allow me to paraphrase His answer to show the brilliance of His response. "Whose inscription is on the coin?" He asks. "Caesar's," the Pharisees reluctantly mutter in response. "Fine. Caesar's image is on it, so it belongs to Him. Give it back. It's not really yours in the first place. In truth, you shouldn't even worry about those little trinkets of metal at all. By the way, God's image is imprinted on you. He made you and you belong to Him. He is the only God, not Caesar. The real question is not whether you should give to Caesar what is Caesar's, but whether you have given back to God what is God's. Are you His servant, or do you still think that you are in control of your own life?"

Brilliant. He defuses the bomb, and gets to the heart of the matter.

The Herodians and the Pharisees struck out with Jesus, their traps snapped on air and didn't catch any flesh. Standing on deck was a group of Sadducees, just waiting to throw their trap out for Jesus. The Sadducees did not believe in an afterlife. The believed, based upon their understanding of the Old Testament, that the soul and the body were one unit and inseparable. When the body dies, the soul dies as well. Because of this belief they put a lot of stock in family blood lines and believed that "eternal life" was experienced through the propagation of the family tree. You could say that they were 1st century existentialists. They believed that it was through the proper obedience to the sacrificial system of the temple that God would shine favor on them and keep the nation intact.

With that in mind, you can see why they were so eager to present their question to Jesus. They were not only trying to trap Jesus, they were also trying to stick it to their arch rivals, the Pharisees. The Pharisees believed that there would be a resurrection on the final day when the dead would rise and their souls AND bodies would live on with God forever.

The Sadducees presented what they thought was an ironclad, logical argument against the absurdity of the resurrection of the dead. First, in the Law of Moses it stated that if a woman's husband died, it was that man's brother's duty to take his widowed sister-in-law in to be his wife, so that she can produce a child for the dead man. From the Sadducees perspective, this law was created because the man's only hope of "eternal life" was to see his family line carried on. So, if a woman followed the God-given Mosaic law of Levirate marriage and had seven husbands, all legal marriages in the eyes of God, and knowing that a woman could not have more than one husband, how could there be a resurrection of the dead? God would be stuck with a moral conundrum of His own creation. Obviously, so the Sadducees thought, there is no resurrection of the dead because God would never advocate a woman being married to seven men in the afterlife. Ha! Gotcha Jesus!

"Hold it right there. That is very clever logic there, boys. There's one problem...you're asking the WRONG QUESTION!!!! Your logic is built upon completely misguided presuppositions. You are wrong about the resurrection. There is one, just read your Bible. But, the Pharisees are wrong, too. They think the afterlife will be like this life. It won't. When the resurrection happens, your bodies will not be the same. You will be glorified into a physical state that is more spiritual than physical. You will be like the angels. Things that are as important as marriage in this life will become petty because they will be so overshadowed by ultimate intimacy with God that you will not even care about them."

So, once again, Jesus demonstrates for us a very important principle; don't get sucked into theological debates that are more about people's needs to be "right" and in control than they are about authentically seeking the truth about God. Here's a little secret. The majority of the theological issues that you hear people talk about in the modern church are controversies, not because they are a debate between "right" and "wrong," but because both sides of the debate are operating from faulty presuppositions. In this postmodern age (meaning nothing more than the period of time after the age of the Enlightenment when human reason was considered the only key to "truth." The time right now when everyone is trying to figure out which direction is "up") it is our job as followers of Jesus to put down our need to be "right" and to enter into the mysterious tension of faith and mystery. Leonard Sweet has a new book out entitled Out of the Question, Into the Mystery. He says that we have spent so much time battling over the rational propositions *about* God that we have forgotten that we are called into a radical, mysterious relationship *with* God. Remember one of the running themes of Jesus' teachings. He said that unless we come to the

163

Kingdom with the faith of a little child we will not enter it. Children don't understand why their Father loves them, or how He provides for their needs, they simply trust that He does because He demonstrates it faithfully to them. They don't worry about it, and in not worrying they are able to experience freedom to play in the presence of the Father.

The Kingdom of God is not about politics or power, or even about being "right" theologically. In the Kingdom of God we are about loving the Father, and loving each other.

Kid's Questions

What does the word "resurrection" mean?

Today Jesus taught that there will be a resurrection of the dead. He said that when we are resurrected out bodies will be different. They will be better. We will be more like the angels, living in an eternal, spiritual life. How does sound to you?

One thing that we can trust in is that if we follow Jesus, then there is more to this life than just this life. No matter how hard our life may be, we can trust that we will be with God for eternity. Isn't that awesome!

Chapter 4 - Session 1: The End of the Age

Pictures of the "Teachers"   Pictures of the "End"

COMING SOON (A.D. 70)

ROME

JERUSALEM

ONLY THE FATHER KNOWS WHEN

TEACHERS

WOE TO YOU!

WATCH OUT!

THEY'RE GOING TO KILL ME FOR THIS

10 Commandments
LOVE GOD
LOVE OTHERS

Kidron Valley

Mount of Olives

BETHANY

Introduction

The sun is beginning to set on Jesus' ministry. This session we hear the closing arguments in the great debate between Jesus and the teachers of the Law. After this He surrenders Himself into the hands of darkness.

In the illustration there are two hills that are separated by a valley. On the left is Mt. Zion, the temple mount upon which is built that beautiful, stone structure that symbolizes the hardened hearts of Israel. It is on this mountain that Jesus stands with pointed finger to expose the true nature of Israel's "holy men" and "most highly exalted teachers of the Law." They are nothing more than a pit of poisonous snakes. They look good and polished on the outside, but inside they are full of the putrid stench of death. They have taken the miraculous mystery of God, the mysterious glory

that appeared to Moses in authentic relationship, and encased it in a stone tomb of death, gilded with gold. And, worse yet, they have led the sheep of God's flock into the pit of death with them.

Between the mountains there lies a valley. The valley is called "Kidron," which means "obscure; making black or sad." In the Old Testament it was also called the valley of Decision. It was the place where the great reformer/kings like Asa and Josiah threw down the pagan idols and destroyed them. It is the place that lies in shadow both when the sun rises in the east behind the Mount of Olives and when the sun sets in the west behind the temple. In both extremes it lies shrouded   in mystery.

It is across this valley that Jesus calls to the people of Israel. He warns them, one last time, that the end is coming. Soon their pretty little temple will become nothing more than a pile of rubble. Everything that they hold to be sacred and secure

165

will come crashing down around them. The end of their world is immanent. Yet, His Kingdom is still open. As Zechariah said He would, Jesus stands on the Mount of Olives and divides it in half, allowing the morning sun from the east to flood into it. His Kingdom has come, and upon the throne of that Kingdom He will sit. He will separate the sheep from the goats. The wise, the mighty, the self-exalted will be turned aside and the meek, the lowly, the diligent, and the humble will be welcomed into His presence.

Jesus calls us all into this place of paradox and mystery that is called the truth. He calls us to walk away from our need for safety, security, and "rightness" and asks us to embrace the mystery of knowing and following Him. No one likes paradox. Mystery is dangerous. The radical who speaks such words must be eliminated or the entire fabric of society may be unraveled. As the perfume is poured on Jesus' head, He prepares Himself for the inevitable execution that awaits anyone who is willing to stand against the power structures of this world order and speak the scandalous, mysterious truth of God' love.

Lesson 1

- Matthew 22:34-44
- Mark 12:28-40
- Luke 20:41-47

Study Questions

What test did the Pharisees give to Jesus?

What was His response?

What was Jesus' counter attack to the Pharisees?

How did they respond?

Food for Thought

At the end of last week we saw that the Jewish leaders were lining up to set traps for Jesus. We read about two of them last week. First the Herodians tested Him with a question about taxes. Then the Sadducees tested Him with a question about the resurrection of the dead.

Today we see the third and final trap in the series. Today it is the Pharisees' turn. The Pharisees prided themselves as being the men of the Word, the Keepers of the Law. While the Sadducees were more interested in the ritual of the sacrificial system and the importance of the physical temple, the Pharisees placed more value on the written word of God that was handed down to them from Moses in the form of the Torah. The Pharisees believed that they had studied the written word of God so thoroughly that they had a firm grasp on the nature of God. They were the Bible answer men. Ask them any question, they would have the answer.

Now it was their turn to trap Jesus on their own playing field; the Law. "Which command is the greatest, Jesus?"

We can learn two very important lessons from Jesus' response. The first has to do with His view of the law and is something that we have discussed a few times in the course of this study. Jesus said that the Law can be summed up in one word – LOVE. We must first love God with our whole self. When our hearts, minds, souls, and strength are completely focused and enraptured in the love of God then we will never break any of the Mosaic Law that warns against idolatry or spiritual adultery.

Notice how I said the "love of God," and not a "love for God." To love God is not to admire Him from a distance the way we would "love" our favorite pop-star or hero. No, to love God is so much deeper than that. God is love. God is pouring out life-giving, redemptive love to His creation every moment. Sin, and the effects of sin, is the result of turning away from this love, turning away from the light of life, and facing into the cold darkness of self-love. When we abandon ourselves and turn to face into the love of God, then we will be sparked back into life and experience the fullness for which we were created. Then, when we are being filled with God's love, we can overflow that love and fulfill all the rest of the commands by simply loving our neighbor. When we love our neighbor through the overflow of God's love in our hearts, we will never covet, lie, steal, slander, or murder.

The second thing that we can learn from Jesus' response is from the counter attack that He launched on the Pharisees. Jesus returned their question with a question. "Tell me, oh wise ones, whose son is the Christ?"

"Well, that's obvious, Jesus. The Christ is the Son of David. The Bible says so."

"Hmmm...that's interesting. I'll agree that the Bible does say that the Christ is the son of David, but, if that is true, then how is it that David, being full of the Holy Spirit, could call the Christ 'Lord?' Which is it, son or Lord? Does the Bible contradict itself?"

The Pharisees had no response.

It is very important for us to catch what happened in that interchange, because it has huge implications for our lives today. The Pharisees prided themselves in their knowledge about scripture. They believed it was through their "correctly dividing the Word of Truth" that they were deemed righteous. Being "right" theologically and having their theological ducks in a row was a badge of honor for them that they used to elevate themselves in society. Being aligned with the proper theologian of the day was very important to them. Jesus cut right through all that crud. He pointed out to them the most vital truth that we, in the 21st century can ever grasp onto. The truth of God is riddled with paradox and enigma. The answer to Jesus' question was, "Yes." The Christ was both son and Lord. That's how it is with all deep truths of God. Jesus is both God and Human. Salvation is both by grace and by works. Justification is both predestined and by free will. The Kingdom of God is both completely present and in an unrealized future. God exists now and in eternity. We will be both physical and spiritual in the resurrection. We know everything and nothing about the infinite, majestic, mysterious nature of the eternal, life-giving, limitless, personal God.

Let me speak clearly (if that is even possible when referring to something that is inherently fuzzy). Jesus invites us into a relationship, not a religion. Relationships are dynamic. They are wild rides of adventure that cause us to delve deeply into the knowing of another person. Religion is a static thing. It is defined by ritual. It is hemmed in by the safety of sameness and "orthodoxy." Unfortunately, the only things that are not dynamic are things that are dead. As soon as you think you are "right" or that you have everything figured out to the point that you can condemn someone, you have sealed yourself in your own sarcophagus. Jesus calls us into the truth of knowing the unknowable God. We are called to know Him fully while, at the same time, realizing that we don't understand Him at all.

In a world that is characterized by skepticism, moral relativism, and general apathy, we, as followers of the dynamic, living, God are called to throw ourselves into God's love and be conduits of God's love to all people. God is the only one who has the right to judge whether another person is right or wrong. We are called to pursue God with all our heart and to love everyone who comes in our path. It's that simple. May we lay aside our obsessive need to be "right" and "holy" and embrace the wonderful mystery of God.

Kid's Questions

Get a big piece of paper and divide it into two columns.

Now look up Exodus 20:1-17. These are the 10 commandments that were written down by Moses.

In the left hand column write down the first four commands. In the right hand column write down the last six commands.

What do the first four commands have in common? What do the last six commands have in common?

Jesus was asked what the greatest command was. What was his answer? What did he say the second greatest was?

Above the left column write the words "LOVE GOD"

Above the right column write the words "LOVE OTHERS"

Here's the secret to living in Jesus' Kingdom. If we focus all of our energy into loving God and loving others, we will automatically keep all the commands. Test it out. See if loving God would cover the first four and if loving others would cover the last six.

Obeying God comes from a heart that is overflowing with God's love.

Lesson 2

- Matthew 23:1-39
- Mark 12:41-44
- Luke 21:1-4

Study Questions

Make a list of all the accusations that Jesus brought against the teachers of the law. Why did He do this?

Why was the widow more highly regarded by Jesus than the rich man?

Food for Thought

Today we have another portrait painted by Jesus to draw attention to the stark contrast between the man-made Kingdom of the Jewish leaders and the true Kingdom of God. Let's step back and watch how the scene unfolds. I think if we observe it this way we will see the real spirit behind the words.

It's like a scene out of an old Bruce Lee movie. Jesus, the hero, has been surrounded by all the bad guys. They've come at Him from every side. The Herodians swing their numchucks of the tax question, but Jesus deflects them and sends them spinning. The Sadducees advance with end over end cartwheels into a flying kick as they ask about the resurrection, but Jesus dodges with grace. Then the Pharisees wield the swords and magnificently twirl them back and forth around their heads with agility and prowess. Jesus, undaunted, and with one flowing move takes the swords out of their hands.

Then, the enemies unite and attack Him. In one burst of energy Jesus clenches His teeth, flexes His muscles, screams "HIYAA" and begins whipping around in a frenzy of agility and speed...

"Woe to you teachers...you are a brood of vipers! You are cup full of filth! You are like a tomb that is bright, shiny, and beautiful on the outside, but on the inside you stink of decaying flesh! You are worse than sinners, you are hypocrites! You condemn everyone around you and accuse them of being law breakers, when you yourselves continually break the first and only command of God...to love! Woe to you. You will be destroyed because of this!"

Then with chest heaving He backs away from His bewildered band of opponents. No one is willing to stand against Him in that moment. As He steps back into the sidelines with His disciples, and the flow of the crowd begins to move into a more normal pattern, it happens. There before Him is the perfect example of everything He has just been ranting about.

He elbows Peter who stands next to Him. "Pete, check this out. Look over there, at the offering box. See that man? Who is he?"

"Well, Jesus, everyone knows that he's one of the richest, most powerful members of the Sanhedrin."

"How much is he putting in, can you tell?"

"Of course I can tell; he's counting it out loud as he's clinking it into the coffers. Whoa, that's a lot of money."

"OK, fine. Now, look over there. She's just coming around the corner. Who is that woman?"

"I have no idea."

"Exactly. You have no idea who she is. She's a nobody. She is a widow woman that everyone has forgotten about. How much is she giving?"

"I can't really tell. She doesn't seem to want anybody to notice. I think it's only a couple cents. That's barely worth putting into the coffer. What difference will that make?"

"Stop right there, Pete. I'll tell you what difference that makes. Do you know how much that woman just gave? She gave everything. Her faith in God is so great that she realizes that she has nothing to lose and is willing to put her complete trust in the Lord.

That is a perfect picture of everything that I've been trying to teach you guys for the past three and a half years.

Rich guy...not the Kingdom.

Widow....she's the Kingdom.

Until you become like her...nothing...you will never see the true Kingdom. If you operate by the rich guy's system you will be jacked into a dangerous illusion, being a blind man who thinks you can see.

I'll tell you what. The day of the rich guy is quickly coming to and end."

We'll talk about that in the next lesson.

Kid's Questions

Go get a plastic cup and take it to outside. Find a nice piece of dirt and spend some time filling the cup with mud. Roll the cup around in the mud and make sure it is covered inside and out.

Now, dump the dirt out and bring the dirty cup into the kitchen.

Would you want to drink out of this cup? Why?

Wash the outside of the cup, but be sure to not get any water inside the cup. Get the outside really clean.

Would you want to drink out of this cup? Why?

Put the cup under the faucet and let the water run into it in a steady stream until it overflows. Let this happen for a couple minutes. Observe what happens. Clean the cup thoroughly.

Would you want to drink out of this cup? Why?

Jesus said that the teachers of the Law were like cups that were clean on the outside but were full of filth on the inside. What he meant was that they pretending to be good people by doing all the right things like going to church, giving tithes, and wearing the right clothes. Yet, they did not have loving hearts.

Jesus reminds us that if we focus on letting his Spirit flow into us and overflow out of us, then both the inside and the outside of our lives will be clean and people will be able to see the Kingdom of God in and through us.

Lesson 3

- Matthew 24:1-51
- Mark 13:1-31
- Luke 21:5-38

Study Questions

What comment did the disciples make that sparked Jesus' message?

What prediction did Jesus make about the temple?

What must happen before the end will come?

How did Jesus say His followers would be treated? How were they supposed to respond to that kind of treatment?

How are we supposed to interpret wars, rumors of wars, and natural disasters?

Who knows the day or the hour when Jesus will return?

In light of the above answer, what attitude is the disciple of Jesus supposed to have in the meantime? Why?

Food for Thought

Let's admit something. We like things that shine. Deep inside each of us there is a place that likes the sparkly things in life. When that one particular kind of car drives by, it turns our head. When we enter a particular kind of house, our mind envisions our family there. When a particular kind of body type walks by, we track with it. As much as we hate to admit it, we like the big and the powerful and the important. We like the big church building that sparkles when the morning sun hits it. We like the name plate that glistens in the light, telling everyone who we are and how important we are to our society.

The disciples were no different. After three and a half years of living with the Teacher, they still had an eye for the shiny. After the big showdown with the Herodians, Sadducees, and Pharisees, Jesus and His disciples were heading out the east gate to retire to their lodging in Bethany. On the way out they passed by the magnificent building called the Temple as its gold was glistening in the setting sun.

"Jesus, you have to admit, it is beautiful, isn't it?"

I wonder what went through Jesus' mind in that moment.

"Beautiful, yes. But let Me remind you of something, guys. Very soon that big old building will be nothing more than a pile of rubble. Then what? Where will the Sadducees find significance then? In what will the Pharisees take pride then?"

Having been silenced by Jesus' sobering reminder they walked across the shadowy valley (Kidron) to the Mount of Olives. As they reached the top, they built up the courage to ask Jesus, "Tell us what the sign will be of your coming and the end of the age?"

Here we enter into one of the most difficult passages in the New Testament, and into one of the hottest topics of the past century. When will Jesus return? What will the signs be? Will there be a rapture? Will there be a literal Millennial Kingdom?

Many well-intentioned people have spent a vast amount of time and energy studying the books of Daniel, Revelation, 1 Thessalonians, and passages like this one from the Gospels, in order to map out a timeline of the end times. I'm sure that you, too, have wondered if such a thing is possible. I bet you'd like me to tell you the answers to these questions, wouldn't you? Well, I can't. Oh, it's not that I'm being ornery or elusive. I'm telling you the simple truth that Jesus told His disciples when they asked Him the same question. I can't tell you the answer because no one knows the answer. Only the Father knows, and He's not telling.

The next logical question would be, "If Jesus didn't give an answer, then why are there so many words printed in red after the question was asked. He said something to them. What was it?"

Let's walk through this passage (traditionally called the Olivet Discourse) and find out exactly what Jesus said about the end of the age.

vv. 4-14 I'm not coming back until everybody gets a chance to hear the Good News and enter my Kingdom. Jesus warned the disciples that many people would try to convince them that He had returned or try to predict the date. As wars and natural disasters run rampant around the world people will point to them and say, "See, this has to be the end of the world." Well, it may seem like the end of the world to the person who is watching their beloved homeland being ravaged by war, but it is not a sign of the return of Jesus. It is just the unfortunate and heartbreaking byproduct of sin that has been present since the day Cain murdered Abel. And natural disasters are just that...natural. They've been happening since the day God's brush first swept across the cosmic canvas. Volcanoes erupt, geological plates shift, hurricanes cycle and cool the atmosphere. It's how it was created, so don't get in a panic. Yes, life will be difficult, especially if you stand up for the name of Jesus, but if you are faithful you will be saved.

vv. 15-35 A terrible destruction is coming on Jerusalem, but that is not the sign of My return. In A.D. 70 the Roman army destroyed the city of Jerusalem. When Jesus spoke these words that horrific event stood 40 years in the future. This destruction would be very similar to the events of Jeremiah's life when he watched the systematic devastation that was brought upon Jerusalem at the hands of the Babylonian emperor Nebuchadnezzar. Jeremiah warned them that it would happen, but the people didn't listen. God warned Solomon that it would happen on the day he dedicated the temple. God said that if the people wandered away from Him that He would not hesitate to knock down that puny little brick house that Solomon thought was so impressive. For three years Jesus had been warning the people of Jerusalem that God had not changed His ways. Just because the temple had been rebuilt that didn't automatically mean that God was pleased with His people. The time was quickly coming when the Father would, once again, allow devastation to fall on His people in order to break through their hardened hearts.

Jesus told His disciples that the days surrounding those events would be terrible, but that they were not associated with His coming. In v. 23 He said, "at that time if anyone says to you, 'Look, here is the Christ!' or, 'There He is!' do not believe it."

vv.36-51 No one knows when I will return (not even Me) so watch and be ready.

There are some key points for us in this section.

1. **Jesus' return will be obvious.** In v. 27 Jesus said that when He returns it will be as obvious as a flash of lightning across the sky. Don't let anyone dupe you into thinking that He came last night and you missed it, or that you have to be on a certain mountain top to be able to discern it. It will be as plain as day when it happens.

2. **No one knows when it will happen.** Did you catch that...no one. Not even Jesus knows. So, here's my question. If Jesus doesn't even know when He's coming back, then how in the world could a simple human calculate the date? Here's a good rule of thumb; if someone whips out an end times timeline chart and/or a secret decoder ring for the hidden messages of the biblical text, run away!

3. **Jesus doesn't know.** Does that strike you as odd? Let's address the question that is lurking in the back of your mind, "If Jesus is God, and if He is one with the Father, then how can the Father know, but the Son not know?" That's a great question. The answer to that question is actually the point of this whole text... "I don't know." Catch this. Jesus did not come to give us clear cut answers. Jesus didn't draw us into answers, He drew (and draws) us into relationship. He draws us into a mystery. God is not the object of our science experiment. He is not a substance that can be dissected and quantified. He is the enigmatic mystery that is the source of all life. Jesus came to demonstrate what it means to have a relationship with such a person. Throughout Jesus' life He lived by these simple rules; trust the Father, obey the Father, and glorify the Father. That's all He did and that is all He is asking us to do. To define the Father or understand the Father is a simple impossibility.

4. **The point is to be ready.** The one thing Jesus did know was that He would return at some point. On that day God would make all things new and settle accounts. He goes on to give some parables to drive this point home, so we will look at those tomorrow.

At this point you may be wondering why I started today's thought talking about shiny things. It is because "sparkle-addiction" is the temptation that I believe Jesus was warning against when He gave this message. The Jews were enamored by their beautiful temple, their sacred rituals, their grasp on "rightness," and their self-exalted state. So, Jerusalem was destroyed and for 2,000 years it has never been rebuilt. We run the same risk today. Just as the elders of Israel were supposed to be servants in the field, so too have we been entrusted with God's Kingdom. If we, too, get caught up in the shiny buildings and the powerful positions, then the end of our age could come as well.

Notice how I said the end of *our* age and not the end of *the* age. Like the Jewish elders, we can tend to become very ethnocentric and think that our particular form of culture or flavor of Christianity is the only right way. Then we enshrine our forms in religiosity and worship at the temple of our own design. When we do that you had better bet that God will bring it smashing down. When He does it will seem like the end of the world and we will probably write books to prove that it is. But it's not. It's just the end of our world...and that world needed to be torn down for our own good.

So, here in the early days of the 21st century, what are we to make of this Olivet Discourse? Think about it; when Jerusalem was destroyed I'm sure it seemed like the end of the world to them. How could they possibly go on after that? Yet, the sun did come up the next day. Why? It came up because the Kingdom of God was not destroyed with the crumbling of a building or the shattering of a few men's egos or the deconstruction of certain systems of worship. The Kingdom of God is and always has been, in the hearts of His people, not in the external forms of culture. Jesus took the Kingdom, planted it in the hearts of His disciples, and sent them into the whole world to plant the seeds of God's Kingdom everywhere, in various cultures, in multicolored wrappings, in every language. We are still workers in those fields. Some of us are cultivating mature fields that are bearing fruit each season. Others of us are forging new ground and sewing seeds in yet unreached fields. We each have our task and we all are simply servants, tending the fields until the Master sees fit to return. Watch, be patient, stay humble, trust, and keep working. That's all there is to it.

Kid's Questions

What is a fire drill? Why do they happen?

Does anyone know when a real fire might happen? Why?

What would happen if no one ever did fire drills or had smoke detectors? What would happen if one day your class decided to stack all the furniture in front of the doors and windows in order to do something in the middle of the room? Then, a fire started and the room filled with smoke, what would happen? Why?

Jesus said that someday he would return and bring judgment on the earth. He told us that no one knows when that would happen. We need to be ready.

What do you need to do to be ready for the day Jesus returns? If he returned tomorrow, would you be ready? Why?

Lesson 4

- Matthew 25:1-46
- Mark 13:32-37

Study Questions

What was the oil for in the lamps? Why did five of the virgins not have oil?

What were the servants supposed to do with the money that the master left with them? What happened to the one who did not do it?

What criterion was used to separate the sheep from the goats?

Food for Thought

I must confess that much of my formative years were spent in a very large Baptist church in Detroit, Michigan. I learned a lot of great things there and I am unlearning a lot of things from there as well. One thing that we Baptists did a lot of was sing. In the youth group we sang one song that seemed a bit sacrilegious to me.

> Give me oil in my lamp keep me burning, burning, burning,
>
> Give me oil in my lamp I pray,
>
> Give me oil in my lamp keep me burning, burning, burning,
>
> Keep me burning till the break of day.

Now, that verse wasn't bad. After all, it comes right out of our reading from today. The following verses got a little suspect, however....

> Give me gas in my Ford keep me trucking for the Lord,
>
> Give me gas in my Ford I pray,
>
> Give me gas in my Ford keep me trucking for the Lord,
>
> Keep me trucking till the break of day.
>
> Give me wax on board, keep me surfing for the Lord...you get the idea.

At the time I thought we were being silly junior highers who were pushing the edge of rebelliousness. Little did I know that we were actually waxing eloquently as profound theologians.

Let me explain. Today Jesus follows up on His Olivet Discourse and explains what it means to watch and be ready. He does so with three parables: The ten virgins, the talents, and the sheep and goats.

Of Oil and Money

The first two parables really teach the same thing. In both instances there are a group of people who have been entrusted with a responsibility by an authority figure and have been told to wait for his return. The virgins were to keep the lamps burning until the Bridegroom returned, so they needed to have a good supply of oil. The servants were given financial resources to manage and grow until the master returned. In both scenarios the message is obvious. Those who took the words of the master seriously, were diligent, and were faithful were found worthy upon the master's return. Those who were foolish, thought they knew better than the master, did not take the proper precautions, and squandered their time were left scrambling on the day of reckoning. The faithful ones were welcomed into a state of relationship with the master and the foolish ones were sent out into the cold. The simple message for us as followers of Jesus is: work hard with what you've been given and always be prepared for His return.

Great, you may be thinking, but what does that look like? What exactly is the "oil in my lamp?" What are the "talents" that I've been given? How do I know if I'm using them properly so that when He returns He will be pleased?

Of Sheep and Goats

It's as if Jesus heard your questions and answered them in the very next story. When Jesus returns and sits on his glorious throne He will separate the sheep from the goats. The sheep are the 5 virgins who had enough oil and the servants who multiplied the talents. "Good job, virgins and servants. You were good sheep, come over here and enter into my pasture. I've got fresh, green grass, cool water, and plenty of sunshine for you."

"Wow, Lord, that's amazing, but we have one question. What was my oil? What was my talent?" (Sound familiar?)

Here it is...

When I was hungry, thirsty, lonely, naked, sick, and in prison, you took care of Me. When I was the underdog, the "unshiny," "non-sparkly" outcast of society, unable to pay you back or sing your praises, you looked past all that and helped Me because you had the Kingdom of God authentically in your heart."

Now for the goats. Go over there, into the darkness. After all, that's the place you prefer, isn't it?

"But, Lord, when did we miss the boat?"

"When I was there, hungry, thirsty, naked, lonely, naked, sick, and in prison you glanced right past Me. You saw Me as a stain on your "holy garb". I was bad for publicity. I was messy and difficult, and you didn't want Me to foul up your perfect little plan. I came to you everyday and you ignored Me. You preferred the darkness of the sparkly over the light of truth. You lived in the Kingdom of your own design and called it mine, but I never knew you. Now, go, live in your own Kingdom forever."

Of Gas and Wax

So, you see, my junior high songs were profound theology. OK, so they weren't really that profound, but they did teach us one important lesson. When Jesus went away, He didn't ask us to do anything "super," He asked us to do the mundane. In our everyday lives, whether we are driving our Ford, or surfing the waves, or walking through the grocery store, we are to be storing up oil and multiplying talents for the Kingdom of God. Each day we need to stop and evaluate whose kingdom we are building. Are we erecting a shrine to our own importance and gilding it with the fool's gold of false pretense? Or are we taking time, in each moment to listen to the soft promptings of the Holy Spirit that tell us to spend time with the life of another person.

What does oil look like? What are the talents? When we take the time to actually sit and listen to our children when they desperately long for our affection; that's a drop of oil. When we go out of our way to help the widow down the street get her groceries; that's a talent multiplied. When we break out of our comfort zone and build a bridge to the poor, homeless, and imprisoned in our neighborhoods and around the world; that is the wool of a sheep.

Kid's Questions

Make a list of the things that the "sheep" did. Who did they do it for?

What did the goats not do?

As you look at that list, what are some real-life ways that you could do the "sheep" things in your life?

Lesson 5

- Matthew 26:1-16
- Mark 14:1-11
- Luke 22:1-6
- John 12:20-50

Study Questions

Why did the woman anoint Jesus with perfume? What was Jesus' attitude toward this action?

What did Judas do? Why?

How did Jesus explain the need for His death?

Why did the leaders who believed Jesus not act on their belief? What was Jesus' attitude toward them?

Food for Thought

What is one of the biggest fears we share in our culture? We fear death. We caricature it in horror movies as a hideous thing. We spend billions of dollars on it in the medical and health industry, trying to push it back. We suppress it in our conversation by not talking about it at all or shrouding it in euphemisms. Yet today, we need to look death square in the eye. Today we observe as Jesus prepared Himself for His death.

Here are some observations.

1. **Jesus was fully aware of His coming death.** When the woman anointed His head Jesus knew that she was preparing Him for burial. He knew that no one who speaks out against the status quo the way He had done would ever be allowed to live. You see, the status quo cannot handle change or accept correction or tolerate the exposure of their heart. The rebel must be silenced.

2. **Death is necessary.** The key phrase to this section is found in John 12:24, "unless a kernel of wheat falls to the ground and dies, it remains only a single seed. But if it dies, it produces many seeds." This is another one of Jesus' enigmatic, paradoxical truths; life cannot happen without death. Jesus had to die in order for the power of His Kingdom to be unleashed. Do you know why He had to die? Was it because blood had to be shed as a sacrifice for the payment of sin? That's part of it. Was it to pay a ransom to Satan? Perhaps, but that is giving a lot of credit to that over-inflated angel. One of the major reasons that Jesus had to die was because if He didn't, then His Kingdom would be just like everyone else's Kingdom in the world that had been constructed by the human will and taken by force. The only way for the Kingdom of God to flourish is for the citizens of that Kingdom to completely die to the trappings of humanly constructed power-structures. As the leader of this Kingdom, Jesus had to be the first to die. He did not play the powerful King card. He did not manipulate a political coup and take the city by storm. Instead, He humbled Himself, willingly gave up every right that He had, allowed Himself to be misunderstood, ridiculed, tortured, and then handed over for execution. He allowed Himself to be stripped of everything that the world says is important. Then, and only then, would He be free to unleash the Kingdom of God.

3. **It's all about glorifying the Father.** V. 18 gives us the key to unlocking the Kingdom

and following the path of death. The only way that we can truly die is when we realize that it isn't about us. We are not the hero of the story. It is all about the Father. When we realize that only God deserves the glory and honor, then we can stop needing attention. We can stop being disappointed all the time when people let us down or when we don't get credit for things we have done. The greatest "achievement" that we can attain is when our lives become so transparent that when people see us they see only the glory of the Father shining through us and forget that we were there. If our motives are not aimed 100% at bringing glory to the Father, then we are drifting into creating an idol that is erected to ourselves. May it never be.

4. **It takes more than agreeing.** In 12:37-40 John tells us that some of the leaders of Israel actually believed Jesus. Yet, they did not follow Him because they lived in fear of the other leaders. After all, what would people think if they, the great teachers of the faith, admitted that Jesus had been right all along? They would be thrown out of the synagogue. Jesus said that a person who hears Him (the literal meaning of "hears" is "understands with comprehension") but does not do anything about it, will be judged by the Father in the end. Do you see what kept the leaders from the Kingdom? Fear. They were afraid of what they might lose if they followed Jesus – respect, power, privilege. But the truth of Jesus' Kingdom is that when you die you lose everything, that's the point. Then, once you lose everything, you no longer have anything to lose and have everything to gain.

Today's lesson can be summarized by one of my favorite quotes from Paul's first letter. In Galatians 2:20 he said, "I have been crucified with Christ and I no longer live, but Christ lives in me. The life I live in the body, I live by faith in the Son of God, who loved me and gave himself for me."

Again, in Colossians 3:1-5, 12 he said, "Since, then, you have been raised with Christ, set your hearts on things above, where Christ is seated at the right hand of God. Set your minds on things above, not on earthly things. For you died and your life is now hidden with Christ in god. When Christ who is your life, appears, then you also will appear with him in glory. Put to death, therefore, whatever belongs to your earthly nature... therefore, clothe yourselves with compassion, kindness, humility, gentleness and patience."

There are two questions for you today. These questions are for you, even if you have been a follower of Jesus for 50 years.

1. **What still needs to die in you?** What part of your sinful nature are you still clinging to as a "safety net" in case this Jesus thing doesn't really work out? What cherished sin is still nestled snuggly in the depths of your heart? Are you still looking for accolades and "atta boys" from people in order to fill up your self-worth tank? Are you still harboring bitterness or unforgiveness toward someone (this, by the way, is just another form of pride, since bitterness is the need to be proved "right" in whatever situation it is)?

2. **Are you willing to hang on the cross with Jesus?** It's one thing to say you want the beast out of your life, but it's another thing to nail it to the cross and watch it suffer and die. That's painful. Jesus endured excruciating pain in order to let go of everything. He calls us to do the same. Until you actually take the plunge and let go of it all, you will not be free to experience the Kingdom.

Beginning next sessions we will explore the "Passion of the Christ" and walk with Jesus to the cross. I invite you to spend the next two weeks opening up your heart to God to show you the parts of your life that need to walk, step by step, beside Jesus, to be exposed, humiliated, and executed. Then, and only then, will you be able to experience the freedom of the resurrection.

Kid's Questions

What is a seed? Where does a seed come from?

In order for a seed to fall from a flower, the flower must first die. When a flower dies it releases hundreds of seeds, and so produces many more flowers in its place.

Jesus said that he had to die in order to his Kingdom to Come. Why do you think that is?

Jesus said that if we want to follow him and enter his Kingdom, then we need to die to things like pride and envy. It is only when we become completely humble that we will be able to have the Kingdom of God live in us.

What are some things that might keep you from wanting to give up the things you have?

Jesus was not afraid to look stupid in front of the whole world. He was willing to be treated like a criminal in order for his Kingdom to Come. Do you think we would be willing to do that for Jesus? If we let him, Jesus will give us the courage to do whatever he asks us to do.

Introduction

There is nothing like a quiet, safe place after a long day of noise, traffic, and the bustling mobs of modern life. If you work in an area that is anywhere near civilization, then you know how comforting it can be to step into the sanctuary of your own bedroom or den, pull the curtains, and simply cocoon for a little while. That is what our study is like this session. For the past few weeks Jesus has been on a rampage, attacking the Jewish leaders and interacting with the wild mob. Now we get to take a break, climb up some back stairs to a nice room that is prepared for an intimate meal, let our hair down, and recline at the table with Jesus and the gang. In this upper room, we will get to reconnect to the positive, life-giving words of Jesus that we came to love at the beginning of His ministry. In this session we will recline at the dinner table and be nourished by Jesus' words of life.

The text for this session is not just a simple meal however. John 14-17 is a very important passage. If you were forced to condense Jesus' teaching into its bare bones form – to create "The Essential Jesus" – I believe you could do so by combining two passages: Matthew 5-7 and John 14-17. Matthew 5-7 is the famous "Sermon on the Mount" that is delivered in the early days of Jesus' ministry. That sermon is designed to explain the transition from the Old Covenant to the New Covenant and is targeted at Jewish listeners who desire to understand what the Kingdom of God is all about. It was a very public address, heard by thousands, and designed to give broad strokes of truth. In John 14-17, on the other hand, Jesus speaks within the boundaries of intimacy. While reclining at the table, sharing bread, wine, and the Passover meal, He explains to His dear friends what it will be like to live in the New Covenant after He is gone.

I need to warn you right now that this passage is, in

my opinion, one of the most important passages in the entire Bible, and I can get very excited about it. It will be everything I can do to not write hundreds of pages about it. For now, as we play the part of the fly on the wall and eavesdrop on this wonderfully intimate, theologically rich, and spiritually empowering conversation, I will restrain myself and try to point out only the major highlights and leave the rest for another day.

If you will observe the illustration, you will notice that there are four major sections.

First, Jesus washes the disciples' feet as a demonstration of true servant-leadership.

Second, there is a very physical act of sharing a meal. During the meal Jesus redefines the Passover Feast and Judas Iscariot sets the wheels of Jesus' demise in motion.

Third, in the big bubble above their heads, there is the abstract teaching that Jesus gives His disciples in which He explains the key to living in the New Kingdom.

Fourth, in the upper right corner, we get to listen in on an intimate conversation that Jesus has with His Father. In that prayer He prays for his 11 disciples, and He also prays for all the disciples that would come after them. That means He is praying for you!

In lesson 2 and 3 of the study we will be exploring Jesus' teaching. It will be helpful for us in the introduction to...well, introduce it.

As is the case in all good teaching, this was not a dry lecture that Jesus presented to the disciples; rather, it was a discussion that volleyed back and forth between them. Jesus made an opening statement which raised many questions. As each disciple raised a question, Jesus would respond.

In order for us to grasp the flow of the teaching let's lay out the outline of the conversation in its entirety. In the study this will be broken into three parts, so I want you to see the big picture up front.

Jesus: I'm leaving now, so love one another. Your love will be your witness.

Peter: Where are you going? Can I come?

Jesus: Not yet.

Peter: I'll go anywhere.

Jesus: Actually, Peter, you'll betray me before dawn.

Don't be upset, guys, I'm going to Dad's house to prepare your rooms. I'll be back for you later.

Thomas: How do we get there?

Jesus: I am the way.

Philip: Just show us the Father.

Jesus: I've been here all along. He's in Me and I'm in Him. Here's how it works. You see the Father through Me. I will send the Spirit to you to show you the truth about Me and the Father. Then you will really see.

Judas (not the traitor): Why don't you show yourself to the whole world, not just us?

Jesus: Be patient. If you love Me, you see the Father, it's that simple. When the Holy Spirit comes He'll help you to see the big picture. But first, I have to get on with this nasty business of dying. That's what love really looks like, by the way...doing exactly what the Father says. It's called obedience.

[At this point interpreters disagree on what happens. Notice in 14:31 he says, "Come now, let us leave." Some say they left and headed toward Gethsemane. On the way they passed by a vineyard. Seeing the grapevine, Jesus used the opportunity to illustrate His previous point. Others say they didn't leave quite yet, but Jesus just popped up the illustration. I like to think of them actually touching and seeing a vineyard as He is saying the next piece.]

Oh, guys, look at this. A grapevine. That's what it's all about. Obey My commands, remain in Me, then you will bear fruit and be in the Father's love.

Oh, yes, one more thing. The world will hate you for this. They might even kill you. But don't worry; the Holy Spirit will be with you to empower you to be My witnesses. In a little while it will all be made right.

Disciples: How long is "a little while?"

Jesus: "A little while" has many meanings. When I'm gone it will hurt, but one day you will fully know the Father and your grief will turn to joy. In that day you won't need Me because you will have direct access to the Father. In that day...you'll see.

Here's the clear truth about Me...I came from the Father, lived in the world with you, now I'm leaving the world and going back to the Father.

Disciples: Oh, now we get it!

Jesus: Finally, you believe in me. Prepare yourselves, because your journey through this world will be hard. But don't stress, I've overcome the world!

Lesson 1

- Matthew 26:17-30
- Mark 14:12-24
- Luke 22:7-38
- John 13:1-30

Study Questions

Why did Jesus wash His disciples' feet?

What meal were the disciples sharing with Jesus? What did this meal represent?

What explanation did Jesus give for the meaning behind the cup and the bread? How was this different from what it used to mean?

Why did Judas leave the meal?

Food for Thought

There are three very important events that happen in today's reading:

1. Jesus washes the disciples' feet.
2. Jesus shares the Passover meal with the disciples and redefines it.
3. Judas leaves to betray Jesus.

1. **Jesus washes the disciples' feet.** The message here is clear. One of the running themes in Jesus' teaching came in response to the selfishness and power-lust He found in the disciples. He was continually telling them that if they want to be great in the Kingdom they had to become servants. In this act of foot washing it's as if Jesus stopped and said, "No, really I mean it." Imagine what the disciples must have thought as they watched Jesus take off His clothes and wrap a simple towel around His waist. How uncomfortable they must have felt as they watched their Messiah crouch before them like a common slave and rub their grimy feet between His hands. "Unless you do this, you will have no part in my Kingdom. Do you get it now?"

2. **The Passover Meal.** Every spring these 13 Jewish boys had sat at the family dinner table with their own fathers and reconnected to that foundational story of Moses and the midnight escape from Egypt. Each year they would remember the little lamb that had been killed so that its blood could be smeared on the doorposts in order to keep the death angel away. Each year they would break the bread and raise the glass to symbolize God's provision for them. They would play and laugh as they were sent to find the hidden afikomen and get a treat, sing hymns, recite scripture, and share intimate times with kin.

This year it was different. This year they were not with their human father. Instead, they were sitting at the table with their spiritual mentor. When He raised that familiar glass of wine that represented the covenant of faithfulness that God had made with Abraham, He shocked them. He said, "Now this glass has a different meaning. Now it is My blood that you remember, not the blood of the little lamb. Now it is not Egypt from which you are escaping, but from a far greater darkness. My blood, spread on the doorposts of your heart will keep the angel of spiritual, eternal death from entering in. Drink it in. Now this bread has a new meaning. No longer is it the "quick bread" of haste that sustains you on your trek through the desert. Now it is the bread of life that is found in My body. It is found in both

My physical body which will be broken for you, but also in My spiritual body, of which you will be the parts. Participate in My body, the community that forms around me. If you do, you will have strength for the long journey ahead. Eat it!

Let's pause for a moment and make one very important observation about this text. Notice that nowhere does Jesus say, "OK, from now on, every time you meet, you have to break up crackers into little pieces, pour grape juice into shot glasses, get really somber, and say a profound thought." Jesus was not establishing a new temple ritual when He had this meal. He was simply breathing new life into an old tradition. If there was any ritual that we could extract from this text, to be absolutely true to the intent, it would be this, "When you celebrate the Passover, remember Me instead of the Exodus." That's it.

So, what am I saying? Am I attacking the centuries-old Christian sacrament called Eucharist by some and communion by others? Well...yes, I am. (Horrified shock ripples through the pews!) Hopefully, by this point in the study, after so many weeks of watching Jesus tear down empty ritualistic religion, it is clear that He would not turn around and create a new, external ritual in its place. On the contrary, at this evening meal, Jesus, the master teacher, was simply entering into the deep cultural moorings of His disciples and attaching an eternal truth to an already established symbol.

The point of His teaching was not to have millions of people place all of their spiritual energy into the physical act of eating a piece of bread and drinking a sip of grape juice. I can't imagine that He envisioned generations of His followers coming to blows over who could and who couldn't eat the bread or participate in the "holy sacrament." I'm sure He never envisioned the table fellowship to be a space where throngs of onlookers watched passively as one man ate bread and drank wine because He was the only one holy enough to do it. Jesus was way more simple than that.

I'm not saying that it's bad to have communion when the church gathers. It's great. Tradition and ritual are good and necessary as teaching tools. What I am saying is that we need to always remember the real point. Here's what I think Jesus was saying that night,

"Friends, you are all welcome at the Father's table. He wants you here. He wants you to be well fed and to feel like you are part of his family. The food He offers you is life itself;

eternal life. That food is what I can provide for you. When they kill Me I will be conquering death itself. If you love Me and obey My commands, then you will eat of My bread and drink of My blood and the life and love of God will flow through your innermost being and overflow in your thoughts and actions. You will truly be set free from slavery when you sit at this table."

So, what should communion look like in the church? I think the church is communion. We are His body. As we obey His command to love one another and authentically enter into each other's lives and speak the truth in love, carrying one another's burdens, then we are feasting at the Father's table. If it has to be concretized into some kind of tangible form, then I think communion should be a community meal served at a house church each Sunday. Each week the small, intimate house church gathers in the name of Jesus, through the unity of the bond of peace that comes through the power of the Spirit, breaks the bread of His word, drinks the cup of His spirit, shares in intercessory prayer, loves on each other, and then shares a good, hearty meal together. That's communion, if you ask me.

3. **Judas betrays him.** As Judas Iscariot sat and listened to Jesus' esoteric words about bread and blood and the spiritual Kingdom, his blood must have begun to boil. This was not what he had signed up for. Where was the power? Where was the mighty King that the people shouted for just a few days earlier? Who would overthrow the Romans? Jesus was such a disappointment. It had been three and a half years, and things didn't change. His message was becoming increasingly intolerable. The Pharisees were right all along. I must turn Him in and officially separate myself from Him before I get caught in the heat of the leader's condemnation.

"Here Judas. I know you don't grasp the significance of this piece of bread that I'm handing to you. To you it's just bread. To you I'm just a kind, but misdirected dreamer. I'm sorry you feel that way. I'm sorry you had to be the one to fulfill the prophecies. But, your heart is hard and your eyes have been blinded to the truth. Now, go quickly so we can get this over with."

As Judas walked out the door that night, he slipped back into the darkness of the comfortable and familiar patterns of his culture. Let's not be too quick to criticize

Judas. How many times have we caved under the pressure of Jesus' radical truth? How many times have we given in to the pressure of status quo and sold out our convictions for fear that we might be ostracized, misunderstood, or even persecuted? Every day we sit at the table with Jesus. Every day we have the choice to eat the bread or to walk out the door in search of our thirty pieces of silver. What choice will you make today?

Kid's Questions

List some of the reasons it is fun to have a family meal together.

Did you know that communion is supposed to be like a family meal? God is our Father and he invites all to sit at his table and eat his food and enjoy his love.

Do you know what his food is? It is Jesus body and Jesus' blood. How does that sound? Does that mean that we are supposed to be cannibals? No. When Jesus died on the cross he was showing us what real love looks like. Real love is when we are willing to lay down our lives for someone else because we care more about them than we do about ourselves. The way that we eat Jesus' body and drink his blood is not to pass bread and juice around on Sunday mornings. Eating Jesus food is the act of loving each other.

Every time Jesus' disciples (you and me) get together it is an opportunity to have "communion" because we have a chance to love each other.

What are some ways that we can show love to each other?

The next time your church has bread and juice for communion, ask yourself, "Am I really showing love to everybody, or am I just having a snack right now?"

Lesson 2

- John 13:31-38
- John 14

Study Questions

What was Jesus' new command? What was the purpose for this command?

What did Jesus predict that Peter would do?

Where was Jesus going and what was the way for the disciples to get there?

Who is the person who loves Jesus? In other words, what is the demonstration of love?

What will the Holy Spirit do for the disciples?

Why must Jesus hand Himself over to the prince of darkness?

Food for Thought

I warned you in the introduction that I was going to have to restrain myself. Leading you through this passage is like taking you to Disneyland, but only having an hour to do it. Where do I begin? What is the most important thing to pick out?

After wrestling with this, I have decided to drive past all the cool word studies and background stuff that would build my case and get right to the punch line. Wave "hello" as we pass them by.

I'd like to present my thoughts on this passage in the form of a dialogue. Remember, Jesus was not preaching a sermon; He was having a conversation with his friends over dinner. By recreating the dialogue, but putting it in my own words, you will see, hopefully, the application points for us today. Where necessary, I will interject some explanation in [brackets].

There is one definition that must be stated before we begin. We need to look at the word "glory." When you think of the term glory you probably have images of powerful lightning bolts and thunder claps, right? That makes sense since that is how God's glory is described when He appeared to Moses on Mt. Sinai. Without getting into all the word study behind this conclusion, I'd like to propose that the word "glory" is not about the magnificent light show of God. Rather, it is about the intimate relationship of God. When Moses encountered God on the mountain it was the people who saw the awesome thunderstorm and were terrified by it. Moses, on the other hand, went up into the storm and came into the presence of God. He spoke with Him. He had a relationship with Him that superceded the Law or the tabernacle. He was a friend with God.

The relationship that God had with Moses, (and Abraham, and Joshua, and David, and all the great men of the Old Testament) is what God does and has always desired to have with His people. It was why we were created. Adam and Eve were clothed with God's glory; they walked with Him in the garden. When they disobeyed Him they turned their backs on Him, hid in shame, and lost the glory, the relationship, the friendship, they had with God.

God's personal interaction with His people has always been His glory. But, when you think about it, to interact with the infinite God is a terrifying and mysterious experience. It is a transforming experience, much like what metal encounters when it is passed through the fire of a crucible. It changes it and purifies it. Most people don't like intense heat. Instead, they like to watch it from a distance, like we do when we burn some logs in the fireplace. That's how we have treated God's glory throughout history. We have rejected His actual presence, and replaced it with a manageable hearth fire that seems like God, but is safe and domesticated.

This pattern is very evident in the story of Solomon's Temple. When Solomon built the temple God placed His "glory" there, but warned Solomon, in the context of intimate relationship, remember, that if the people turned away, He would remove His presence from the Temple. Well, that's what they did, and that's what He did. The people placed a fire in the fireplace of the temple (ritualism and idolatry), watched it from a distance, and called it God. So, God removed His glory (intimate relationship) from the temple and allowed the people to worship the fire of their own creation. This condition persisted in Israel to the point where God destroyed the Temple at the hands of the Babylonians. Then He allowed them to rebuild the Temple and try it again. 400 years later the hearth fire was burning in the fireplace, but the glory of God was long absent.

For the past few weeks we have listened to Jesus explain how the Jews had turned away from the glory of God and exchanged it for the pseudo-glory of a shiny temple and external rituals. They thought that God's glory and the nation's glory was in their political power and adherence to the external rituals of animal sacrifice, ceremonial cleansing, and rigid adherence to the meticulous details of the Law. Jesus spent a great deal of energy trying to expose this shortsightedness to the people and reconnect them to the true glory of God.

Now, in this warm, safe, upper room, the arguing is over. Now, the demonstrations of His miraculous authority and power are over. Now, in the safety of a quiet room, with close friends, the glory of God can be revealed.

Jesus: I am demonstrating the glory of God in My relationship with the Father. I have to go and demonstrate extreme love, so I will be gone for a little bit, and you can't come with Me. For now, obey My command to love one another, because that will be the demonstration to the world that you are My disciples.

Peter: I want to come.

Jesus: Later.

Peter: I want to come now! I'd die for you.

Jesus: You don't even know what you are saying. You are still sitting at the fireplace. You aren't quite ready to come up on the mountain with Me,

into the fiery presence of God, but you will be. First, you must go through the painful humiliation of betraying Me, being completely destroyed, and then rebuilt in the truth of God's glory. You see, that's just it. You think you can follow Me in your own strength, but you can't. The only way that I can go to the Father is through death. The same is true for you. When you die to yourself and all your "abilities" and strength, then you can follow Me.

Look, guys, there is plenty of room in God's heart for an intimate relationship with all of you. It's like He's got a big house with lots of rooms. I'm going there to get things ready for you.

Thomas: But we don't know the way to get there.

Jesus: I am the way. I have demonstrated with My life, My teaching, and, soon, with My own death, that the only way that you can get to the glory of the Father is to die to all the trappings of life and self. You can do this, and you will do it. If you love Me, and obey Me, then you will be on the path of intimacy with God and will be interacting with the Father.

Philip: Why don't you just show us the Father?

Jesus: Don't you get it? I am showing you the Father. The Father is not some big statue or object that I can parade down the street. He's not a being that can live in a temple. The Father is so much more than that. My love and obedience to the Father IS the Father being demonstrated to you, right before your eyes. Unfortunately you still can't see it. It won't be easy to see, so I will send the Spirit to come alongside you and walk with you every step of the way as you, yourselves, enter into that mysterious place of God's glory.

Oh, the world will only see lightning and hear thunder, and they'll think you're crazy, but what does that matter if you are in a dynamic relationship with the Father? If you follow Me, interact with Me, obey My command to love each other, then you'll see the Father.

Judas: Why just show the Father to us? Why not to the whole world too?

185

Jesus: Did you not hear what I just said? OK, I know you can't understand this right now, so you just have to trust Me. When the Holy Spirit comes He'll help you understand what it means to be in the glory of the Father.

Cheer up. I know you're sad that I'm leaving, but if I didn't leave, you wouldn't meet the Spirit and none of this would ever make sense to you.

Right now I have to demonstrate love to you. I have to show you that love is radical obedience to the Father. I have to hand myself over to the enemy, empty Myself of Me, and die. When that happens, then you'll understand what I'm talking about.

Come on, let's do this thing.

In this dialogue Jesus is demonstrating to us that the ultimate goal of life is to be in intimate relationship with the Father. The only way that we can know that kind of love is through the path of radical obedience. Only when we die to the idea that we are in control of our own destinies, and give ourselves sacrificially for another, can we be reborn in the freedom that comes from absolute love. That is the Father's glory and when we love one another as Christ loves us, then the Father is glorified and the light of His glory shines to the world around us.

Kid's Questions

When is your family the happiest together, and you are proud to be part of it?

When is your family struggling and you wish you could be somewhere else?

A happy family is one where everyone really loves each other. It is when they spend time with each other playing and laughing. It is when they can be honest with each other and not get mad at each other. It's when there is genuine love. It is easy to feel proud of a family like that. That family has a certain Glory to it, doesn't it?

When a family is fighting and bickering all the time, it can get pretty hard to feel good about it. There is not a lot of glory in a family where no one trusts each other and everyone is always picking on each other.

Today Jesus taught us that God's glory is when his people love each other and when they love him. That's why Jesus said that his new command was to love one another. The best way that we can honor God and really make his family shine is by loving and forgiving each other all the time. If we do that, then the people who don't know God will notice that we are different and want to know how they can have the same kind of joy that we have.

Lesson 3

- John 15
- John 16:1-6

Study Questions

Who is the vine? Who are the branches?

What must the branch do in order to bear fruit?

What does this look like in real life? What did Jesus ask the disciples to do?

How will the world feel about fruit-bearing disciples? Why?

Food for Thought

Today we continue with part 2 of our three part conversation. When last we met our hero and His band of unmerry (they were sad, remember) men, they were leaving the upper room and heading out of the city.

Remember the simple message that He taught was this:

To experience the Father's glory/love, we must die through radical obedience to Him. When we do, then we will be free from self, glorify Him, and shine the light of His glory to the world around us.

Let's continue the dialogue.

[As they pass by a vineyard...]

Jesus: Check this out. See that vine? That is a perfect picture of what I'm talking about. What is the purpose of a vine? To produce grapes, right? Whose job is it to produce the fruit? Is it the branch's job, or the vine's job? It's the vine's job. The branch's responsibility is to stay tightly connected to the vine so that the nourishing sap can pass into it, through it, and produce luscious fruit. As soon as a vine thinks to itself, "I can produce my own fruit," and separates itself from the vine, then it dries up and stops bearing fruit. When the farmer finds a dried up branch, what does he do? He cuts it off and uses it for firewood.

Do you see the picture? I am the vine. You are the branches. The Father is the gardener. If you want to experience the things that I've been talking about – to produce fruit – then you need to follow the code of the branch; stay connected to the vine.

How do you stay connected to the vine? You obey my command.

What is my command? Love each other, like I love you.

Do you see what I mean? This isn't obedience like a slave obeys a master. You aren't My slaves, you are My friends. If you want to experience the glory of the Father, then you need to love Me, be filled with My love, and overflow that love to each other. That, by the way, is the fruit. When the Father's love is flowing through your branch and being evident as luscious fruit, then the whole world will see the Father and be drawn into His glory as well.

The bottom line is that it is all about Love. The Father loves Me, I love you, you love each other, and we all get intermingled in a dynamic, intimate, and selfless, love relationship.

Now, I have to make one thing clear. As wonderful as this sounds, the world hates it. The world loves the darkness of their own prison cell. No matter how much we talk about it or demonstrate it, they will not see it. They love their power and their pride, and they don't want to give it up.

You, along with the Holy Spirit, will be My witnesses of the Father's glory. You will bear this fruit and love others selflessly, but they will hate you for it. Just be ready. Your journey through this life will be difficult and the physical reality will be painful to be sure.

Fruit obsession

Here's the point for us. In our culture we are driven by success. We are a consumerist culture that is driven by the need to produce things and then consume them. We place value on a person or an organization if they are successful and productive. Unfortunately, this mentality has crept into the church and we have become obsessed with being fruitful. We read Paul's description of Spiritual fruit in Galatians 5 and think, "I want to be more loving, patient, and kind, so what can I do to be more like that." Then we work really hard to be loving, patient, and kind.

When we have that mentality we are essentially joining Peter and saying, "Lord, I will follow you anywhere. I can do anything You ask me to do." That is a noble attitude, but is inherently flawed. The truth is that we cannot do anything in our own strength. We are only branches. We cannot produce fruit on our own. Yet, we, as industrious American churches, spend a great deal of time and money on "doing" fruitlike things.

Here's something to think about. If all we do is do, then all it is is doodoo. If we try to manufacture fruit, it becomes wax fruit that is shiny on the outside, but hollow and dead on the inside.

The key to producing fruit is to die. The key is to stop trying to produce fruit and focus our energy on staying connected to the vine. Jesus said that we are to "remain" in Him. This word means to dwell, to abide, to be in community. We need to be in Christ. What we need to do is to be. I call this the do-be principle. When we die to ourselves, admit that we are unable to produce anything good on our own, soak in the Word of Truth, and allow the Holy Spirit to flow through us, then we will be in the Father's love, shine His glory, bear His fruit, and the world will taste and see that the Lord is good.

No more doodoo. Let's do-be. First we die, then we fill, and then we spill over God's glory.

Kid's Questions

What is your favorite kind of fruit? Draw a picture of the plant on which that fruit grows. Maybe it's a tree, or a bush, or a vine.

What would happen if a branch was cut off from the main part of the plant?

Would the whole plant die?

Would the branch continue to produce fruit? Why?

Jesus said that he is like a vine and we are the branches. Our job is to produce the fruit of God's love in our lives every day. He said the only way we can produce the fruit is if we focus on staying connected to him. We stay connected to him by reading the Bible, praying, and being in a good church community.

Look at the picture for this session. See how the Holy Spirit is like the water in the soil. When our branch is connected to Jesus, then the Spirit can be free to flow through us.

Read Galatians 5:22-25 and see if the Spirit is producing that kind of fruit in your life. If there are some areas that need work, ask Jesus to help you to be better connected to Him today.

Lesson 4

- John 16:7-33

Study Questions

What will the Counselor do when He comes into the world?

What was going to happen "in a little while?"

How did Jesus define "in a little while"?

What will it be like for the disciples in "that day?"

What will it be like in the world for the disciples after Jesus leaves? What promise did He make to them?

Food for Thought

Let's continue with part 3 of this 3-part conversation. Last time Jesus ended on a downer as He prepared the disciples that a life of "remaining" and bearing God's glory-fruit would be difficult because it will be rejected and despised by the world.

Jesus: I know it seems like a bum deal that I'm leaving, but you have to trust Me when I tell you that it's for your own good. When I leave I will be able to send to you the Holy Spirit. He's the kind of guy who will come up alongside you when you are limping and carry you on His shoulder.

Here's what He is going to do through you. He is going to shine the light of truth into the dark world and expose [the true meaning of the word "convict"] the truth of the situation. It's kind of like a dark basement that is full of bugs. When the light is shined into that dank place, things happen.

First, He is going to expose the simple fact that the world has been shrouded in the darkness of rejecting the love/glory of the Father [sin]. They've been wallowing in the dank prison cell of self love and the deception of believing that they can experience life apart from the Father.

Now, there are two kinds of bugs in a dark basement. There are moths and there are cockroaches. One is attracted to the light; the other is repelled by the light.

The second thing the Spirit is going to do is expose righteousness by attracting the moths to the light. I am the first moth and I will be leading the way out of the darkness and into the light of the Father's love.

The third thing He is going to do is expose the cockroaches and send them scurrying into the darker cracks and corners of their self-made hell [judgment]. The first among them, the prince of cockroaches, is the great accuser himself who will stay eternally entrenched in his rebellion against the Father's glory.

In order for Me to lead the moths out of the darkness, I have to plunge into the darkness Myself. I'll be there for a little while and you won't see Me. It will seem very dark at that point. But, don't worry, I'll emerge and the Spirit will shine the light and the great moth exodus will commence.

Disciples: When You say "a little while" what do You mean exactly?

Jesus: That's a great question. Unfortunately the answer to that question is not as clear cut as you probably would like it to be.

First of all, let's be honest. During the transition period, it will be painful. It will be like when a woman is in labor. During the pain she's thinking, "Why in the world did I ever want to have a baby? This is the worst thing I've ever experienced." Then, when that miracle of life lies on her belly and begins to suckle and draw life from her, the endorphins kick in and her spirit is flooded with love that washes away the negativity associated with pain. That's what this whole process of the Kingdom of God is like.

Now here's the tricky part. There are really two "little whiles" going on here. The first one will be really, really dark and you will be very afraid. That is when I'll be dead. The world and Satan will think they have won and you will feel alone. That will last for a very little while, then I'll rise and your joy will be restored.

The second "little while" is more complex. You see, I will be returning to the Father and will be sending you the Spirit. During that time it will be your job to be the conduit through which the Spirit can shine the light of the Father's glory into the dark basement. During that time you will be in flux. On the one hand you will be already in the Father's glory and the baby is there. On the other hand you will be living on the stairs of the dark basement and will still be in the pains of childbirth. You will know both joy and pain. This transition time has to happen so that all the moths can fly out of the basement. Eventually, you will be able to step completely out of the basement, we will shut the door, leave the cockroaches in there, and be fully in the light of the Father's glory, living and loving in the joy of his house.

Disciples: OK, now we get it.

Jesus: Finally, I think we are beginning to communicate. You have a tough job ahead of you. I won't be physically with you to walk the path. But you will have the Spirit. He will be your peace as you battle against the darkness. Don't worry though, always remember that I have won the battle. You are simply conduits of light to let the moths come home.

That's where we live. The church is called to be an open conduit of the Father's glory, allowing the Spirit to shine the light of truth into the dark basement. We are like a lens that magnifies the light and spreads it out. Our job is not to shine the light, but to keep the lens clean and pointed toward the light.

Here is one problem that I see happening in churches today. In our zeal for evangelism we have slipped into the idea that it is our job to shine the light and that we are called to transform cockroaches into moths. Well, the only way that you can keep a cockroach out in the open is to dim the light. In many circles we have compromised the truth of Jesus and the Father's glory to the point that we have dimmed the light very low, allowing the darkness to creep up the stairs, and have invited the cockroaches to come in. The parable of the wedding feast comes to mind. When the guest was found at the banquet with no wedding clothes on, he was cast out. You see, a cockroach is a cockroach and will always be repelled by the full light of God's glory. As the church, it is our job to simply be a conduit of the light of God's glory, allowing His magnificent, mysterious, love to shine into the whole basement, letting God decide who is the moth and who is the cockroach. We must never be ashamed of the name of Jesus, or afraid to proclaim the truth, no matter the cost. May we always be a clear lens, correctly focused, transmitting the light to the world.

Kid's Questions

Once I took my kids on a long hike. We went on a six-mile trail up in the mountains. About half way through it we got really tired. It was hard work.

What would have happened if we had given up and just sat down? Would we have made it to the end and been able to get back to camp for dinner? No. We would have not gone anywhere. We would have just withered up and died.

Even though it was really hard work, we knew we had to keep pressing on because we believed that there was an end to the trail.

Today Jesus told his disciples that it would not be easy to be his followers in the world. In fact the world would hate them for loving Jesus. He told them to not give up, because one day they would make it to the end and be able to have dinner with the Father.

If you sometimes get tired of being the "good kid" don't give up. It will be worth it in the end.

Lesson 5

- John 17
- Matthew 26:31-35
- Mark 14:27-31

Study Questions

How did Jesus define eternal life?

Make a list of the requests that Jesus made to the Father for the disciples. What did he ask the Father to do?

Food for Thought

Today we are privy to listen in on Jesus' prayer. There are two parts to His prayer. First He prays for Himself. Then He prays for His disciples that He will be leaving behind, both the present ones and the ones to come after them (you and me).

In vv. 1-8 notice that Jesus recaps His entire teaching from the last three chapters. He asks to be glorified because He has obeyed the Father and has brought eternal life to the disciples. Notice, here, a very important verse. Jesus defines eternal life. Eternal life is "that they may know You." Do you see it? Glory, Heaven, the afterlife, it is not about pie in the sky in the great by-and-by. It is not a place somewhere, out there in the universe where we will sit around a gigantic throne with white robes and harps, singing in an eternal choir. Eternal Life is to know the Father and to know the Son. We know them through the power of the Holy Spirit.

Let's take a brief theological moment. God is an eternal loving community. The Glory of God is the dynamic, eternal, loving relationship that the Father, Son, and Holy Spirit share. Humans were created to participate in this relationship, to be clothed with glory, in Eternal Life. That is what the Garden of Eden represents. After the rejection of God's relationship, and the loss of glory, we have been cut off from life and have existed in the darkness of death, not knowing the Father. Through Jesus' life, death, resurrection, and glorification (being united with the Father) we, too, can enter into eternal life and be glorified (united with the Father).

Like we talked about previously, the process of bringing all the moths out of the darkness will take a little while. So far it has taken over 2,000 years. Who knows how much longer Jesus will wait. But, God is so loving that He will wait as long as it takes until every moth comes home.

Jesus knew it would be difficult for His disciples as they stood on the basement stairs, with one foot in the Father's glory and one foot in the darkness, so He prayed for us.

Jesus prayed four things for us.

1. **Protect them.** As we stand on the stairs we will be hated and despised by our enemy, the Prince of Darkness. He will creep through the cracks, under the line of light, crawl up our pant leg, into our ear, and whisper lies to us. He will try to steal our glory like he did to Adam and Eve. This will be a battle. It will be a battle for our hearts that begins in our mind. He will tell us lies like, "God doesn't really love you. He's making you do all the

work and He gets all the glory. What's up with that? You aren't really a light bearer, look at all the darkness in your heart. If people really knew about your junk they would throw you out. You should just go hide in the corner before you are exposed." He will push every button and exploit every weakness he can find in us.

The key to our protection in this battle is the name of Jesus. In other words, we have been adopted by God as sons and have His name. We have been given full rights as children of God and nothing that the Accuser says will change that. To be strong we need to claim the truth that we are the Sons and Daughters of the Living God, set free from darkness, and living in the light of the Father's glory.

2. **Sanctify them.** The Greek word being translated here is a form of "hagia" which is also translated as "holy." To be sanctified is to be in the process of being made holy, to be set apart for the purpose of God's glory. We are made holy by the truth. The more we are saturated with the truth, the more we will be transformed into the likeness of our Father; just like a child who grows up to become the spitting image of his Dad.

3. **Unify them.** Here we see the real power in the Father's glory. Our love for one another is the glory of the Lord that shines to the world. The only Jesus that the world sees is the love that we, His body, have for one another. How unified are we? What kind of Jesus does the world see? Are we experiencing selfless love for one another, brothers and sisters standing arm in arm as soldiers braced against the darkness? Or, do they see us divided against each other, being dissected by petty arguments and power-struggles? If we are going to shine the light of the Father's glory then we need to lay down our egos and unite in the name of Jesus and spread the love of the Father to everyone, everywhere, all the time.

4. **Fill them.** In His very last line, Jesus summarizes everything. Jesus has made the Father known to us in order that the love the Father has for the Son may be in us and He Himself may be in us. It goes back to the illustration of the vine and the branches. The only way that we are going to be able to fulfill this mission that Jesus has set before us is to be filled with Him continually. We must remain in Him, meditate on His word, soak in the water of His Spirit, and yield our lives to His control, so that He can shine the light of the Father's glory through us.

People of God, we stand on the stairs today, half in the light, half in the dark. The battle rages around us. Jesus calls us to stand strong as we hold the lens up to the light and shine it wherever we can. On our own we will be engulfed in the darkness, but, in the power of the Holy Spirit, we can shine the light of love to the world.

Kid's Questions

Did you know that Jesus prayed for you? In today's reading he was talking to the Father and he said, "My prayer is not for them [his disciples] alone. I pray also for those who will believe in me through their message." That means you. If you love Jesus, then everything he prayed for today was meant for you.

Read through the study for the grown ups. It's for you to. You can feel confident that Jesus loves you and wants the very best for you.

Introduction

Darkness. That pretty much sums up the study for this session. As John told us in the opening paragraph of his story, "the light had come into the world, but the darkness has not understood it." Instead of basking in the life-giving warmth of its rays, the darkness bucked against the light and tried to defeat it.

If you are a science fiction fan, then you will understand when I say that this session's reading is like the second episode in almost every trilogy. In part 1, the good guys rise up and fight against the evil empire and experience great progress and show promise. In part 2 the evil empire strikes back and delivers a crushing blow to the rebels. At the end of this heart wrenching episode it seems that all is lost, the hero has been defeated, and that evil will dominate forever.

That is just where our story ends this session. It seems that Jesus is defeated. First, He is betrayed in His place of peace and prayer by Judas. Then He is brought to trial before the Sanhedrin (you know, the guys He's been tongue-lashing for several weeks now) and found guilty of blasphemy. Next, in an effort to have Him killed, He is dragged before the Roman Governor, Pontus Pilate, and is accused of insurrection against Caesar. Pilate has Him flogged, and, reluctantly, handed over to be treated like the worst of all criminals and to be cruelly crucified. The session ends with the light of the world being snuffed out and stuffed into the dark cave of a newly cut tomb. The disciples are left alone and afraid, unsure of what to do.

Fortunately for them, and for the world, this is only session 14 out of 15. There is still one more session to go. There is still a "part 3" to the trilogy where we get to see a great reversal. But, that is next time. For now we must stew in the darkness, grit our teeth, and observe the ultimate display of man's inhumanity to man. It is this depravity that has kept us shackled in our own darkness, and it was for this that Jesus allowed Himself to be swallowed up into it. He came to set us free from it.

As we study this session we will try to strike a balance between just glaring into the ugly face of brutality and noticing the glimmers of hope that can be found even in this dark hour. If you will observe the illustration, there is one major glimmer of hope that is apparent. Notice what is coming from the base of the cross. When Jesus died, a very physical event took place that had deep spiritual impact. An earthquake shook the city and tore the curtain in the temple in half, moving from top to bottom. Because of His death, the old order was overturned and now, once and for all, the passage to the presence of the Father (to His glory) was flown wide open. Because of Jesus, all may enter. No longer was access to the Father limited to one man, once a year. Now, followers of Jesus, those who remain in Him (John 15) can come to the Father and speak to Him, bringing their praises and petitions.

So, as you move through these pages, watch your step as we travel because the passage is dark. I'll try to hold a torch for you, but you will have to bump and feel your way through it. Don't worry, though, there is a light at the end of the hall and we will be there soon.

Lesson 1

- Matthew 26:36-75
- Matthew 27:1-10
- Mark 14:32-72
- Luke 22:39-71
- John 18:1-27

Study Questions

What request did Jesus make of the Father? What was His conclusion?

How did the disciples disappoint Jesus in the garden?

What accusation was brought against Jesus when He stood before the council? What was the verdict of that trial?

How did Peter respond when he realized the sin of his actions?

How did Judas respond when he realized the sin of his actions?

Food for Thought

There are five major events that happen today:

1. The disciples sleep while Jesus prays.
2. Jesus is betrayed by Judas and arrested in the garden.
3. Jesus is tried by the Sanhedrin and found guilty of blasphemy.
4. Peter disowns Jesus.
5. Judas hangs himself.

As much as it would be nice to do, there just isn't enough time or space in this study to comment on all of these wonderfully rich events. We could talk about the complacency of the disciples and how they fell asleep in Jesus' most intense moment of prayer. We could talk about Jesus' power that was manifest when the soldiers tried to arrest Him. During that same scene we could point out the issues raised regarding the use of violence in the Kingdom of God. And of course, we could discuss the kangaroo court that was set up by Jesus' accusers and how deception was the tone of the event. All of these things were done under the veil of darkness. All of them are treasure chests of truth-nuggets. Yet, we will discuss none of them.

Today, I'd like to hone in on number four and five of the list above. Here we have two "sinners" that take two very different paths. Peter and Judas both turned their backs on Jesus. Judas feared that Jesus' agenda was skewed, so he sold Him out for 30 pieces of silver. Peter was overcome by the fear that, if discovered, he would suffer the same fate that Jesus was enduring. Fear and the distortion of truth led both men to do the worst thing possible; they severed their relationship with Jesus. The branch broke free from the vine.

These stories are very familiar to us. Usually when they are told, Peter is always the good guy and Judas is always the bad guy. We feel sorry for Peter when he gives way to his fear and doubt, but we hiss at Judas when he does the same. Yet, were they really that different? For one brief moment Peter and Judas were actually standing at the same spot. They both had entered a path of rejecting Jesus. They had committed a pretty heavy sin. And, they both had been convicted of their sin. Do you see this point? Both had come to the realization that they were wrong. That is what conviction is; the exposure of guilt. The judge stands up and declares, "Guilty as charged," and the gavel slams down.

Having both come to the same realization, they both stood at the same spot. They stood at a

197

crossroads of decision. They had to choose what to do with their conviction. What would they do with their realization that they were guilty?

Let's bring this home for a moment. Every day each one of us comes to this place in our lives. As much as we hate to admit it, we sin in one way or another all the time. When we sin, we turn our face away from the light of Jesus and look into the cold darkness where the enemy lives. Yet, as we learned last session, the role of the Holy Spirit, out of deep love for us, is to shine the light of truth into the darkness that we have allowed into our heart. He loved Peter AND Judas so much that He exposed the sin in their heart. The question for them was, and the question for us is...what will we do with that exposure?

Peter and Judas demonstrate the two options that lie before us. Peter chose one path, and Judas chose the other. When Peter realized his sin, what did he do? He wept bitterly. He became contrite. Wow, there's a great word...contrite. It means to become humbled. Now, it doesn't actually say that he became contrite, but we can deduce from the fact that he wept bitterly, that he stuck around, that he was later reinstated, and ultimately became a dynamic leader in the church, that he chose the right path. He admitted that he was wrong, turned away from it, and allowed Jesus to bring him back into a right relationship with Him.

Judas, on the other hand, took a different path. When he was faced with the reality of his sin, he became overwhelmed with remorse and shame, ran outside the city, and hung himself to death. The truth of his sin was so shameful to him that he could no longer bear to live in his own skin. So, Satan won the victory in his life.

There you see the two paths that stretch out beyond the crossroads of conviction. Conviction can either bring about self-contrition or self-destruction. Here is the point I'd like to make for you today. The first path is the one that the Holy Spirit is calling you to follow; the second path is the one the enemy would like you to take. The first path says, "Yes, I was wrong and I admit it, but I want to move past this and be reconciled to God." The second path says, "Shame on you, you are a bad person. How could you ever live with yourself after doing such a terrible thing? Run away. God never wants to see your dirty face again. In fact, why don't you just curl up and die right now."

Do you remember what Jesus said when He was talking with Nicodemus? He said that He did not come into the world to condemn the world, but to save the world. He also said that He came to bring life and to bring it to the fullest. Just

last session He said that eternal life is defined as a right relationship with the Father. Jesus is calling you to own up to the truth and receive His grace. Here's the thing. This is not just a one-time offer that only counts the first time when we pray the "sinner's prayer" and receive our fire insurance policy from God. God's mercy is new every morning, and He offers the path to life with Him, basking in the light of truth, every day.

Many times Christians who have slipped up and fallen into sin forget this and they begin to go down the second path. They listen to the whispers that say, "I thought you were a Christian. How could you do something like that? You had better isolate yourself from your Christian friends and hide from God. Throw yourself into you work; medicate your pain with the indulgence of your choice. You might as well, since you are used goods at this point anyway."

If you have found yourself going down this path, I ask you to stop. Stop and listen to the truth. Yes, you sinned. Was it right? Not at all. Should you have done it? No. Was God pleased? Nope. Alright, now that we have that clear, let's continue the truth train. Does God want to throw you away because of it? No way. He wants you to take the path of Peter and become humbled in His presence. He wants you to become humbled to the point that you can receive His gracious gift of love, forgiveness, and restoration. So, please, fallen Christian, don't go the path of Judas. Step into the light of truth and allow God to refill you with joy once again.

Kid's Questions

How do you feel when your parents point out when you are doing something wrong and correct you? How do you react when that happens? Why?

In the story today two men both did something very wrong. Peter and Judas both betrayed Jesus. When God exposed that sin two them, one man responded correctly which led him to a peaceful and loving reunion with Jesus, and the other man responded incorrectly which ended up in his death.

Here's the lesson for you. When your parents correct you, it may seem like they are being mean, and you may feel very embarrassed by it. That's understandable. Nobody likes being told that they did something wrong. Yet, how you handle that correction will make a huge difference in your life. If you get all mad, or if you get to feeling bad about yourself, then you will end up getting sick in your soul. You don't want that. You need to remember that your parents love you, and the only reason that they correct you is to help you learn how to live in a way that will bring you joy and wisdom in your life.

Peter wept bitterly, and then he made things right with Jesus. After that he did great things for God. The next time you are corrected, don't beat yourself up like Judas did, instead remember Peter and simply make things right and move on. It's that easy.

Lesson 2

- Matthew 27:11-26
- Mark 15:1-15
- Luke 23:1-23
- John 18:28-40

Study Questions

According to Pilate, what was the motivation for the Jews to hand Jesus over to him?

What did Pilate offer to the crowd? Why?

What was Pilate's response to the crowds demand to crucify Jesus? Why?

What explanation did Jesus give to Pilate for His lack of resistance?

Food for Thought

There are two places that are ideal breeding ground for Sin to multiply like a swarm of cockroaches. It grows in the dark isolation of a hidden heart, and in the unruly chaos of a wild mob. In today's reading we can see evidence of both at work. First we will look at the mob that cried out, "Crucify Him!" Then we will look at the heart of Pilate.

Ask any police officer and they will tell you that the scariest thing to deal with is a crowd. Anything can happen when a crowd gathers. Mix in a few drinks and you have imminent chaos on your hands. In this passage we see a crowd that had gathered outside the governor's place. There is an interesting thing about a crowd; it can turn at the drop of a hat. Just a few days earlier this same crowd was crowding around the east gate shouting "Hosanna!" and now they are shouting "Crucify Him!" How does a transformation like that take place so quickly? First of all, the crowd really doesn't know what they believe or what they want. They are like the waves of the sea and will be blown in whatever direction is blowing the strongest at the moment. When Jesus rode into town His followers had the platform, so the crowd joined in the chorus. Now, the Sanhedrin was the prevailing wind, and they were blowing the winds of hatred, fear, and sin.

It would do us well to analyze the different aspects of the sin that drove the leaders to transform this crowd into a bloodthirsty mob. Follow me as I detect a progression of sin. By studying this we may be able to detect patterns in our own lives, and, in so exposing the patterns, be able to better avoid them.

1. **Envy**. It was Pilate who really pinpointed the root of all this trouble. The leaders were envious of Jesus. If you do a study through the New Testament you will discover that in all of the lists of sins, envy is always at the top. It is one of those sins that we call a "root" sin. It is out of envy that many other sins are motivated. So, what is envy? Envy is a feeling of discontent in what you have and resentment towards someone else for having what you want to have for yourself. It goes a little further. Envy, in its rawest form, desires for the other person to not have it. When a new person shows up and starts getting the attention that we think we deserve, we can begin to envy that person, and secretly wish that they were no longer present. Given space, the root of envy could grow to become the fruit of crime in which we seek to remove that person; either through slander, back-room manipulation, or ultimately, murder.

Pilate, standing outside of the social system of Jerusalemite Jews, was able to see clearly what was really going on. He could see that the Jewish leaders were simply envious of the attention that Jesus was getting. After all, they were the ones who were born into the right families, carried the correct credentials and titles, and followed all the rules. Who was this Galilean nobody, and what right did He have to come in and start accusing them of being in the dark? Their envy blinded them to the powerful evidence of His authenticity that He demonstrated through the miracles. Their envy did not allow them to accept the overwhelming response that He received from the masses. Their envy, which is ultimately rooted in pride and the need for control, led them to seek His destruction.

Ask yourself a question. Is there anyone in your life that stirs up envy in your heart? Does someone have a new house that you wish you had? Is someone better at your job and receiving a promotion over you? Does your competition seem to be more successful in your industry? If so, how does it make you feel? What thoughts do you have about that person or that group of people?

Listen to this right now. If you have even a single seed of envy in your heart, and if you do not do anything about that envy, it will begin to grow. When it grows it will start sending roots into other areas of your life and before long will control you. It will, like all sin roots, eventually choke out your joy and send you spiraling into a downward cycle of self-destruction which will eventually suck others into its destructive vortex.

2. **Envy in the hearts of the powerful few created a tidal wave of mob rule.** Once the envy had taken over the hearts and minds of the leaders, it overflowed in their actions, leading them to take advantage of their positions of leadership and influence and incite the crowd to defy logic and demand an innocent man's blood. Pilate set before them a choice which, at face value, was a no-brainer. He offered to release back into the general population either a) a man who was notorious for being a trouble-maker and a murderer, or b) a man who had done nothing but heal the sick, feed the hungry, and instill hope into the hearts of the neglected masses. Yet, persuaded by the envy-corrupted hearts of those who wielded power over them, the crowd locked logic in the prison cell of sin, and got caught up in the swell of bloodthirsty vengeance and chose to release a killer and kill a healer.

There is a lesson in this both for the leader and for the follower. As a leader you must always remember the extreme responsibility you have with your position. If you are in a place of authority, a large percentage of people will follow, regardless of the logic or moral stance of your position. A leader will be held responsible for the misdeeds of the mobs that they led into sinful acts. Before you incite the masses, think carefully about the motivation behind the command that you give. Is it coming from God, or is it driven from some inner need or personal agenda that is overshadowing the truth?

As for the follower, be careful to remember that your leaders are flawed people like yourself. Never blindly follow a leader. Always use discernment. Know the truth and know the leader. Make sure that the leader is in line with God's word and is following God's leading before you raise the battle cry.

3. **The fear of a mob and the pressure to pursue political self-preservation will lead a man to deny his convictions and "sell out" in exchange for temporary peace.** Pilate was warned both by the premonition of his wife and by his own moral conscience, that it was wrong to execute Jesus. By all accounts of the Law Jesus was an innocent man. Yet, Pilate did not want trouble in Jerusalem. He was on thin ice with the Emperor as it was, and, if there was another riot in Jerusalem, it would be the end of his political career. So, the life of one innocent and insignificant man was a small price to pay in light of the political peace of the Empire and the preservation of his own reign in the province.

How many times do we get tempted to fall into this kind of ends-justifies-the-means mentality? Oh, it's OK to lie to the staff in order to preserve the "integrity" and "unity" of the leadership. It's OK to cater to certain people and ignore their sin because the community really needs their generous contributions. It's OK to allow a few "insignificant" people to be mistreated and brushed off if it will make it more pleasant for hundreds of others to come and hear the gospel message.

4. **Sin does not only affect us, but is passed down to our descendents.** Notice what the crowd said when Pilate resisted giving in to their demands. They said, "Let His blood be on us and on our children!" When they said this they did not realize how close they were to the truth. They were referring

to several principles that were taught in the Law of Moses. A running theme throughout the Law of Moses has to do with the effects of one generation's behavior on the lives of the subsequent generations. The whole idea can be summarized in the following passage.

Exodus 34:4-7 (NIV)

[4] So Moses chiseled out two stone tablets like the first ones and went up Mount Sinai early in the morning, as the LORD had commanded him; and he carried the two stone tablets in his hands. [5] Then the LORD came down in the cloud and stood there with him and proclaimed his name, the LORD. [6] And he passed in front of Moses, proclaiming, "The LORD, the LORD, the compassionate and gracious God, slow to anger, abounding in love and faithfulness, [7] maintaining love to thousands, and forgiving wickedness, rebellion and sin. Yet he does not leave the guilty unpunished; he punishes the children and their children for the sin of the fathers to the third and fourth generation."

The crowd, through the persuasion of the leaders, believed that they were innocent of sin and were actually demonstrating love to God by condemning Jesus to death. Little did they know that their blindness was opening the door to great evil in their lives that would eventually, in the next generation, bring the destruction of their city.

Here's the point for us. In our culture we have been duped into thinking that we live in the bubble wrapping of individuality and that what we do with our lives in the secrecy of our own heart has no effect on anyone else. So, if we want to open our heart to secret sin, as long as no one gets hurt, then go ahead. Men, if you want to maintain an addiction to pornography, then culture says, "You have the right to do it." Women, if you want to harbor bitterness or engage in "innocent gossip" among friends, then it's your business. Well, the Bible teaches us that it is not. What we do in the secrecy of our inner life will eventually bubble up and overflow into the lives of our children and all those around us. The evil that we cherish and harbor in our hearts will be passed on to our children without them even knowing it. It, being more veiled, will be allowed to fester and grow into something far worse and distorted in them. Within a few generations the sin can become so great and so pervasive that an entire generation of people can be swept away from the path of God and call it "good."

Throughout this whole study we have been looking at the effects of sin. It is an ugly subject, but one that needs to be studied. Sin, left unchecked, can and will completely destroy the person and the culture.

So far we have looked at the effect that sin can have on the mob. Now, let's briefly look at what sin can do to the individual soul. In so doing we will also, incidentally, discover the antidote to this problem.

Notice the interchange that Pilate and Jesus share. In John 18:37 Jesus said to Pilate, "everyone on the side of truth listens to me." Pilate's response seems to come straight from the mouth of a good postmodernist. He replies, "What is truth?" Sounds familiar, doesn't it? That is the mantra today. The mainstream and the dominant thinkers of our culture no longer believe that there is such a thing as truth. They listen only to the voice of the mob. Whatever will bring the greatest level of peace and national unity is "truth." If it's true for you, then it's true; that is the mentality.

In this dialogue Jesus did not answer Pilate's question with words. Yet, as I hope we have seen through this study, Jesus answered it with His life. I believe that Jesus' answer to the question "What is truth?" was this – "you are asking the wrong question. The question is not WHAT is truth, but, rather, WHO is truth." Truth is not a proposition about God, because there is no amount of human language that can adequately encompass the infinite complexities of the eternal creator of the universe. The truth is the person of Jesus Christ. When we come to truth we do not come to a correct statement of faith, we come to an authentic step of faith into a relationship with a very mysterious, yet real person.

The effect that sin had on this individual named Pilate was that he was blind to the answer to his own question when it was standing right in front of him. That is how most of us live. We are so dialed into the thinking patterns of our current cultural value system, and focused on the material circumstances that surround us, that we cannot see the person of Jesus when He stands right in front of us, demonstrating the glory and the love of the Father, inviting us to enter into a relationship with Him.

Today, as you go about your business, ask God to reveal in you any roots of sin that may be present that you are secretly harboring and incubating. If you don't let Jesus flush them out with His truth, you will not only be hurting yourself, you will be passing it on to the next generation.

Kid's Questions

Get a dictionary and look up the word envy. What does it mean?

In our story today it said that the Jews were envious of Jesus. Why do you think they were?

What did their envy lead them to do to Jesus?

Have you ever been envious of someone? Why?

What could you do to help stamp out envy in your heart, before it takes you over?

Lesson 3

- Matthew 27:27-44
- Mark 15:16-32
- Luke 22:63-65; 23:24-43
- John 19:1-27

Study Questions

How did the soldiers treat Jesus?

What warning did Jesus give to the women who were weeping for Him?

What attitude did Jesus have toward His killers? Why?

What promise did Jesus make to the thief? Why?

Food for Thought

Today and tomorrow we encounter the darkest moment in the story. Here we stand, at the base of a rocky hill, looking up at a grisly scene. We cringe as we hear the clang of the hammer and the sickening creak of the nail as it passes through flesh and bone and wedges into the wood beneath it. Our hearts sink into our stomachs as we watch the cross get lifted up above it's hole, and then, THUD, get dropped harshly into the ground, sending His body lurching forward and straining against the spikes in his wrists. Now His body is in full view; naked, bruised, ripped to shreds, muscle and bone exposed, swollen beyond recognition. As we watch, an eerie darkness falls across the sky. The sun seems to go to sleep and nighttime replaces midday. It is cold, and all hope seems to be fleeting away with each strained breath that He eeks into His battered chest.

After 2,000 years it is very difficult for us to truly crawl into that place. The recent craze over Mel Gibson's movie The Passion of the Christ, has allowed us a small glimpse into the horrific events of that day. Yet, it was still latex skin and the magic of Hollywood. How would we have really felt in that moment of darkness? The man that we had spent over three years with, the man that had taught us a new way of love and equality, the man that spoke so boldly about his Kingdom, was now hanging in absolute disgrace, dying the death of the lowest of criminals. How could this be happening? Where was God? What is truth? What will happen to me? What do I do now?

In the middle of this darkness there is a shining jewel. Look at Luke's account of the story. Luke records two statements that Jesus made while hanging on the cross. In these statements the entire message of His Kingdom was spoken.

1. "Father, forgive them, for they do not know what they are doing." Can you imagine that? As He looked up at the bulky body of the Roman guard that was brutally pounding that nail into His flesh, He asks the Father to forgive him. That is love. Could we do that?

2. "Today you will be with Me in paradise." One of the thieves that was crucified with Jesus was "converted" right there in the final moments of his life. The thief confessed that he believed that Jesus was the King and asked Jesus to be in a relationship with him. He said, "Remember me when you come into your Kingdom." What was Jesus' response? Did He say, "Yeah, right, buddy. Nice try, but I think you're a little too late." Or, did He say, "Ooooh, I'd really like to accommodate you, but I'm afraid you haven't been baptized. If

we had a baptismal here, and if you had the time to go through our six-week new believer study, then I could make sure your doctrine was all correct, and, if it was, then I could let you in." No, He didn't. Hmmm. He simply said, "I tell you the truth, today you will be with Me in paradise." The thief was the first real example of the parable regarding the workmen that were hired at different hours in the day. All of us "good" people that have gone to church every Sunday of our lives, have passed all the Bible drills in Sunday school, who have the correct answer to every theological question thrown at us, we all stand up and say, "Hey, that's not fair! How can Jesus let that guy into the Kingdom, he's never even read the Bible!" You see, that is what the Kingdom is all about. Jesus came to save the lost, not to create doctrinally correct clones. Jesus wants everyone who is willing to acknowledge His Kingship and humbly ask to enter to be able to come in. We need to make sure that we do not make it too difficult for that to happen.

The running theme here is forgiveness. In keeping with our overall theme of darkness for the session, it would do us well to stop for a moment and look at this word. Forgiveness. Forgiveness is really the key to the Kingdom of God. Jesus taught us last session that unless we die we will not be able to enter the Kingdom. Unless He died He would not be able make the way for us to enter the Kingdom.

Now, I'm going to make a bold statement. I think it is possible to die without dying. I mean that in two ways. First I think that you can allow your body to be killed, in the name of martyrdom, but not actually die the death that Jesus called you to die. In other words, you could actually become a self-righteous martyr and, as you drew your final breath, say, "Look at how good I am." That would be a death without dying. The other way I mean it is that you could die to self and pride, without having your physical body killed. This is the death that Jesus calls us to and the death that He demonstrated on the cross. It was not as much the fact that His physical body died as it was that He was willing to forgive His killers even in this most heinous acts of injustice.

The only way that we can forgive is when we die to the need for vengeance. That is because the need for vengeance is rooted in a form of pride that states that I have rights and deserve to be treated with favor. Only when we die to that will we ever be free.

Here is a truth that you must hear. Your unforgiveness will destroy your soul and rob you of all love, joy, hope, and peace that are part of the Kingdom of God. Who are you angry with? Towards whom do you harbor bitterness? Did your parents abuse you? Did your children disappoint you? Did a stranger violate you? Did an opponent slander you and destroy your reputation? Did God allow a natural disaster to take something, or someone from you? Who is it, what happened? I realize that these events are soberingly real and devastating. Every fiber of your natural self demands justice and vengeance toward the perpetrators of these heinous crimes. Yet, please indulge this cold logic for a moment. Let's say that the perpetrator was prosecuted in the extreme way that you see fit. What will it change? Will the event go away? Will the effects of the event be reversed? No. Here's the truth. The bitterness that you harbor toward that person is killing you. It is embedded in your soul like a cancerous tumor and is bubbling up in your life in the form of anxiety, physical illness, depression, anger, and the inability to love. You are in a prison of darkness, and you didn't do anything wrong. The only way out of that prison is to follow Jesus to the cross and authentically repeat His words, "Father, forgive them for they know not what they do." "Aha," you may protest, "that is where my situation differs. My perpetrator knew exactly what he/she was doing." Did they? When you look at Jesus' situation you could make a strong case to say that the Jews and the Romans knew exactly what they were doing. They were killing an innocent man because they didn't agree with Him. So, what did Jesus mean, then? I think He was saying, "Father, forgive them, because they are sin-sick people who are so blinded by their own pain and ignorance and are so deluded that they are behaving irrationally." To forgive your perpetrator, you need to realize that he/she was just a sin-sick person who was operating out of his/her own pain and delusion.

Jesus knew that God was ultimately in control of everything, even this dark moment of His execution. He knew that if He did not love His killers in the way that God loved them, then He would be no better than them. Earlier in His ministry He said that to hate someone was just as bad as murdering them, so if He harbored hatred toward those who were crucifying Him, then He was actually crucifying them back and was no different. In other words, when you harbor bitterness, hatred, and unforgiveness toward someone, no matter how much or how little, you are actually treating them in the same way that they treated you and it becomes a vicious cycle of destruction. The only way to stop the cycle, and to be set free from the darkness of that sin and the physical, emotional, and spiritual affects of it is to forgive. To forgive is to die to the need for vengeance and to open the gate of love that is the path to the Kingdom of God. Only when we die like this can we be brought into the new life of love, joy, peace, and hope that flows from the Kingdom of God. This is death without dying.

Kid's Questions

This is a very sad, and can be a very scary, scene in the life of Jesus. If you were Jesus, and you had done nothing wrong, but the people were nailing you to a cross, how would you feel toward those people? Why?

How did Jesus feel toward those people? What did He say? Why?

Is there anyone that you are angry toward? Has someone done something to you that hurt your feelings or hurt you physically? The message of today is this – the only way you are going to be set free from your bad feelings toward them is to forgive them.

Jesus said that we are to love our enemies and pray for those who persecute us. Spend some time asking God to show you if there is someone you need to forgive today, and pray for that person. It will do your heart good.

Lesson 4

- Matthew 27:45-56
- Mark 15:33-41
- Luke 23:44-49
- John 19:28-37

Study Questions

Make a list of the statements that Jesus made while on the cross. What did they mean?

What happened in the temple when Jesus died?

Who was present to witness Jesus' death?

Food for Thought

There are four observations from the dark hours that brought an end to Jesus' life.

1. **He worshipped God.** At first glance the statements that Jesus made from the cross may seem like the desperate cries of a dying man. Yet, at closer inspection we find that they are actually small openings into a large cavern that is full of precious gems. Let's look at three of these statements, two from Luke and one from John. Jesus said,

"My God, my God, why have you forsaken Me?"

"Into your hands I commit my Spirit",

and,

"I am thirsty."

Each of these statements is actually a quote from a Psalm. The first comes from Psalm 22, the second from Psalm 31, and the third from Psalm 69. It is very likely that Jesus was actually quoting these Psalms as He was dying on the cross and that either a) the people around Him only heard these phrases, or b) only these phrases were recorded as a sort of shorthand to indicate the Psalm He was quoting. In either case, Jesus was referring back to these Psalms and connecting them to the event of His death. We can safely come to this conclusion because John said, in reference to the comment about being thirsty, "in order that the scripture be fulfilled."

So, what's the big deal? Why are these statements important? To find that answer we must understand these three Psalms. If you have the time, it would do you well at this point to stop and read these Psalms for yourself. Each of these Psalms was written by David when he was in a time of great suffering. All three of them can be basically paraphrased like this.

> Oh, God, why are you letting me suffer so terribly?
>
> My enemies are torturing me and gloating over it.
>
> But, I know that you love me and are in control of every situation.
>
> I will praise you, even now.
>
> You will glorify yourself and all the poor and lost will find their hope in you.

Now do you see? These statements were not the desperate cry of a dying man. They were the worship songs of a suffering man whose faith was completely in the sovereignty and love of God, even in the darkest and most severe circumstances. Even in death He was able to sing praise to the Father.

How often are we able to pray to God in this way? Jesus, and David, poured their hearts out to God. They admitted their pain and did not hold back from God their emotions regarding that pain. They expressed their confusion and their human desire for retribution toward their enemies. Yet, they ultimately, through the process of confession and intimate communication with the Father, were able to come to a place of peace as they acquiesced to God's plan and purpose for the pain they were experiencing. Imagine what our lives would be like if we could have that level of communication with the Father, being honest to God, and placing our lives in His hands.

2. **He really died**. When Jesus said, "It is finished" He was indicating that His earthly life and ministry was now complete. It was over. He was going to die. To drive that point home, John includes the detail of the piercing of Jesus' side. When the blood and water flowed from His side that indicated that His heart had, indeed, stopped beating and that the fluids had already begun to pool in His chest cavity. He was dead...dead as a doornail.

Why is this important? In the decades following Jesus' life and the book of Acts, there was a group of people that claimed that Jesus had not actually died, but had simply appeared to die. Some call this the "Swoon" theory, stating that He had only slipped into a coma and that the resurrection was simply his revival. So, it is important that John included the detail of the blood and water to put this heresy to rest. If Jesus had not died, then the whole thing would be pointless. Because of Jesus' death we can know that

- Jesus was an actual, physical human.
- He really died and gave up everything for us.
- His resurrection was a literal reversal of physical death.

3. **Women were exalted**. Throughout the gospels, the women of Jesus life play a special role. From our perspective, on this side of 20th century women's lib, the gospels don't seem very female-friendly, but, in the 1st century context, they were radical, pro-women texts. When the women are mentioned in the story, it is always in the most positive light. Early in His ministry it is indicated that the women were the ones who were financially supporting this roving band of disciples. Today we see that, when the men had scattered and even denied Jesus, the women stood there, watching Him in His most difficult hour. Way to go, ladies! Jesus came to set the captives free. In that day, the women were captive to a male-dominated society. Through the liberating ministry of Jesus, both men and women are equally servants of Christ. Just a thought and an observation.

4. **The curtain opened**. Notice what happened when Jesus died. In the temple, the curtain that divided the Holy of Holies from the Holy Place was torn from the top to the bottom. Some have interpreted this as an indication of God's judgment on the temple and a foreshadowing of its coming destruction. That may be true, but I think there is something deeper than that. The Holy of Holies was a physical representation of the very presence of God, in all His glory and holiness. In the Levitical system only one man was allowed into that space, only once a year, and with much fear and trembling. Now, because of the self-sacrifice of the Son of God, the dividing wall (or curtain) that stood between the Holy Creator and the unholy creation has been torn in two. Now there is reconciliation between these estranged partners. Now, we, who are the ones that deserve to be hanging on the cross, actually have access into the Most Holy Place, without fear, and can receive the fullness of life in the Father's presence. Now that this deed is done, we can rejoice with Jesus as we join Him in singing the Psalm,

From you comes the theme of my praise
in the great assembly;
before those who fear you will I fulfill
my vows.
The poor will eat and be satisfied;
they who seek the LORD will
praise him—
may your hearts live forever!
All the ends of the earth
will remember and turn to the LORD,
and all the families of the nations
will bow down before him,
for dominion belongs to the LORD
and he rules over the nations.

Kid's Questions

We are going to do a little play acting. You will need some simple supplies: the biggest piece of paper you can find, and a pair of scissors.

Fold the piece of paper in half and crease it like you were going to tear it into two equal pieces. Don't tear it.

Now place a cut about ½ inch long at the top of the crease. This will serve as a guide cut.

Now we can begin the enactment. You need two people for this.

Have two people stand up and face each other. One person will represent God and the other person will represent humanity.

Have the God character hold up the piece of paper with two hands, one on each side, and hold it in between your two faces so that you cannot see each other.

Now have each person make faces at each other. Can you see what the other person is doing? Why?

Now have the God character pull out on the paper so that it rips down the crease and splits

into two parts. Pull them apart so that you can see each other's faces. Now, can you tell what the other person is thinking by looking at their face?

This demonstrates what happened when Jesus died. When He died the temple that covered up the Holy of Holies was torn in half from the top to the bottom. This showed the world that, just like your paper was ripped, God was making it possible, through Jesus, for us to come into his presence and know Him personally.

Spend some time thanking Jesus for opening up this door to God.

209

Lesson 5

- Matthew 27:57-65
- Mark 15:42-47
- Luke 23:50-56
- John 19:38-42

Study Questions

In whose tomb was Jesus buried? Why?

Why were the Roman guards placed at the tomb?

Why was Jesus' body not prepared right away?

Food for Thought

Silence. Sometimes silence can be deafening. Silence is the presence of nothing; the absence of something. It comes in between the something.

When I was in high school I played football. During the fall the world revolved around Friday night. All week we would focus our energy toward the conflict that would happen on the field that night. The coaches prepared their strategies. The players prepared their bodies. The cheerleaders prepared the school with decorations and school spirit. The pep band prepared their music. Then the event took place. Bodies crashed into each other, risks were taken, cheers roared, the band blasted, a victory and a defeat was taken. Then there was the post-game party where everyone gathered to relive the moments and soak the night for every ounce of experience it had to offer.

Then it happened. Inevitably you were back in your home, the lights were turned off, and it was silent. No more cheering, no more high-fives. It was just you and the dark ceiling above you. On Saturday morning it was just another day with trash to be taken out and mundane tasks to be done. It always seems most silent after a big climax.

There is another time that things become silent. Having grown up in the Midwest, I am very familiar with the storms that blow across the plains in the late spring when the warm air invades the cold. Something happens just before the storm. The sky turns green, the air seems to become electrified, and...it gets very quiet. In that silent moment you stop and realize, "Run for cover!" and then, BOOM, it hits like a Mack truck and the winds begin beating relentlessly against the ground. The twister forms and cuts a swath through the countryside, leaving devastation in its path. It always seems to be most silent just before the storm.

Saturday must have been the most silent day that Jerusalem had ever experienced. The Sanhedrin lay in bed that night staring at the ceiling, wondering what had just happened. The three years of bantering were over; Jesus was dead... now what? The disciples were stunned. Their master had been locked tight in the tomb of one of the members of the Sanhedrin, and the Romans had placed a guard in front of the entrance, just to assure that there would be no monkey-business. When the dawn broke, would the soldiers be coming for them? Was all that Jesus had taught a big sham? Where was God? Where were the miracles? Where was the power? It seemed as if heaven was shut tight, if it existed at all.

Have you ever been in one of those places? Have

you ever experienced the post-climactic let down, when all the hype faded and you were left all alone with your own heart? Were you lonely? Or, perhaps you have been in a season of your life when it seemed that God could not possibly be present in light of the terrible circumstances that had just taken place. In either case it was silent, and the silence left you feeling alone, vulnerable, cold, and scared.

The silence of Saturday was the kind of silence that fit both descriptions we discussed earlier. It was a post-climactic let down, and it was the silence before the storm. On Sunday everything would change. On Sunday the Kingdom of God would storm the world, blowing away the chaff and bringing in the wheat. It would be a bright new day of hope and glory. On Sunday that would happen, but today is Saturday. Here's the key. Sunday can't happen without Saturday. There can't be a resurrection without a burial. There can't be a sudden blast of hope, without a precursor of silence.

As Christians in the 21st century we live in a shadow land, a borderland, a place of Saturday/Sunday. We live in the reality that Sunday morning happened and Jesus did raise from the dead, but we also live in the reality that the big Sunday morning, THE resurrection of the dead has not yet happened. Jesus' resurrection was just the first fruits; the preview of coming attractions. We live in a time when the darkness of Friday night is still dominant, and the light of Sunday morning is still a glow at the end of the tunnel. We live in the nexus of Saturday. Sometimes Saturday is silent. Sometimes we wonder if God is speaking. We toggle back and forth between the glory of Sunday and the silence of Saturday.

The message for today is simple. It's Saturday, but Sunday is coming. No matter how bad things may get, no matter how silent Heaven may seem, never forget that God is in control and the hope of resurrection is not a vain desire, but a promise from a faithful Father.

Kid's Questions

How do you feel when you are all alone and it's dark and completely quiet? Why?

Let's say you are lying in your bedroom, and all the lights are off, and there isn't a sound in the house. How does it feel? When the light comes on downstairs and you hear your parents talking or the TV on, how does that make you feel? Why?

When Jesus died he was buried in the ground and was there for at least one whole day on Saturday. How do you think the disciples felt that day? Why?

The silence of Jesus' burial was kind of like what it feels like when you are alone in the dark. The great thing was that Jesus turned the light on the next morning when he rose from the dead.

As Christians, we can always know that, no matter how dark and quiet things may seem to get, God is always there with us. And, someday, we will be with him where there will be no more darkness or silence at all.

211

Finale : Walk into the Light

Introduction

Daybreak. Light on the horizon. New Life. Hope. These are the key ideas of this final session in our study of Jesus' life. Last session we watched in horror as darkness seemed to rule the day. Now we can breathe again as the hero breaks the bonds of the oppressor and rises to victory, once and for all time.

There are four basic sections to the illustration. First we see the empty tomb which is flanked by the "Men in White," (you know...M and G... God's special agents.. Michal and Gabriel). The tomb is empty. Jesus is no longer dead. His body has been resurrected; brought back to life; re-animated. This single event is the hinge upon which all of cosmic history swings. Jesus has reversed the effects of sin and has brought the hope of eternal life with God back to the world.

The second section deals with the interaction that Jesus had with the disciples while He walked on the earth, before He returned to the Father. He needed to spend this time with them in order to substantiate the reality of His physical, bodily resurrection and to alleviate any doubts they may have had.

Thirdly, we see one of the most touching and intimate moments recorded in the Bible. Jesus welcomes Peter back into fellowship and reinstates him as a key leader in the New Kingdom that the disciples would introduce to the world. In this story we see the healing power of love, forgiveness, repentance, and reconciliation at work.

Finally, Jesus has lift off as He ascends back to the Father. As He leaves He commissions His disciples to take the Kingdom of God to the entire world, guiding people into the transforming relationship that awaits them with their heavenly Father.

213

Lesson 1

- Matthew 28:1-10
- Mark 16:1-8
- Luke 24:1-12
- John 20:1-9

Study Questions

How did the guards react to the "Men in White?"

How did the women react to them?

What message did the "Men in White" bring?

How did the disciples interpret these events?

Food for Thought

Have you ever noticed that Christians have a cross fixation? We build giant crosses and place them on top of buildings. We wear crosses around our necks. We hang them on the wall.

How would we feel if we went into someone's house and saw a big, gilded noose hanging on the wall? Or a bronze statue of a man being hanged by the neck from a tree? What would we think if we were having dinner with someone and the centerpiece was a guillotine with a severed head in the bucket, right next to the salt shaker? We'd raise our eyebrows in suspicion about these people while old reruns of the Adams Family started running through our memory.

Yet, as Christians, we have done exactly that. In the first century, the cross was nothing more than a means of cruel execution for the basest of criminals. To the Roman mind it was a symbol of disgrace, death, disgust, and despair. So, if a Roman were to come into your home and see the cross on the wall, they would probably be alarmed.

Now, don't get me wrong. I'm not trying to bash the symbol of the cross. For the Christian, the meaning of the cross was transformed the day Jesus died on it. For us the cross symbolizes humility, self-sacrifice, and the extreme love that God has for us, as well as the high calling to cross-carrying discipleship that Jesus set before us. It is a good and powerful symbol, to be sure. However, I'd like to suggest that there may be a symbol that has been underplayed, but is of even more significance than the cross.

If a jeweler were to make the best object for you to wear around your neck that would symbolize the power and significance of the Jesus that you follow, it should be a rock with a hole in it. The empty tomb is the real symbol of Christianity. Think about it; anyone can die. Anyone can offer themselves over to be executed. In fact, many great religious leaders have done just that. But, they are still dead. Everyone dies eventually, because death is the result of the sin-sick world in which we live. As Christians we should use the empty tomb as our symbol because Jesus is no longer dead. He has risen! The only reason the symbol of the cross is significant is because of the symbol of the empty tomb where Jesus broke the chains of death, reversed the effects of sin, walked out of the darkness of the tomb, and stepped into the light of the eternal Kingdom of God.

As you were reading the four accounts of the resurrection you may have noticed that they were fairly short, straightforward records of what happened. The stone was rolled away, the guards got knocked out, the "Men in White" appeared and declared that Jesus was risen, the women saw the empty tomb, and John and Peter witnessed the deserted grave clothes. It was simple reporting, and then the story moved on. We must remember that the gospels are the story of the events, but they do not necessarily explain the meaning behind them for us. Even though these are quickly told stories, they are actually of paramount importance. The resurrection event is the hinge upon which the history of the cosmos swings. Sunday morning in the garden tomb was the morning that light penetrated the darkness and ushered in the Kingdom of God. It was the morning toward which all Old Testament prophecy was pointing and from which all New Testament history has flowed. Ever since that day every generation has had to come to grips with the resurrection's reality, its significance, and its implications for life.

Since the gospels merely tell the story, it is important for us to look elsewhere in the Bible to understand the deep significance of the resurrection. This affords us the opportunity to briefly look at the purpose behind how the New Testament is laid out. The New Testament is divided into two basic sections: The Story of what happened (Matthew – Acts), and the letters to the churches, called Epistles (Romans – Revelation) The gospels tell the story of what happened and the Epistles demonstrate how the first generation of Christians interpreted and applied the events and teachings of the gospels in everyday life. In light of this it would be beneficial for us to take a moment and look into the writings of Paul (the one who wrote the most epistles) so that we can understand the depth of meaning that the event of the resurrection had for the early church, and for each of our lives today.

In Paul's letter to the church in Corinth (1 Corinthians 15) he spends a great deal of time explaining how vitally important it is for a Christian to have a strong belief in the resurrection. If you have time, read the whole chapter. For now, read the following verses:

> ...And if Christ has not been raised, your faith is futile; you are still in your sins. Then those also who have fallen asleep in Christ are lost. If only for this life we have hope in Christ, we are to be pitied more than all men. (1 Corinthians 15:16-19)

In Paul's introduction of himself to the church in Rome, as he defines the core of the gospel, he notes that it is through the resurrection that Jesus is demonstrated to be the Son of God.

> Paul, a servant of Christ Jesus, called to be an apostle and set apart for the gospel of God—the gospel he promised beforehand through his prophets in the Holy Scriptures regarding his Son, who as to his human nature was a descendant of David, and who through the Spirit of holiness was declared with power to be the Son of God by his resurrection from the dead: Jesus Christ our Lord. Through him and for his name's sake, we received grace and apostleship to call people from among all the Gentiles to the obedience that comes from faith. (Romans 1:1-5)

In the following three verses we can see that Paul clearly understands that the very power that we possess as Christians comes through the resurrection of Jesus.

> I want to know Christ and the power of his resurrection and the fellowship of sharing in his sufferings, becoming like him in his death, and so, somehow, to attain to the resurrection from the dead (Philippians 3:10-11)

> We were therefore buried with him through baptism into death in order that, just as Christ was raised from the dead through the glory of the Father, we too may live a new life. (Romans 6:4)

> And if the Spirit of him who raised Jesus from the dead is living in you, he who raised Christ from the dead will also give life to your mortal bodies through his Spirit, who lives in you. (Romans 8:11)

You see, the power of our faith goes far beyond the cross. Yes, Jesus had to die for our sins. Yes, His death was the ultimate example of God's love that was set before us to follow every day. Yet, without the resurrection, the cross would mean nothing. It would just be the story of another good man that was needlessly murdered for his starry-eyed idealism. No. We know it was so much more than that, because our power comes from the resurrection.

Today, as you walk through the paths of life, winding your way through the darkness, remember that you have, living inside of you, the very Spirit that brought Jesus out of the grave. You are no longer bound by the darkness of sin and death, but have received the victory over those things through Jesus' resurrection and you are invited to walk in that victorious stance each and every moment of your life. May you experience the resurrection power in your life today!

Kid's Questions

Let's reenact this scene. You will need at least three people to do this.

Parts:

> *Jesus*
>
> *Men in White (one or two people)*
>
> *Roman guards (as many as you like)*
>
> *Women (if you don't have enough, you can double up as guards and women)*

Have Jesus lie down on the ground and pretend to be dead. Put a couple pillow on the ground to represent the door to the tomb with a stone in front of it. Place the guards at the entrance of the tomb.

Earthquake!! Everyone starts shaking.

The Men in White show up and point at the guards. The guards are so afraid they fall to the ground. The Men in White roll the stone away.

Jesus gets up and walks out of the tomb, and into another room.

The women come to the tomb and see that it's empty. The men in white say,

> *Do not be afraid, for I know that you are looking for Jesus, who was crucified. He is not here; he has risen, just as he said. Come and see the place where he lay. The go quickly and tell his disciples: 'he has risen from the dead and is going ahead of you into Galilee. There you will see him.*

Jesus comes back in the room and says,

> *Greetings.*

The women fall down and worship at his feet.

Jesus says,

> *Do not be afraid. Go and tell my brothers to go to Galilee; there they will see me.*

Spend some time thanking God that Jesus in no longer on the cross or in the grave. His is alive and well, and sits in power over the universe!

Lesson 2

- Matthew 28:11-15
- Mark 16:9-14
- Luke 24:13-49

Study Questions

Who were the two disciples on the road?

Why did they not recognize Jesus?

How did the disciples interpret the events of Jesus' death and the reports of His missing body?

What did Jesus teach them as they walked?

What action triggered the disciple's recognition of Jesus?

Food for Thought

At the very least, Luke 24 is a wonderful piece of storytelling. If this were a movie we would be sitting on the edge of our seats, squirming with unrest and excitement, wanting to yell at the screen, "Come on you numbskulls, can't you see it's Him? Get with the program."

Jesus, in his newly resurrected body, slides up alongside two unsuspecting disciples, and has a little fun with them.

"Hey, boys, what's up? Whatcha talkin' about?"

"Where have you been? We're talking about what everybody within 20 miles of Jerusalem has been talking about all weekend; Jesus' execution, of course."

"Sounds interesting, tell Me about it."

With a condescending look, the disciples indulge the ignorant visitor, "Well, first of all, we've been following this Man for over three years now. He was amazing. We're sure He was a prophet sent by God. He did all kinds of miracles and taught with such authority...oh, man, you should have heard Him speak! We thought for sure He was going to be the one to take the leadership reigns of Israel and finally do something about these nasty Romans. That's why we are so sad and so confused. One minute Jesus is entering Jerusalem like a king, and the next minute He is surrendering to the guards and allowing Himself to be executed. That's the part we don't get, why did He voluntarily surrender to them? It just doesn't add up. To muddy the waters even further, some of the women folk have started spinning a wild tale about Jesus' tomb being empty and seeing men in bright clothing who said He was alive. We just can't figure any of it out."

"Wow, you guys are pretty slow and thick-headed, aren't you? Isn't that exactly how the Bible said things would go down when the Messiah showed up?"

"Huh?"

"OK, let Me explain it to you. Let's start with Moses... [then, for the next few miles, Jesus walks them through a step-by-step explanation of how the entire flow of Israel's history and the preaching of the prophets explained that the Messiah would first come to suffer for the sins of the people, and then be exalted to a place of power from which He could lead all people into the Kingdom of God.]

"Whoa, that's some pretty intense teaching. Why don't you stay and eat with us while we try to sort all this out."

Over dinner Jesus reenacted two very significant

events from His ministry. As he broke the bread He relived the time when He fed five thousand and declared, "I am the bread of the world," and that night, in the upper room, when He took the Passover meal and said, "This is My body, eat it."

BOOM, just then, as they sat in the presence of the bread Himself, all the pieces popped into focus. This was Jesus. The women weren't whacked. He had risen from the dead. He is alive! POOF! Then He was gone.

The crowd slumps back in the theater seats in a satisfied narrative delight.

Of course, this is so much more than a well told story. In this story we see the process of discipleship. As we explore these three points we will see the process of the journey that each of us must take as we "travel toward Emmaus."

1. **Their misguided presupposition was blinding them to the truth of the facts that were clearly laid before them.** Everyone has ideas about how things are. We may not be aware of where we got those ideas, or be able to articulate them well, but we still have them nonetheless. These ideas that we carry with us are ideas that came previously in our upbringing -- they are pre-ideas; commonly known as presuppositions. Here's a little insight into presuppositions – they're almost always wrong, at least in part, they hinder our ability to correctly interpret data, and they always need to be tweaked. The two disciples in the story were unable to correctly interpret the events of Jesus' death because their presupposition was incorrect. They expected the Messiah to behave in a certain way, so when He went outside of their expectations He disappeared from their view. It's like polarized sun glasses. One day I was pumping gas with my sunglasses on and I was not able to see the numbers on the screen. I got a little frustrated, thinking that the pump was broken. Fortunately, I tipped my head back and looked at the screen underneath my glasses and, almost like magic, the numbers appeared. When I looked through the lenses, they disappeared instantly. Knowing a little bit about polarization, I did an experiment and slowly tilted my head to the right. As I did it was like a fade in on a movie scene. The farther right I turned, the brighter the numbers became. When I turned my head back to the left, the numbers faded back to black. Polarized lenses are designed to only let a certain pattern of light penetrate the lenses, thus cutting down on the glare from the sun. The pattern of the numbers on the screen was polarized in the opposite pattern as my

glasses and was rendered completely invisible. That's how it is with presuppositions. When we have pre-constructed an idea of how we think things should be, we have created a grid that only allows us to see the data that we want to see. If the data doesn't match our presupposition, then it becomes invisible to us, leaving us unable to construct an accurate understanding of reality.

When we encounter the "Jesus data" most of us have great difficulty understanding it and/ or believing it. Depending upon our training and our life experience, we have certain ideas of what God is and isn't, and how things should be. Perhaps we have experienced a great deal of pain and we can't believe that a loving God would allow this to happen, so we have dismissed the idea of a God who can be known. Perhaps we have been trained as a naturalistic, scientific thinker and have categorically dismissed the notion of the supernatural as a stone-aged superstition. Or, perhaps we have been brought up in the church and have been taught a very narrow and rigid doctrinal stance on the nature of God that constricts our minds and leaves us unable to process certain apparent paradoxes in scripture. Whatever the case may be, we all have on a pair of lenses that blocks out at least some aspect, or distorts some aspect, of the reality of Jesus, and it needs correcting. As we begin our "walk to Emmaus" we need the next two steps to happen in our life in order for the light of truth to break through to our eyes.

2. **It took a "Walk through the Bible" to make sense out of things.** The first thing Jesus did with the disciples was to give them a macro-perspective, a bird's-eye view, of the big picture of the Bible in order to demonstrate how God has been working throughout history to bring about His plan. The Bible is the one objective revelation that God has sanctioned to communicate truth to his people and to exemplify how He interacts with different people, in different cultures, in order to reveal Himself to them in a way that they can know Him and be transformed by His presence. If we are going to grow spiritually then it is vitally important that we have a solid, working knowledge of the Bible in its entirety. Too many times Christians adopt a few pet sections of the Bible and camp out in them, never delving into other areas. We like the passages about love and joy, but stay far away from the war sections, and, heaven forbid that we ever read from the Old Testament prophets. Let me tell you right now, as difficult

as the OT prophets may be to read, if you don't have at least some working knowledge of them, you will miss the full impact of the New Testament. Jesus' teaching, His life, and His resurrection are the fulfillment of these prophecies. When I say fulfillment, I don't mean simply that they predicted certain events that would happen in His life. This is a true aspect of it, to be sure, but Jesus' fulfillment of the prophets goes much deeper. Jesus functioned in the role of a prophet. The things He said and the way He said them were parallel to the preaching ministries that those Old Testament mouthpieces of God had during their ministries. The Wisdom literature of the Old Testament as well, Job, Song of Solomon, are portions of the Bible that are pregnant with Messianic messages that are intrinsically woven together with the life and teaching of Jesus. Simply put, if you want to grow spiritually it is a necessity that you get on a serious, comprehensive study of the whole Bible and learn how all the pieces fit together.

3. **It wasn't until they were "at the table" that they could see the truth.** Notice that the cognitive understanding of the scripture was not enough. Don't get me wrong, I didn't say that it wasn't necessary. It is essential, but it is not enough. To merely fill your head with the knowledge about God from scripture is not what is needed for life transformation. It wasn't until the disciples sat down to the dinner table with Jesus and broke bread with Him that their eyes were opened to the mystery of His presence. Throughout this study we have emphasized the importance of "table fellowship" in the spiritual life. To have dinner with someone is a symbol of being in intimate relationship with them. To share a loaf of bread with someone as you sit across the table with them is a picture of being united and sharing more than logical understanding, but sharing a heart passion and unity with one another. This is a supra-rational place of emotional bonding that takes place. If we are going to remove the polarized lenses, then we need to first have them corrected through teaching, but also be removed through an intimate encounter with the person of Jesus. We need to not simply learn about Him, we need to meet Him and eat with Him. Then we will see, we will understand, and we will be changed.

The process of discipleship happens when the informational instruction of Biblical truth is combined with the ignition of the mystical presence of God that brings about illumination and transformation in the life of the disciple. It is like a jet engine. When air is pulled into a jet engine it is compressed and fuel is injected into it. The compression is the educational process and the fuel is the Word of God. These things are vital components to the propulsion of the engine, but on their own they amount to nothing. It takes a spark to ignite the fuel and transform it into energy. The spark is the Spirit of God; the mystical, mysterious presence of Jesus, through the Holy Spirit, that illuminates the teaching and empowers the learner (this is the meaning of the word "disciple") to be transformed and utilized for the Kingdom of God. Fuel injection (teaching) without ignition creates nothing more than a flooded engine. Ignition (the spiritual experience) without the fuel simply makes flashy sparks without power. When the two come together and educated people are ignited by the Spirit of God, then a powerful jet engine can propel the Kingdom of God and thrust it deeper into the world of darkness to establish new beacons of light for the world to see and find their way home.

Each one of us is on this walk to Emmaus every day. The journey is what our life is all about. As we progress, we reach new levels of awareness and understanding about the nature of Jesus. It is possible to have many "aha" moments throughout our lives as new layers of understanding are unveiled before us. With each layer of "revelation" the same process is required. We need to learn and we need to eat with Jesus daily. As we walk on this road to Emmaus this process repeats itself over and over, igniting us anew for power in the Kingdom of God. Happy Journey!

Kid's Questions

Why do you think the men on the road did not recognize Jesus?

What did they think Jesus was going to do when he entered Jerusalem? What did he really do?

What did Jesus have to do for them before they could understand the truth about him?

This is a good reminder to us that it is very important to study our Bibles all the time. The more we understand the Bible, the easier it will be for us to recognize the truth about Jesus.

Lesson 3

- John 20:10-31

Study Questions

What emotion was Mary experiencing when she encountered Jesus?

How did He reveal himself?

What emotion did the disciples experience when they saw Jesus appear?

How did Jesus convince them of His reality?

What did Thomas demand before He was convinced of the truth regarding Jesus' resurrection?

What purpose does John give for writing His gospel story?

Food for Thought

When the story began this week the disciples were in a deep pit of darkness. They had locked themselves in a dark room, shuddering in fear and uncertainty. The running theme of this week is the process that the disciples went through to emerge from the cave of darkness and step into the victorious light of the power of Jesus' resurrection. In the same way that Jesus was buried in a dark tomb and walked out of it, so too did the disciples need to follow the same path.

Yesterday we focused on Luke's version of the emerging process as Jesus walked on the road to Emmaus with them. Today we will focus in on John's version. It has three scenes.

The first scene is at the entrance to the garden tomb. Mary Magdalene is all alone in the garden, grieving deeply for the loss of her liberator. When she encountered Jesus it was her grief that impaired her ability to recognize Jesus. She was so full of despair that her ears could not recognize His voice when He spoke to her. Yet, all it took for her was for Him to speak her name, "Mary." That one word must have been dripping with compassion, for with that one intimate utterance Mary's world was changed. She spun around and saw Him, and, in seeing, she believed. He was alive.

In the second scene all the disciples (except for Thomas) were present and Jesus showed up in their presence. Unlike Mary, they saw Him, but their sight did not initially convince them. Their first response was one of fear. We can deduce this because His first words to them were "Peace be with you!" I don't think he was just saying "Wassup?" He was saying don't be afraid, be at peace. Perhaps they thought He was a ghost, much like they did the night He walked on the water. To belie their fears He showed them his scars. He demonstrated to them that, even though He had suddenly appeared, He was still made of flesh and bones. He still bore the scars of the crucifixion He had just endured. In seeing this evidence, their fear was replaced with joy, and Jesus was able to breathe the Holy Spirit into them and commission them to enter the world with power and authority so that they could usher in the Kingdom of God.

There is one more scene. Thomas was not privy to this event. When the disciples told him what happened, he would not believe them. Even though they were his closest friends, and they had no motive for deceiving him, he would still not believe their testimony. It wasn't until he saw Jesus for himself and touched His scars and His side that his doubt was transformed into belief.

221

Mary grieved, but a compassionate voice delivered her from grief. The disciples lived in fear, but the visual evidence replaced their fear with joy. Thomas was shackled with doubt, and the physical, tactile evidence allowed him to exchange his doubt for trust. Grief, fear, and doubt. These are three prisons of darkness that each one of us experience in our lives. The question is, have you encountered Jesus in a way that has removed that darkness and exchanged it for joy and belief?

John concludes this passage by giving his purpose statement for writing his gospel story. He said, "these things are written that you may believe that Jesus is the Christ, the Son of God, and that by believing you may have life in His name." Life. That is what it is all about. God created life and desires for you to experience it. I like to define life as **L**iving **I**n the **F**ather's **F**ellowship **E**ternally. L-I-F-E. The gateway to this kind of eternal life is belief. If you want to know the joy of living, right now, and experience the hope that comes from knowing that your relationship with God is eternally sealed through a covenant (a promise) that is as binding as that of adoption and marriage, then all you need to do is believe in Jesus. Believe that He came from God, that his teaching is from God, that He died for your sin, and that His resurrection is real and can give you the power for life. Jesus is a doorway that stands wide open, inviting you to step into the Kingdom of God that is full of light and truth and life itself.

Many of us are living in a walking death. We are in the bondage of grief, bitterness, fear, and doubt. These things hang around our necks like thick chains. They drag us down and bind us to the dark places. Even those of us who have placed faith in Jesus can still be dragged down by these chains as we allow the enemy to penetrate our armor and allow tendrils of these weeds to worm their way into our hearts, stealing the joy that is ours to experience. Whether you have never before stepped into the light of life that comes through trust in Jesus, or you are struggling against the weeds of darkness in your emergence process, today is a reminder that you can be free from it and experience the joy and empowerment of God's love.

The journey to this light is different for everyone. All Mary needed was to hear His voice and she believed. The disciples needed to see it. Thomas needed to touch it. Depending on your pathway and personality, you will need to find the evidence that will convince you. It may be a logical argument that brings you into the Kingdom of God and convinces you of the unavoidable truth of the reality of Jesus' resurrection. If that is what it takes, then know that the evidence exists. Books like Mere Christianity by C.S. Lewis, Evidence that Demands a Verdict by Josh McDowell, and The Case for Christ by Lee Strobell are just a few examples of rational material that will provide the case for belief for the intellectual pathway. Or perhaps logic is not enough. You need to see it to believe it. You need to see miracles. You need to see love and healing in action. If you open your eyes, you will see these things all around you. And, to the church, ask yourself if you are being the love in action. Are you the nail-scarred hands, and the spear-pierced side that is the incarnation of Jesus that the Thomases of the world need to see? Regardless of your need, the evidence is there. Open yourself today and step out of the dark pit and into the light of life.

Kid's Questions

How did Mary feel when she went to the tomb? Why? How did she feel after she saw Jesus? Why?

How did the disciples feel when Jesus appeared to them? Why? What did it take for them to believe that he was really alive?

What did it take for Thomas to no longer doubt? What does doubt mean?

Do you have any doubts about Jesus? It's OK if you do. It would be better to honestly discuss them now than to go through life pretending to believe just to please your parents. Ask your parents the questions you have and, together, investigate the answers.

Doubt is a natural thing. If you doubt, know this. There is an answer to your question, and if you are willing to investigate it, Jesus will make himself real to you.

Jesus is real, and he did rise from the dead. Because he rose from the dead, he conquered death itself. If we believe in Jesus, then we will never have to fear death. Isn't that great?

Lesson 4

▪ John 21:1-14

Study Questions

What does Jesus ask the disciples to do on the boat?

How do they respond to Him?

What has Jesus prepared for the disciples when they come off the lake?

How many times does Jesus ask Peter if he loves Him? Why do you suppose He says it that many times?

What does Jesus tell Peter to do?

Food for Thought

As we watch this final scene in John's gospel where Jesus shares a breakfast with the boys, we see that John is presenting two concluding commentaries on the purpose and significance of the Jesus story.

1.   God is the God of do-overs. Peter is back in action.

It must have taken a long time for Peter to pick all the feathers out of his teeth after he ate such a huge crow. He was so full of pride and self-confidence when he promised Jesus that he would never leave Him and that he would die for him. Then, only a few hours later, he was cursing and swearing that he never even knew Him. Peter must have thought that it was all over for him. All those years of training with Jesus were lost. All he was good for now was to be a two-bit fisherman up in Galilee.

If it were up to us, that is probably how we would have treated Peter if had he betrayed us like he did Jesus. Fortunately for Peter, and for us, Jesus isn't like that. Jesus, and the Kingdom of God, is all about do-overs. Peter blew it, that's for sure, but Jesus was willing to give him another chance. Jesus extended grace to Peter, opened His arms, and trusted him all over again.

Perhaps you need to hear this message today. You may be on either end of this equation. Perhaps you have blown it, again, and you think God could never use you. He can. If you are willing to repent from your mistake and start following Jesus again, He will take you back and give you a do-over. He will throw your sin into the sea of forgetfulness and wipe your slate clean. That's called Grace.

Or, perhaps you were on the receiving end of a Peter-like betrayal. Someone has hurt you and you have every reason to be justifiably guarded against them. Ask yourself whether it is doing you any good to harbor resentment toward that person. Especially if that person is repentant, we need to follow Jesus' example and open up our hearts to be willing to receive and trust again. This is the path of life.

2.   This is a summary of the process of discipleship. In this final chapter, John uses this story to recap the process that the first disciples went through and the process that must be repeated in every generation and every individual life that follows. That includes our own.

▪   The disciples are fishing. We begin the journey toward discipleship and maturity by being "out to sea." The disciples were fishermen. That was their trade. It was their physical means of supporting themselves through their own efforts. We all live and work in the physical reality of survival and have each developed varying degrees of proficiency in supporting ourselves through different vocations. No matter what we do, or how well we do it, we all start out in the chaotic sea of survival, just getting along in the world with no real purpose or direction.

- Jesus calls them. In this story, Jesus reenacted the moment when they first met. He asked them to do something that defied logic. He asked them to throw their nets in after they had been unsuccessful all night. He got their attention, and, through performing a miracle, caused them to be intrigued enough to pursue Him. That's how it works with us. Generally speaking, it takes something to get our attention. Sometimes it is a tragedy that wakes us up to the deeper realities of eternity. Sometimes it is intellectual pursuit. Sometimes it is the demonstration of overwhelming compassion through the life of someone who is already following Jesus. Whatever it is, Jesus is the one who initiates the courtship and calls out to us. Then we are left with a choice. Do we respond to the call, or do we turn away and push out into deeper waters, farther away from the shore.

- The disciples respond. Peter and the others responded. Their hearts were quickened when they heard His voice and they were drawn to Jesus. Notice how their responses were different. Peter, being inclined to brash emotionalism and abrupt action, jumped out of the boat, abandoning all caution, and plunged headlong toward Jesus. James and John, on the other hand, tended to the nets and, because of their more level-headed approach, were able to haul in the miraculous catch of fish that Jesus had given to them. Both responses were valid because they were authentic. The point is that they all responded and moved toward Jesus. They said, "Yes, we hear Your voice and we want to follow You." That's the first step.

- Jesus feeds them. When they got to the shore, Jesus had a little breakfast cooking for them. Notice that He did not have a white board and a PowerPoint presentation ready to instruct them in the doctrinal significance of their decision or to map out a strategic plan for growing the Kingdom. No, He had a meal prepared. Once again we encounter the image of sharing in a meal with Jesus. This meal represents the three and a half years they had

spent with Him; walking, talking, laughing, crying, watching, learning, and bonding with Jesus. The first step in becoming a disciple is to feed with Jesus. We need to eat the Word of Truth and drink the wine of His Spirit. It is the combination of cognitive learning and emotional intimacy that is the source of nourishment and power for the growing disciple.

- Jesus commissions them to feed others. When Jesus reconnected to Peter, He gave Him instructions to feed His sheep. The feeding was described in two ways, using two similar, but different words. One was, literally translated, "to graze" them, or to lead them to good food, to feed. The second was "to shepherd" them, meaning to nurture, protect, and guide them. In essence, Jesus was telling Peter that his job was to do for others what Jesus had done for them. He was sending them out in His name to be his representatives, having learned from the Master, to repeat the process in other's lives, so that they can then pass it on to others. And, thus, the Kingdom of God is expanded.

- Jesus reminds them that they are simply followers. The final word is a caution to Peter, reminding him that he is not in control of his life. Basically, Jesus said, "Look, Pete, to be a shepherd for me is not to be a high mucky-muck, but is to be a simple follower. I'm the only real shepherd. You are working for Me and you do what I say. If you keep that straight then we won't run into the same problem we did before. Got it? If I lead you to be crucified, and I lead another disciple to live a long life, you have to leave that up to Me and not worry about it. You focus on Me and no one else, and let Me handle everyone else's deal."

This story leaves two questions for us to ask ourselves.

1. Where are you in this process? Are you still in the boat? Are you making your first steps of response to Jesus' call? Are you in the feeding process? Are you being commissioned to go and do something in the Kingdom? Are you in the ongoing process of learning to follow and listen to no one else's voice except Jesus? No matter where you are, remember to keep moving. There is more to learn and more room to grow. Find the place where you can be equipped and follow Jesus well.

2. As a church, are we providing the resources for all the disciples at all places on the journey? People at each level have different needs, much like children at different

developmental stages require different kinds of tactics in training them up. As the church, it is our job to edify, or to build up and equip, people to be able to grow from their current developmental stage into the next. Let's ask God to show us how we can create good food for everyone, at every level, so that everyone can grow and become reproducers of God's Kingdom.

Kid's Questions

Let's say you had a best friend that you really enjoyed playing with. One day you both were at school and a group of kids decided that they didn't like you; they thought you were weird, and they teased you. Then, when they saw your best friend, they started picking on him and saying, "Hey don't you hang out with that loser?" What if your friend said, "What? That loser? I wouldn't be caught dead playing with him."

How would you feel?

Would you want to be that kid's friend anymore?

What if your friend felt really bad and asked you to forgive him and wanted to be friends again, would you do it?

That's what happened to Jesus. Peter denied even knowing Jesus at the point when Jesus most needed a friend.

In today's story, what did Jesus do for Peter? Why?

We need to follow Jesus' example and not hold a grudge against someone who is really sorry for what they've done and wants to make things right.

Lesson 5

- Matthew 28:16-20
- Mark 16:15-20
- Luke 24:50-53

Study Questions

How did the disciples respond when they saw Jesus on the mountain?

What place does Jesus have in the universe?

What did Jesus tell His disciples to do?

How were they supposed to accomplish this instruction?

What promise did He make to the disciples?

Food for Thought

Well, it's hard to believe that this is our final day -- the 75th day -- in our study. It is interesting to observe how the gospel writers chose to conclude their stories of Jesus' life. They each end with a beginning. The end of Jesus' story is actually the beginning of our story. Luke is the writer who takes this to its greatest extreme. He takes the end of Jesus' life and actually springboards from it into an entirely new narrative that describes how the disciples began to spread the Kingdom of God to the world. This is the story found in the book of Acts, Luke's sequel to his gospel. It will be the subject of another study, for another time.

For now, the most concise version of Jesus' final words is found in Matthew's account in Matthew 28:16-20. Just before Jesus leaves His physical ministry, He commissions the disciples to be His witnesses. These instructions are for us as well. Let's observe Jesus' final words.

1. **Jesus is the supreme victor.** He said that all authority is given to Him, both in Heaven and on Earth. This is a vitally important truth for us to grasp. Many people envision the Christian life as a cosmic struggle between the forces of good and the forces of evil, like the yin and yang of eastern cultures, where two equally opposing forces are engaged in battle. Nothing could be farther from the truth. Jesus has conquered death. Evil is not a force that can defeat Him. He has authority over the people of Earth and the spiritual forces of evil in the heavens. As we take the standard of light and truth into the darkness we can rest in the confidence that His authority gives us. We are not fighting in the hopes that light will win, we are simply doing reconnaissance and rescuing the refugees that are still trapped in the deception that darkness is all there is to reality.

2. **As you journey...** At this point we need to stop and have a short, but important, Greek lesson. When you read this passage in English it sounds like Jesus is barking out orders. Go! Make! Baptize! Teach! This is not true in the Greek. The technical term for a direct order is an imperative. A verb that is written in the imperative, in the Greek, can be translated as a command. However, there is only one imperative in this passage; the word "Disciple!" – or make people into disciples! All of the other words are participles (that means that they have –ing at the end and are used as adverbs to describe how the main action is to be carried out). The word "go" in the English is actually the participle that should be translated, "as you are on your

227

journey." Unfortunately, when this verse is seen purely as a sending out, it has been used as a call for people to go overseas in some sort of specialized foreign mission. Now, Jesus' instructions definitely encompass that as one form of "as you are going," but if it is exclusively understood in this way it may leave 95% of the church thinking that they are either not called, or are off the hook to make disciples. The correct reading of this – as you are going – widens the scope to be for the entire church. All of us are going. We are all on a journey. We are all growing and walking with God. So, as we are going, doing whatever it is that God has called us to do; we are to obey His command.

3. **Make disciples!** That's the imperative. All of us, as we are going are called to make disciples. The word "disciple" literally means "learner." It is not necessarily a spiritual term, since all great teachers and leaders - good or bad - have disciples. Hitler's disciples were called Nazi's. The Rabbi Hillel's disciples were called Pharisees. Jesus' disciples are called Christians. Making disciples, or the process of discipleship, is the process of bringing people into a learning and following mode, so that their hearts and minds are focused on Jesus, and they are becoming more and more like Him as they learn and practice His ways. That is what the church is called to do. According to Jesus this happens in a two-pronged process, which are found in the next two points.

4. **Baptising them.** The ritual of baptism was more than a ceremony that got people wet. Remember, Jesus was not about to build another ceremonial institution after having just torn one down. Baptism was a symbol of repentance. It was a process of dying to one's old ways of life, being cleansed from the decaying process of sin, and being raised to new life and empowered to walk in a new direction. The Greek term is "baptizo" and has the sense of being immersed in something so thoroughly that you are transformed by it. When a cucumber is baptized in vinegar it becomes a pickle. Its nature is altered. The first prong of discipleship is to bring people into an encounter with the power and the spirit of God so that they become fully immersed in His presence, repent from their sin, and commit to a total follower mode of existence, bringing their life under the authority that is rightly Jesus'.

5. **Teaching them to obey.** The ways of Jesus run counter to the ways of the world that are ingrained into our minds from a young age.

Ideas like "the first will be last," "love your neighbor," and "you must die to live," are concepts that must be carefully explained and demonstrated through a process of both propositional and experiential training. In the end, Jesus gave us only one command, to love one another. Within the seed of that one command is the DNA for the entire Kingdom of God. Without the love of God, we cannot love one another. Through the love of God we can die to ourself, fill up with the love and truth of God, and then overflow that love to everyone around us, including our enemies. When we love out of the overflow of God in us, then we will be able to obey Jesus' commands. This is what we are to teach as we make disciples.

6. **He is with us.** As we find out in the beginning of Acts, Jesus kept his promise and poured out the life giving fire-water called the Holy Spirit. Through the presence of the Holy Spirit -- who empowers us, corrects us, teaches us, guides us, and unites us – we can step into this commissioning with a sense of expectancy and confidence. Jesus is with us, He is the authority, and we are ready to go.

As He ascended to the heavens He left us to carry the torch. Today, in the 21st century the commission is still the same. As we go, we are to make disciples of everyone, from every walk of life, calling them to submission to the authority of Jesus, repentance, life-change, and teaching them to be filled to overflowing with the love of God so that everyone we meet will be touched by the Kingdom of God on Earth.

Kid's Questions

What does the word "disciple" mean? Look it up in the dictionary.

According to Matthew 28:18, what is Jesus?

What did Jesus tell the disciples to do?

How were they supposed to do it?

In what ways could you make disciples around you today?

Epilogue

The tour bus has pulled up to the station. It's time for me to take off my tour guide hat. A while back I invited you to travel on this journey with me as I played the role of part tour guide and part traveling companion. As we encountered this story together, it was my prayer that we would be changed by it. I invited you to come as you are and be open to the possibility that you could be changed. I hope you have been. I have to confess that sitting here, writing this epilogue, I am not the same man that I was when we began. I have been changed through the process of studying Jesus' life again. For that I am grateful.

The big question for us is, "Now what?" What do we do with it? I will leave you with the two concluding remarks, one from John, and the other from Matthew, that sum it all up. John said,

But [this story has been] written that you may believe that Jesus is the Christ, the Son of God, and that by believing you may have life in his name.

My desire for you is that you know life and know it to the fullest.

Then Matthew recorded Jesus' words, which I will paraphrase...

Now that you've got it, go give it!

Let's be the kind of people that know Jesus so well, that are so connected to the vine, that the fruit of the Spirit is popping out in luscious abundance in our life, available for all people to taste and see that the Lord is good!

More titles from Vibble Books

The Overflow Principle

a 7-week introductory small group Bible study that explores how
to grow in the love of God and overflow God's love to the world.
The study explores how to obey Jesus' commands to love God
and love neighbor. We love God with a whole heart - the mind,
spirit, and body. Then we overflow God's love to the natural
spheres of relationship that surround us; first to our comfortable
neighbor, and then, most importantly, to our uncomfortable
neighbor.

Acts

a 12-week, 5-day per week study that will guide you through the
book of Acts. This is the story of the first generation of Jesus-
folowers as they spread from Jerusalem throughout the Roman
Empire.

Paul's Letters

a 16-week, 5-day per week guide through all of the letters that
Paul wrote both to churches and individuals. Through these
letters we have a model of how to contextualize Jesus' message
for specific cultural issues.

View all the titles at www.vibblebooks.com

The learning adventure doesn't stop with the printed studies. Visit www.VibbleSpace.com and witness the Vibble in its natural habitat. At VibbleSpace.com you can watch teaching animations and interact with others who are using Vibble Books material.

Workshops and Seminars

Steve is available to provide workshops and seminars for your church as a suplemental resource to the group studies.

Contact him at info@vibblebooks.com to learn more.